THE FLAME OF LOVE
OF THE IMMACULATE HEART OF MARY

The Spiritual Diary

Elizabeth Kindelmann

THE FLAME OF LOVE OF THE IMMACULATE HEART OF MARY

The Spiritual Diary

The Flame of Love of the
Immaculate Heart of Mary Movement

On June 6, 2009, the original Hungarian Spiritual Diary of Elizabeth Kindelmann received the Imprimatur number 494-4/2009 from Cardinal Péter Erdö, Archbishop of Esztergom-Budapest and Primate of Hungary.

The cover image representing the **Virgin Mary of the Flame of Love** is a creation of the Austrian artist Erwin Schôppl of Regensburg, Austria, 1977.

First Edition

The Flame of Love of the Immaculate Heart of Mary, Inc.
Montreal, Canada

ISBN 978-0-9879765-4-3

The Flame of Love Movement in Canada
P.O. Box 21111, Postal Station Jacques-Cartier
Longueuil, Quebec J4J 5J4
www.theflameoflove.org
holymary@theflameoflove.org

The Flame of Love Movement in the U.S.A.
8 St. Albans Ave.
Newtown Square, PA 19073
www.flameoflove.us

CONTENTS

ELIZABETH KINDELMANN

Budapest, Hungary

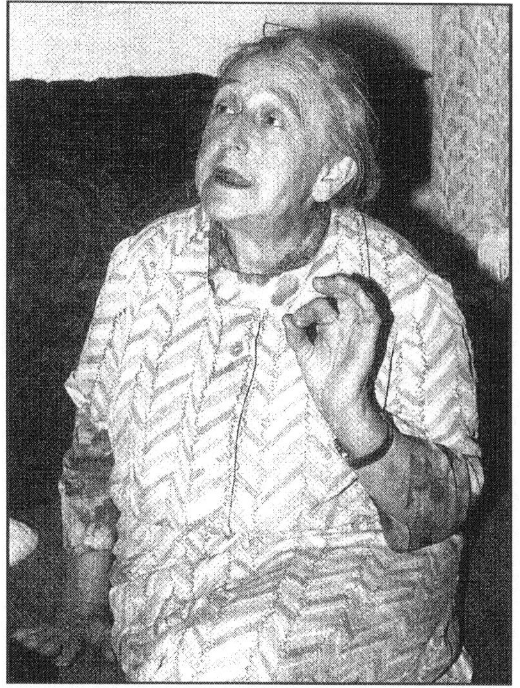

BIOGRAPHY

Elizabeth Kindelmann, maiden name Szántó, was born on June 6, 1913 at Saint Stephen's Hospital, in Kispest, Hungary. She was baptized on June 13, 1913.

From the posthumous writings of her spiritual director, who died in 1976, we learn that she came from a poor family. Her parents were Joseph Szántó, printer (1871-1917) and Ersébet Mészáros (1878-1924). Her father was Protestant and her mother Catholic. The children were educated and raised as Catholics.

Elizabeth had twelve brothers and sisters, six pairs of twins. She was the thirteenth child, the only one not a twin. She was the only child to make it to adulthood. Seven of her siblings died during the Spanish Plague of 1919. Two died in the aftermath of diphtheria and two more died accidentally. Another brother died as an infant, and Elizabeth never got to know the cause of his death.

"Following my father's death, and from 1917 to 1919, I was raised by my maternal grandparents in Seresznyéspuszta, in the countryside. Because of my frail health the physician advised me to live in the countryside. From that period of time, I cannot recall being taken to the church of Szekazard located some fourteen kilometers away. All I can remember is that my grandmother always wore a Rosary around her wrist even while she was feeding the chickens and the hogs.

From September 1919 to June 1923, I attended the elementary school for girls on Pannonia Street, in Budapest."

As part of an international assistance initiative, on November 8, 1923, Elizabeth was sent to Switzerland, to the family of a wealthy agricultural machinery manufacturer in Willisau. "From the weak child that I had been, I became a young girl under the care of French and German governesses growing in weight from twenty-one to thirty-eight kilos."

"In November 1924, purely out of love, I came back to Budapest to look after my ailing mother who was seriously ill and bedridden. Towards the end of 1924, my foster parents of Willisau wanted to adopt me and take me back to Switzerland. I was to meet them at ten o'clock at the Graz railway station (Austria). I got there at 10:00 p.m. as opposed to 10:00 a.m. when they were actually expecting me. Incredibly, it is this mishap that changed the course of events affecting my life and leading me to fulfill my mission in Hungary. At the time, a young Hungarian couple took me back to Budapest.

By the age of twelve, I was working in the household of my maternal uncle in Vajta for the period running from Easter up to the corn harvest. I simply could not stand the crass laziness of my cousins, three boys and a girl and I slipped out without a word and I went back to Budapest.

From November 1925 to June 1926, I was working as a maid in the countryside for the mother of a man of significant influence. I had to work from morning to evening having to survive on a single meal for the whole day. My social condition was indeed pitiful, suffering from severe hunger. So, I packed up my things and simply left for downtown.

Under the carriage port of a small, dilapidated house, I noticed a not so friendly older woman holding an empty siphon (bottle) of Seltzer water. She looked at me and called me over. She asked me to go buy her a bottle of Seltzer water at the bar across the street. She gave me the money and watched to see whether I would comply with her request. Upon returning with the Seltzer, she proceeded to question me. Then she let me into the house and gave me breakfast. I was hired to look after her small garden in exchange for meals. There were very strange visitors living there. I actually had to fight off with considerable loud yelling a young man who frequently came to the house. I left the same day and kept on wandering with my meager belongings.

On August 10, 1926, I went to the Church of Perpetual Adoration on Ülloi Avenue. When the time came to close the church, I went on wandering until I found a bench on Matyas' Place. The policeman patrolling the area had pity on me and did not send me away. When morning arose, I went to the Church of the Sacred Heart of Jesus, where I slept through the Mass. Once warmed up, I went out roaming around looking for work.

Close by the church of Jozsefvaros, there was a creamery and on the door a note that they were hiring people to distribute bottles of milk. I introduced myself and was hired on the spot, but I was also told I could only start three days later, the time when the current carrier would leave the job. What would I do meanwhile? On Koszuru Street, I came across a factory hiring people on the spot to crack nuts. The employees would sit alongside a table each with two baskets. The nuts taken from one were shelled and placed in the other. Each employee's production was weighed. They paid four fillers[1] an hour, and for ten fillers I could buy myself five croissants at the Teleki marketplace, the cheapest in the city.

1. From 1925 to 1946, one hundred fillers equalled one pengo, Hungarian currency.

Later, I strolled to the Franciscan Fathers who gave me a small amount of money and I shared my bread with a starving woman. We ate it right away sitting on a bench at the marketplace. The Franciscans suggested that I see the Sisters on Maria Street, who effectively gave me shelter for one pengo. Hunger drove me to steal and I was ashamed of myself. I went to confession. The priest who heard my confession was moved to tears and he assured me that I had committed no sin, for misery was what had forced me to steal. Later, the Sisters would charge me nothing for lodging."

"In my misery and deprived of any human support I had to go from employer to employer for any additional remuneration and improved conditions. For the same work in a creamery on Baross Street, the Eighth District of Budapest, I was given six pengos and free lunch. The third creamery, also on Baross Street, in effect provided me with a satisfactory livelihood for almost a year. Materially, this job turned out to be the best one I ever held. I was earning eight pengos and working only from 5:30 a.m. to 11:30 a.m. I spent all my free time praying most often at the Church of Perpetual Adoration. I attended the office of Perpetual Adoration regularly. To earn more, I worked in a factory peeling potatoes, that payed two fillers for ten kilos of production. In three hours, I could earn twelve fillers. Further, I was supplementing my income by selling sweets in a small suburb cinema. I did not pay attention to the projections, I would simply take an available seat and meditate on God. The managing lady often borrowed small sums from me and once her indebtedness rose to twenty pengos, she simply fired me.

I also became an occasional grocery bag-carrier at the local market in the Ninth District. Early at 6:00 a.m., I would go to the local market offering my services to the ladies doing their shopping. Once we got back to their house, many times I would be invited to stay for breakfast. This is how I met a middle class family in Budapest and thanks to whom I was able to take classes at the school of nursing on Dohany Street in the Eighth District. However, it would be another ten years before I would put my nursing skills to actual practice at the Hospital of the Franciscan Sisters and at a hospital on Tarogato Avenue, dedicated to patients afflicted with tuberculosis.

I kept my activities at the market even once I had landed a job in a small family factory making brushes. I was paid sixty pengos a month and the family gave me lunch. That provided me with the means to rent a room and I settled down on the first floor at 10 Magdolna Street. My cost was twenty pengos a month and my working hours went from 8:00 a.m. to 4:00 p.m.

Throughout this struggle for survival and daily bread, I wanted to make people aware of the Lord. The necessity to teach about religion was forever a pressing desire in my perceived mission in this life.

By the age of fifteen, I decided to join the nuns. I had in mind the religious order of Perpetual Adoration. The Congregation was founded in Paris by the Countess of Oultremont. I would spend hours silently contemplating the Blessed Sacrament exposed for the faithful in adoration. In so doing, my heart would fill up with the love of God.

One day, I went to the convent to ask the receptionist Sister about how one could be admitted to the order. She replied that I needed a letter of recommendation and handed me a large printed sheet of paper listing what was to be provided to the convent upon admission. Besides the detailed list of needed personal clothing, it was also pointed out that each candidate should provide a certain amount of money according to the individual's capacity to pay.

I was stunned reading the document, it was clear to me that I could never raise such a small fortune. As a result, I concluded that my abject poverty should be the basis for making that project vanish altogether from my mind. Despite that, my desire to become a religious missionary was continually growing deep in my soul. There was no way I could suspect that God had other plans for me."

Autumn 1928. "At the Perpetual Adoration which I often attended, there was an elderly lady whose name I can't recall and in whom I confided about my dream to become a missionary. She gave me the address of the Missionary Sisters on Hermina Street whose mission was to educate orphans and send nuns out on various missions.

When I got there, I asked to speak with the Sister responsible for admissions to the order. It is then that I heard the word Superior for the first time. The receptionist nun led me to the guest room. The Superior came in and invited me to sit down, because I was used to just keep standing up. I told her about my wish to go to missions to make people know about God. After telling her I was an orphan and my earnings, she stood up and said: 'My child, I will tell you why you want to be a nun. You don't have the vocation, you are an orphan without a home and this is motivating you to join a convent.'

That terminated the conversation. I was totally shattered. I told no one about this encounter, except the lady who had given me the address. She listened to my story and said: 'Go to the Mother House on Menesi Avenue and see the Provincial Superior.'

I took the streetcar to Pest across the Franz-Joseph Bridge. Buda and Pest are separated by the Danube River, cutting the city in two parts. I asked to see the Provincial Superior and I had to wait some five minutes, which felt like a painful agonizing moment.

The Provincial Sister spoke to me with such kindness that I felt quite relaxed. I told her everything in total honesty. She took my hand like a mother and said: 'Let us ask the Lord Jesus what His will is and He will tell us what we must do. Everything will be according to His Will.' We went to the chapel but I stayed in the back standing beside the pews. I kept watching the Provincial Sister speaking with the Lord Jesus. She came back, took my hand and we returned to the guest room. We sat down and she placed her hand on mine, took a deep look into my eyes and said: 'My child, the Will of God is different.' I almost fainted. 'Do you know what the Will of God is? He wants something else for you. He will entrust you with another mission. That mission will need to be fulfilled as best you can.'

The Provincial Sister walked me to the door, kissed me on the forehead, blessed me, and I left. God has another plan for me. Following that encounter, it was like everything inside of me was disintegrating. I was quite distraught. My soul was tortured for a week. I wasn't yet aware at the time that this torture was in fact the work of the devil.

I went to Father Matray for confession (he later became my confessor for many years). The darkness of doubt in my heart had dissipated."

1927-1930. "Praying and knowledge were my only desire. It was difficult to express my thirst for study to broaden my knowledge base. Within six months I learned by heart the textbooks of the first two years of the Superior Elementary School. However, since I didn't have the money to write the exams, I continued studying the books of the third and fourth years with the results that I had done the studies without a certificate to show for it.

In the fall of 1929, my life took a significant turn. Since I was gifted with a fine voice and a good ear, I was admitted to the Community Church, Christ the King Choir in Jozsefvaros. The first tenor was Karoly Kindelmann and I was the first soprano. He asked me to marry him and so we did. I was quite young at sixteen while he was thirty years older. His main occupation was as master chimneysweeper, a well-remunerated trade at that time. We got married on May 25, 1930, on Pentecost Sunday. He had a four-room house built on the outskirts of Budapest.

Between 1931 and 1942, we had six children. The Angelus and the Rosary were an integral part of our family daily life. A few years later on April 26, 1946, my husband died. My social status as a widow with six children made it particularly difficult. Following the devastation of the war, I was able to survive with my children only by bartering our possessions. The closets were being emptied and almost all our belongings changed ownership. The nationalization of 1948 brought my family to the edge of ruin. I became a waitress at the military academy working twelve hours a day. The meal leftovers provided food for my family. However, I was fired six months later for political reasons. Somehow, they discovered I was keeping a statue of the Virgin Mary and candles in my home."

November 1950 to May 1951. "I was quite destitute and in a truly desperate situation. Unbearable money problems were forcing me to be more and more distant from the Lord. This got to the point of being completely dazed and wandering aimlessly from street to street and district to district without any definite purpose. It is during one of those aimless walks that I came across the Eötli foundry in the district of Kobanya, which had changed its sign to the new name of Gábor Áron. The benevolent personnel manager saw fit to hire me as the Technical Piecework Supervisor. That literally saved my family from dire starvation. Further, my children were doing craft work at home. My two elder daughters were making stockings with a knitting machine while my sons were making sieve cloth on a weaving loom.

Soon after, the factory was reorganized and along with other employees, I was back on the street looking for a job.

On December 26, 1951, Cecilia, my oldest daughter got married.

While browsing through the classified ads in a local paper I found work in a stove factory. The pay was at starvation level and I had to get back looking for yet another job opportunity. In the fall of 1953, I was hired in a gas equipment factory. My work came to a halt one month before the national uprising of 1956."

Christmas 1955. "Valery, my second daughter got married."

Summer 1957. "My next employer was a dyeing shop, Lazlo Harangi, in the Seventh District. Following that job, I became quite busy in a cooperative doing handicraft work, more specifically making silk scarves."

June 1957. "Maria, my third daughter got married. In June 1958, my son Karoly got married. In 1959, the lodging problem for the four families was resolved."

1960. Material hardships having subsided, Elizabeth Kindelmann registered at the public university to study psychology and astronomy, yet another project like so many others bound to fail dismally.

"On July 13, 1960, three days before the feast of Our Lady of Carmel I had a wonderful spiritual illumination. It lasted three days from dawn to dusk. If I spoke to anyone or conversely anyone spoke to me, it disappeared. This blissful sensation would create a serene peace in my heart. That experience was absolutely overwhelming. It is only several weeks later that I could determine that it represented the silent introduction of the Lord's presence, something that literally defies one's capacity to express intellectually."

Christmas 1961. Jozsef, the second child, but the eldest of three sons, got married at the age of twenty-six. Over the following six years they had three sons. Unfortunately, following the birth of the third child, the mother died of breast cancer. The grandmother on the father's side took charge raising the young orphans.

As Elizabeth was edging towards her fifties, she thought that she would enter a calm and peaceful period, having lived through a difficult life. However, that wasn't to be. The Lord Jesus and His Blessed Mother began speaking to her.

1962. "Prior to receiving messages from Jesus and the Virgin Mary, I received the following inspiration: 'You must be selfless, for we will entrust you with a great mission and you will be up to the task. However, this is only possible if you remain totally selfless, abjuring yourself. That mission can be bestowed upon you only if you also want it out of your free will.'

After a period of serious doubts and torments for my soul, I accepted that the Will of God be done. My soul was so overwhelmed with grace that I was unable to utter a single word."

Very deep inside she could hear their words. She could clearly distinguish the voice of the Lord Jesus from that of the Virgin Mary or the angel.

On April 11, 1985, Elizabeth Kindelmann died at the age of 72, after a long illness that she bore with patience and was comforted by the Sacrament for the Dying. She was buried in Érd-Ófalu, about twenty-four kilometers South West of Budapest, on the banks of the Danube. In 2001, the remains of Elizabeth were transferred to the family crypt located in the Church of the Holy Spirit in Budapest, a place she used to visit every day.

Before she became the instrument of the Lord and the Virgin Mary, she had suffered many trials and tribulations that she overcame with exceptional resilience and courage.

She remained totally unknown to the public for years after her departure.

PRONOUNCEMENTS OF CARDINAL PÉTER ERDÖ

Pronouncements of His Eminence Cardinal Péter Erdö, Primate of Hungary, Archbishop of Eszertom-Budapest, concerning the Association "Flame of Love of the Immaculate Heart of Mary Movement."

1. Quotes taken from his homily given on June 1, 2009 at Máriaremete, on the Feast of Pentecost.

"...I personally believe that the completion in the spring of this year of the revision of the Spiritual Diary of Elizabeth Kindelmann and of the Rule of the Association of Prayer 'Flame of Love' is a sign of the life giving Holy Spirit. This Movement now functions in many dioceses of the world with the approval of the bishops and also prospers here in Hungary, the country of its origin. We have found that it brings an authentic Catholic spirituality and devotion toward the Virgin Mary that is in total conformity with the Catholic faith. May this recognition given in our diocese contribute to the spiritual renewal of our community of believers and of our people. This Saturday (June 6 at 11:00 a.m.) we will solemnly promulgate this approbation in the Church of the Sacred Heart of Jesus, in Kispest."

2. Pronouncement of Cardinal Péter Erdö in the Church of the Sacred Heart of Jesus in Kispet (June 6, 2009) at the Tenth National Conference of The Flame of Love (of Hungary).

Cardinal: "Praised be Jesus Christ"

Faithful: "Let Him be eternally praised. Amen!"

"Thank you very much for the kind words of introduction given by your pastor and by the leaders of the 'Flame of Love Movement'. Certainly the Holy Spirit will work in the Church until the end of time. Frequently, the entire community of the Church accepts inspirations that originally came forth from the heart of a Christian person who was completely dedicated and deeply believing. After examining these impulses, the successors of the apostles eventually welcome them as gifts of God for the whole Church.

For many centuries, the Church institution and charismas were seen as two distinct realities, as if opposed to each other. On the contrary, the Church's history shows that truly authentic charismas (those special Divine Gifts given to believing persons for the benefit of the Church) and the institutional structure established by Christ's Will, are in strict correlation with each other.

The most beautiful example of this is the history of religious orders. The great founder of an order is a truly charismatic person, as was St. Francis and St. Ignatius of Loyola. They were an extraordinary phenomenon in their own age. The Church rejoices so much in the value of their spirituality and of that form of life that it represents, that the Church shouts to the founder, 'Do not go away.' We want this form of life to remain and this charisma to last in the Church. In this way, the religious orders and their charisma become part of the institutional Church.

I will say even more. Christ Himself, His person and His mission, travels along the road of Church history. Jesus said to His disciples, "As the Father sends Me, so I also send you." (Jn 20:21) Therefore, the Church on earth, as a visible community, carries on the mission of Christ. It follows that the Church is not merely an external human organization. Rather, she lives within the world. Also, the Church is not just some invisible, mysterious reality of grace. The same Church is both an invisible reality and a visible society. These are not two distinct things. Sometimes human frailty and human history produce an obstacle. However, at a given moment of history, there appears in the Church something beautiful, a new possibility for the Church. I believe that this is true of the "Flame of Love Movement".

A believing woman, Elizabeth, prays and hears voices in her soul. She perceives that these wonderful voices come from the Virgin Mary. No one asks – since this is not important – what is the nature of the experiences that she describes in her Spiritual Diary. This is not the task which the Church has undertaken in these years of judgment. It has not tried to discern some special happening or supernatural phenomenon. What we have deeply and seriously studied is the content of the message.

While we could not yet officially deal with this matter in Hungary, this spirituality spread to many countries throughout the world and has produced positive fruits. Before making this decision in Budapest, we have spoken with bishops, priests and people from other countries. We have also talked with pastors of souls in our own country. They have testified that the Flame of Love produces fruits in the lives of individual persons and of communities. These testimonies were very positive and we know that a good tree produces good fruits.

After this, we established a commission. Various priests examined the written documents, including the Spiritual Diary itself, the documentation from foundations outside of Hungary and the recognitions that local bishops in many parts of the world (from Brazil to Mexico) have given to this Movement as a private association of the faithful. Just a short time ago, this investigation was finished. As a conclusion, our Church recognizes as authentic, in accord with the Catholic faith, all of the material contained in the Spiritual Diary. Also, this archdiocese considers that the activity, life and rule of this community is in accord with all that characterizes movements of spirituality and authentic communities of the Catholic Church.

At this point, the entire Church receives this charisma as a gift from God. Instead of forgetting about this gift, we ought to place it on the lampstand so that it lights up everything in the house. Having already seen the effects of grace poured out in many other countries, we pray that this charisma shine upon the entire country of Hungary. For this reason, I have asked the senior director of the Archbishop's office to read this decree."

Excerpts from the official Decree

(Read by Canon László Süllei)

Our Lady of Hungary, pray for us!

With these words, I establish in the Archdiocese of Esztergom-Budapest the 'Flame of Love of the Immaculate Heart of Mary Movement', as an ecclesial association of the faithful in Christ. It is a private association enjoying a juridical personality.

At the same time, I also approve for this Archdiocese the Statutes of this Association as accepted in San Paulo, Brazil, on August 15, 2008 and as approved in the Archdiocese of Hermosillo, Mexico, on December 11, 2008.

I ask God to give His abundant blessings for the life and activities of this Association. May your activities serve the spiritual renewal of our homeland!

Budapest, Palm Sunday, 2009

With my blessing as pastor,

Péter Erdö
Cardinal, Primate and Archbishop

FOREWORD

Letter of Cardinal Bernardino Echeverría Ruiz

With great devotion and emotion, we have read this book, Flame of Love, translated [into Spanish] by Father Gabriel Róna, S.J., and presented for approval prior to its publication. We must confess, with due sincerity, that we have found in the pages of this book the most beautiful and profound lessons of spiritual life, so much so that not only we believe it is appropriate to give the requested authorization, but also to recommend this book, which will contribute to deepen the demands of the Christian life.

Flame of Love is a new name given to that immense and eternal love that Mary professes to all human beings, for whom Christ offered His Life and shed His Blood. Likewise, Flame of Love is the name that expresses the love that Mary has for her children. Flame that enlightens, flame that warms up, flame that burns, flame that, while burning in the heart of Mary wants also to burn in the heart of her children, especially on Thursday and Friday, the days chosen for the prayer of reparation.

With this Flame of Love, which is the Immaculate Heart of Mary, we discover the innumerable treasures of the five wounds of Christ, which are not only the refuge of the soul, but also the lesson of the Cross we need to understand when we make the sign of the Cross repeating one of the most simple and profound prayers. By the Holy Cross, He delivers us from our enemies. The Cross is the most powerful weapon to defeat the devil, the evil spirit, who dominates the world more and more every day.

The Flame of Love must be ignited to save all Christians and to save families. It will save fathers and mothers, and will help to sanctify priests. They will have a more effective ministry as they grow more like Christ. This Flame of Love should illumine every moment of the Christian life – the moments of suffering, of illness, of agony and of death. Even after death, this Flame of Love will continue to light the hope of those in Purgatory.

While giving the authorization to publish this beautiful book of love, we express the most fervent wishes that it will reach many and become an instrument drawing all closer to God, unceasingly enlightened by this eternal Flame of Love, which is the Immaculate Heart of Mary.

Bishop Bernardino Echeverría Ruiz
Archbishop of Guayaquil, Ecuador
June 1989

INTRODUCTION

The following text was written in 1989 by Father Gabriel Róna, S.J., and constitutes the introduction to the Spanish version of the Spiritual Diary

The Diary was written by a humble woman named Elizabeth Kindelmann, who lived in Hungary from 1913 to 1985. During most of those years, the Catholic Church lived under a regime of persecution in that country.

The Diary eventually came to Western Europe through a Hungarian religious, Sister Ana Roth. Making herself acquainted with the pressing message of the Most Holy Virgin – which forms the main contents of this Diary, Sister Roth published the most important texts in 16 page booklets, and later 60 pages. These were translated into many languages and became widespread. In 1985, in Germany, the whole Diary was edited in Hungarian.

- Content of the Diary

The Diary begins with a description of a terrible Dark Night. Through the Blessed Virgin's help, Elizabeth returns to Divine Light. She begins to hear the voice of Our Lord Jesus Christ and of the Blessed Virgin Mary by interior locutions, words which she heard clearly in her soul.

The Diary contains not only noble spiritual thoughts, but also a message of great importance, and even more, an initiative of grace by the Most Holy Virgin, of the greatest importance, that may be summed up as follows:

Satan intensifies his efforts to ruin souls. His eternal opponent is the Most Blessed Virgin Mary. We know that "where sin abounds, grace abounds even more" (Rom 5:20). She obtained from the heavenly Father, by the merits of the Passion of her Most Holy Son, an outpouring of graces so great as have not existed since the Word of God became Flesh (the words of our Most Holy Mother). She will blind Satan with the Flame of light and grace which bursts forth from her Immaculate Heart. This Flame must enkindle all the hearts, even those who do not belong to the Catholic Church. She tells us what we must do to collaborate with her in this great endeavor. The Most Blessed Virgin Mary cries, begs, exhorts. She asks us for prayers, sacrifices, holy hours in the family, and fasting to help her in this fight against evil.

Someone could ask, "What is new in this book? Does it add anything to what the Church believes and does to venerate the Most Blessed Virgin?" We respond that these writings put before our eyes the Virgin Mary as she feels and acts in the present hour of our history – her immense spiritual motherhood and that incredible preoccupation with the salvation of her children's souls. Let us listen to her words:

"Take this Flame... It is the Flame of Love of my heart. Ignite your own heart with it and then pass it on to others."

"With this Flame full of graces that I give you from my heart, ignite all the hearts in the entire country. Let this Flame go from heart to heart. This is the miracle becoming the blaze whose dazzling light will blind Satan. This is the fire of love of union which I obtained from the heavenly Father through the merits of the wounds of my Divine Son." (April 13, 1962)

Dear reader, the Diary which you hold in your hands has received the approval of my Order, the Society of Jesus. I have the pleasure to transcribe it here in full:

1- The subject treated is useful.

2- The Spiritual Diary goes beyond the average quality of many autobiographies and testimonies.

3- It agrees with the doctrine of Faith and Tradition, as taught by the Magisterium of the Church, the spiritual authors and the sense of the faithful.

4- It contains nothing that would cause offense to anyone. For these reasons, this work seems worth of publication.

Dear reader, I leave the Spiritual Diary in your hands. May it fill your heart with love for our Blessed Mother and with the burning desire to respond to her urgent pleas.

Father Gabriel Róna, S.J.

* * *

FATHER GABRIEL RÓNA

Father Gabriel Róna, S.J. is a resident of Budapest, Hungary. He used to live in Ecuador for thirty years. Providentially, it was at that time that he received the writings of Elizabeth Kindelmann. They were the heavenly messages speaking of the Flame of Love of the Immaculate Heart of Mary.

Father Róna invested himself heavily to the task of translating these writings from the Hungarian language to Spanish. Thank God for his perseverance and dedication, it became possible for large numbers of people to become acquainted with the messages from the Virgin Mary who has been doing so much for the souls of our time.

Father Róna assumed the role of International Coordinator of the Flame of Love Movement until August 2008 and Spiritual Counselor until April 2012.

ígyekezzetek lángomra!!!

Közel az idő mikor szeretetlángom kifog gyulni és abban a pillanatban is rabbá lesz a sátán, melyet érezteni fogok veletek, hogy bizalmatokat fokozzam és ez nagy erőt ad nektek. Ezt az erőt mindenki fogja érezni kihez csak el jut Mert nem csak a nekem ajánlott országba, hanem az egész föld kerekségén kifog gyulni és az egész világon elfog terjedni még a legmegközelíthetetlenebb helyeken is, mert a sátán előtt nincs megközelíthetetlenség meritsetek erőt és bizalmat én eddig még soha nem látott csodákkal segitem munkátokat mely észrevétlenül szelíden csendben fog terjedni Szentfiam engesztelésére.

Kérem a Szent Atyát, hogy Szivem Szeretetlángjának ünnepét Gyertyaszentelő Boldogasszony napján február 2 án tartsátok.

Nem kívánok külön ünnepet!

Egy alkalommal sok elfoglaltságom miatt reggeltől késő délutánig nem gondoltam [illegible]. Mikor magamra maradtam az Úr Jézus igen panaszos szavakkal így szólt hozzám. Látod mily rossz már megint magad vesződsz ügyes bajos dolgaiddal miért nem hozod hozzám, úgy teszel mintha egyedül is tudnál valamit tenni, tanuld meg már végre, hogy bizalmamba férkőzve a mások számára is elérsz mindent. Szedd össze felebarátaid nehézségeit, a családod zökkenőit és Én elintézek mindent neked. Higgy hatalmamban!! Ha nem hozod Nekem ugye-

Black and white image of page 85 of the Spiritual Diary handwritten by Elizabeth Kindelmann.

Dear readers,

The translation of this edition of the Spiritual Diary wanted to preserve, to the greatest measure possible, the particular style of the author with her own turns of phrase, inversions, repetitions, the originality of the description of her different states of soul, etc.

We therefore did not attempt to improve the syntax into a literary form of English.

The Editor

THE SPIRITUAL DIARY

1961-1981

Chapter One

1961-1962

MY SPIRITUAL STRUGGLES

DARK NIGHT

The Lord is leading us through ways that never end; we alone deviate from them. I too have gone astray. I was a widow, with many worries and exhausting work, which destroyed my spiritual life.

Little by little, I distanced myself from God. The continuous task to survive consumed my soul. After a long battle, my spiritual life faded. Even my faith itself was endangered. This continual fight to exist made me question: "You see, I have always told you, why have a large family?" Because of this questioning, everything that had been sacred and had meaning to me seemed like empty foolishness.

When they fired me from one job, I had to seek others. Then misery became even greater and the temptation much stronger. The evil enemy continually bothered me: "Why are you telling yourself stories? You're well aware that you would have given up the struggle a long time ago, but you do not know what to say to your children. You do not know how to tell them about the things you do not believe in anymore. Remove you mask and you will feel better because your children will soon discover what you are hiding."

Then I came to a dead stop and for a brief moment the clouded face of God appeared before me. A great battle began within me. I implored God. It was beyond description, words fail to express the intensity of the spiritual combat beginning in me. It was long, dreadful and nerve-racking.

I was still attending Holy Mass, but it seemed so empty and tiresome. At the time, I was working two shifts at the factory, even on Sundays. My children went to Sunday Mass in the morning while I went in the evening. It was better that way for they did not see my lack of devotion. At Mass, I was so bored that I kept yawning instead of praying. One day, I just decided to stop going. Little by little, I had the feeling that my conscience had eased into accepting that situation.

One Sunday, I started to do the weekly laundry. I sent the children to Mass and then kept doing the wash all day. When evening came, my children warned me, "Mommy, it is five-thirty." I felt uncomfortable but I kept working. Finally, a few minutes before six, one of my children said, "I beg you, please hurry." That shook me up and I went. However, in my emotional state, I did not know how to talk to God. My thoughts wandered. I thought: "I am foolish. Why do I keep the fast of the Third Order of the Carmel? It is insane. I will leave all of that behind." So, I decided that I would no longer deprive myself of eating meat since my nourishment was of such poor quality. I always observed the fasting without any difficulty but only out of straight routine.

When I returned home, I couldn't recall how I came across the little Psalter of the Blessed Virgin Mary. I opened it and began to pray. In the past, these prayers always rose from my heart towards God, now it seemed to be an empty whisper. I reached for my old book of meditation, but my efforts were in vain… A dark, frigid and mute silence surrounded me from all sides. I burst into tears: "God no longer wants to have anything to do with me."

During one particular week when I was on the morning shift, and the following week on the afternoon shift ending late, I experienced an intense internal anguish. Such thoughts came to me that to reveal them would be blasphemous against God. In the midst of this harsh struggle, the Evil One uttered horrible words within my soul: "I have permitted this to convince you that it is useless to fight on."

This terrible battle lasted about three years until the day when my daughter C said: "Mommy, hurry. Today at 2:00 p.m. is the burial of Doctor B." It was already 1:00 p.m. My heart was so overwhelmed by these words that I got dressed in a great hurry, without thinking, so as not to be late. When I entered the funeral parlor, I began to sob: "He is now happy where he is. He has been a true Carmelite and has led a holy and exemplary life... but me… will I ever get there?" – "Don't cry!" It was his gentle and soft voice that only holy souls would have you hear. "Go back to the Carmel."

The next day was a Sunday, July 16, feast of Our Lady of Mount Carmel, patron saint of our church. I arrived early in the morning and stayed until the evening. I walked with heavy steps towards the confessional. My soul was consumed with a great dryness and I felt no sorrow in my heart. I said my penance mechanically and thought: "All these people are praising our Most Holy Mother." But the idea did not occur to me that I was also praising her. I kept thinking about Brother B because this brought some relief to my soul. It was him who had directed my steps towards the Blessed Virgin, "Go and prostrate before her." I did that but I still couldn't find peace.

When I arrived home late that night, I experienced a strange feeling, as if I had left my wounded and wasted soul at the Carmel. Although I had not eaten the whole day, I felt no hunger. The Evil One took place near me once again. "Why such foolishness? What use is all that to you? Get a good rest and pay no attention to these things."

With a heavy heart, I went into the garden and in the silence of the night I wept abundantly. Under the starlight, in front of the statue of Our Lady of Lourdes in our garden, I began to pray with great fervor.

In the morning, I quickly went to the small chapel where I used to go as a young mother accompanying Brother B at the Table of the Lord. Once again today, it is the empathy I had for him that I felt was driving me there. Along the way, I met people who remembered me as a model young mother. That worried me because I felt that the Evil One was tempting me with vanity. I implored: "Dear heavenly Mother, I do not want to ever be unfaithful to you. Do not abandon me, hold me tight. I do not trust myself. My steps are so unsteady."

During Holy Mass, I was praying the Lord Jesus continually, "Lord, forgive my sins." I did not dare go to the Lord's Table even though the person next to me took me by the arm and said, "Come on, let's go."

THE LORD IS KNOCKING AT THE DOOR

During these days, I received extraordinary graces the Lord reserves only for the weak and the convalescent. A nun kneeling next to me said: "I am kneeling by your side because I also want to be a saint." Oh, I knew she perceived the Lord's presence in me.

Many times I was walking around with teary eyes. My love for the Lord Jesus filled my eyes with tears of repentance. I did not want to turn my eyes towards the world ever again. I sought only silence so I could continually hear the Lord's voice, because from that day on, He was the One speaking to me. How simple were these intimate conversations!

I'VE BEEN WAITING FOR YOU FOR SUCH A LONG TIME

I begged Him to allow me to immerse myself in the ocean of His graces. I insistently asked the same graces for my children and I asked Him to draw them near to His side. He promised to grant that request if I kept asking Him with perseverance.

While I was adoring Him, immersed in a deep devotion, the demon said: "Do you think that He can do this? If He had the power, He would do it because that would be pleasing to Him."

What a horrible blow! My heart sank... Then Our Lord's Sacred Face appeared before my spiritual eyes. He said:

Jesus: "Look at My disfigured Face and My tortured Sacred Body. Didn't I suffer to save souls? Believe in Me and adore Me."

At that very moment, I made acts of faith, hope and charity begging Him to never allow that I be separated from Him. Let Him chain me to His Sacred Feet so I would always be united to Him. Thus I would always feel sheltered. He then asked me to renounce myself because I tend to be distracted and worldly.

Jesus: "I do not force you. You have your free will; only if you want it."

I tried with all my strength. Afterward, everything fell into place drawing me closer to Him. He kept urging me.

Jesus: "I want to give you great graces, but you must renounce yourself completely."

These were harsh words for my reason. This is why I asked Him, "Am I capable of doing this?"

Jesus: "You must only will it; leave the rest up to Me."

All this gave rise to new struggles, but the Lord enlightened my mind and guided me step by step. I had to make these sacrifices within my family responsibilities.

Since my youngest child lived with me, the meaning and importance of these sacrifices were not clear to me. In my house, I had to tighten still further to make room for my children who based their families. This was very difficult. I had a four bedroom home with modern conveniences. I still had the large dining room at my disposal. Nevertheless, I gave it up also even though it came at a great cost.

As I gave up the dining room, both happy and sad memories invaded my thoughts. Many familiar memories came to mind. There were the Christmas nights, the weddings and the baptisms of the grandchildren. I remembered the poor food in my years of need. For several years, we had only a piece of bread smeared with butter for breakfast, or vegetables without sauce. For years, the poor vegetable platter remained very plain, but I took care to place a nice shiny apple next to each plate. I made the table with great care so the children would not think we were poor. I had enjoyed being with them and was always preoccupied with their food. The dining room was difficult to give up because it was a part of my heart. I moved to the children's room, thinking I would have a place filled with memories and my soul would be at peace. I would be changing my room for the last time.

Shortly before this, however, my youngest boy got married. Now, I had to help him get a bedroom. So, I gave up the children's room. I felt that the Lord was asking for this sacrifice, so I would be totally poor. Many memories came to mind – the nights that I spent at the bed of a sick child, the joyous moments, the prayers at night and the intimate family readings. When I thought of these, I experienced great pain, like something you love being ripped from your heart.

And the Lord kept urging me.

RENOUNCE YOURSELF

Jesus: "Renounce yourself completely."

So that nothing would tie me to this world, I gave away everything to my children. Later on, I felt that I had done the right thing. Now, I had nowhere to rest my head peacefully. Our Lord kept urging me.

Jesus: "Renounce yourself."

Everything around me seemed dark and sad. What can I do with my life? The Evil One came with his big smile: "Don't be discouraged. You are not so old. Take it easy. Dress well. Enjoy yourself. And if you have a chance, get married! This would not be shameful. You will have a home and will belong to someone. Your conscience will be at peace because you have completed your work as a mother."

The blood rushed to my face because I truly felt abandoned. The next morning, I prostrated myself before the altar of the Lord. "Lord, You know that I chained myself to Your Sacred Feet and I do not want to move from there. Lord, why have You left me alone?"

Jesus: "For the good of your soul. In the hours of My agony, I was alone. Does this small sacrifice seem difficult for you? Accept all that is still to come."

After this, I placed my daughter C in charge of the house: "From now on, you will be the little owner of this house and I will not cook any more." She was surprised and asked what I would do. "Whatever you ask, I will do and I will eat whatever you give to me." – "Mother," she said, "you are acting like a hermit."

At that moment, my youngest daughter M, the mother of two small children, came in. She said: "I have to look for work because one salary is not enough" (her husband is a teacher). I decided to help her. I gave up my good paying work at the cooperative (which consisted of painting plastics), so that she did not have to leave the two small children alone in the house. This was my final sacrifice. All of this happened in just a few days. I made these sacrifices because the Lord urged me.

Jesus: "Your will is free. I do not force you. You must accept also. The only thing of value in My eyes is for you to entrust yourself to Me with complete confidence. Do you not believe that I can repay you? What great riches lie in store for you!"

AT THE SCHOOL OF THE DIVINE MASTER

I completed all these urgent sacrifices on Saturday, February 10, 1962. The following day was the feast of Our Lady of Lourdes. Early in the afternoon, my soul longed for silence, so I fled the noise of family life. Now, I had no home and the Lord Jesus desired this.

AT THE CHURCH

On this beautiful Sunday, a large crowd came from the Máriaremete Sanctuary (Hermitage of Mary Sanctuary) to visit our church dedicated to the Holy Spirit. There, I was kneeling in the midst of the crowd. Following a brief moment of adoration, I said to the Lord: "O Jesus, You have me here. I have separated myself completely from the world, just as You wanted, so that absolutely nothing can come between us. Do I please You? O my God, how miserable I am! How much these sacrifices have cost me! Do You know how humiliating it is to live this way?" Then I heard the Lord's voice in me.

Jesus: "You must live this way from now on, in the greatest humiliation."

Hearing these words, my soul was plunged into His eternal thoughts. I asked, "Do You now accept me?" The Lord did not answer but my soul experienced a great silence. Bowing my head, I was only looking at Him. What will He say to me? I felt this self-surrender had moved me closer to the Lord. Nothing disturbed the silence in my soul. While kneeling, my soul was filled with profound repentance and gratitude towards Him. I awaited His words more than ever. After a long moment, I broke the silence: "Are You happy, dear Jesus, about all these devout souls who have come to You?" He replied in a sad tone of voice:

Jesus: "Yes, but they are in such a hurry. They do not give Me time to grant them My graces."

I understood and how I would have loved to console Him. "O sweet Jesus, I live for You, I die for You, I am Yours forever." While attempting to console Him in His deep sadness, I remembered the legend of the little bird that tried to remove the thorns from the Sacred Head of Christ. While trying to do so, the bird's breast became red with the Precious Blood of the Lord.

After being there for a long time, I was getting cold. I wanted to go home. Then I heard His voice deep within my soul.

Jesus: "Do not go yet."

I remained. A few minutes after, I heard a sweet voice in the silence of my soul.

MESSAGE OF THE MOTHER OF GOD

Mary: "My dear little Carmelite!"

When I heard her voice, a great river of repentance flooded my soul. When I heard this sweet voice two more times, tears of sorrow for my sins flowed out. Then the Blessed Virgin spoke in my soul, as if holding back her tears.

Mary: "Adore my Divine Son and make reparation. He is so often offended."

I pondered these words. They could not come from the Evil One since he would not say, "Adore and make reparation." However, I experienced unrest in my soul, "How could I bring this about?" Although I stayed a little longer in the church to get my thoughts in order, darkness covered my mind. On my way home, I asked the Blessed Virgin: "Heavenly Mother, if you are the one asking me to do this, then direct my steps toward your Divine Son."

The next day, this thought stayed in my mind. During Holy Mass, I asked fervently: "Heavenly Mother, what do I have to do? You will be at my side, won't you? I am so small and weak without you." After Holy Mass, I felt a strong impulse to get the key to the house of the Lord to be able to get in freely. I asked the Sister sacristan, telling her my situation at home. She said that she needed the priest's permission. Two days later, she gave me the good news. I got the key I had asked for. The same day, I went to open the church door with my heart beating fiercely. I felt that the Lord was sharing His house with me, giving me a replacement for my own house. How I loved this church! As I entered the side door, I stopped at the altar of the Blessed Virgin, patron saint of the Hungarian people. I greeted her: "Hail Mary, my sweet Mother, I humbly implore you, keep me under your special protection. I am your unfaithful Carmelite daughter. I know I am not worthy of that title, even if I were to labor for centuries to gain it. Come, Mother, and lead me to your Divine Son."

THE FIRST HOLY HOUR

Being alone in the big church, I went to Jesus' feet and asked, "Are we not alone?"

Jesus: "Unfortunately."

I heard His sad voice in my soul.

Jesus: "Make great efforts so we can become many."

What gratitude and sorrow broke out in my heart! "O sweet Savior, how blindly I have walked until I came to You. Now that You have removed the external hardness of my soul, I feel Your graces flooding me. O my Jesus, You remove my great faults by the blows of Your chisel. This hurts me but it does not matter. I ask only that You recognize in me the work of Your hand when I come before You after death.

My beloved Jesus, I want to repent of my sins and to love You more than any repentant sinner. My beloved Jesus, in the future, I ask that not one day goes by without my love causing me tears of repentance. Humble me, Lord Jesus, every moment of my life, so I always see myself as poor and sinful.

O my Lord Jesus, my heart shudders when I think that I can live with You on this earth and then, after my death, be separated from You for a short time because of my sins. Tell me, O sweet Jesus, what will I do with my innumerable sins?"

An unimaginable anguish came over me. I implored the Lord. He made me feel that my sins would be taken away in His merciful love. I would have remained longer at the Lord's feet if the Sister sacristan did not tell me that the doors closed at 7:30 p.m. At that time, I did not yet have a key. Since I could not separate myself from the Lord Jesus, I asked Him to accompany me. I sensed the Lord's presence as I went home by a longer route that was quieter. We spoke no words. His presence was so strong that I wanted to prostrate in the street.

After He gave me such a big house, I visited Him every night with a humble and repentant heart, moved by gratitude. In accordance with the Blessed Virgin's desire, I adored Him and made reparation. What joy! He is always there and waiting for me. It is impossible to describe those intimate hours.

The year 1961 went by in the midst of these conversations that I did not then put in writing. I wrote them only after the Lord asked me. When the beloved Savior holds a brief conversation with me, I write it word for word. During the hours of adoration, the ideas frequently went directly to my intellect and I could not express them. On one occasion, He promised me an eternal refuge.

Jesus: "You also, My little Carmelite, assure Me of an eternal refuge. You feel, do you not, how much the two of us belong to each other? Your love must never rest."

One time, He asked me to pray on Monday night for priests in Purgatory.

One day, I visited a friend's house which had a chapel. When I finished, I did not visit the chapel to say goodbye. In a sweet tone, He reproached me my indelicacy towards Him. I told Him: "Forgive me, my beloved Jesus. Did I not ask You to destroy the rough features of my soul?" He answered with a mild voice:

Jesus: "My little daughter, you must love Me night and day."

One time, I asked Him to allow me to feel His glorious and majestic presence. He said:

Jesus: "My little one, do not ask this for yourself. I give it to those for whom you have made a sacrifice or have offered prayers."

"Forgive me, my Jesus, You see how selfish I am." He said:

Jesus: "My daughter, I know your imperfection and your sinfulness, but this must not lessen your future efforts. This is a greater motive to abandon yourself and to rely on My love."

Chapter two

1962

CONVERSION OF SINNERS

March 4 to 7, 1962

I do not know what happened in the country. During these days, almost every five minutes, the Lord urged me to kneel down and offer Him reparation.

The following happened in the first week of March. During my housework, I was continually overwhelmed by His presence. I asked Him if I could participate to the greatest degree possible in His work of Salvation. Then He began to speak to me.

Jesus: "Ask for abundant graces. The more you ask, the more you will receive. Ask for others and do not fear that you ask for too much! I am happy when I give more. Even your desires make Me happy. Accept faithfully the sacrifices that I ask of you for My Cause. Many ask repeatedly to share in My works, but when they must accept a sacrifice from My own hands, they are afraid of Me.

Do not deny Me your sufferings, and help for the conversion of sinners. If you act this way, you will have a great reward. A time will come when you do not just hear My voice quietly in your soul, you will hear it aloud and it will bless you.

My daughter, you will have to suffer much. I will give you no consolation that will tie you to the earth, but I will always give you My fortifying grace. Also, the power of the Holy Spirit will be with you. You must get rid of all that entices you to evil, and live according to My pleasure. I can help you to find the right path. Immerse yourself in My teaching."

"In spite of all my efforts, O Lord, I see no progress in myself."

Jesus: "Do not worry! Begin anew each day. Our Mother will help you, ask everything from her. She knows how to please Me."

Many times, Jesus said to me:

Jesus: "My daughter, renounce yourself. I keep insisting on this because you can only share in My work of Redemption if you live united with Me at every moment. There must be no interruption...

Offer this to My Father at all times, without any interruption, also for those who have consecrated their lives to Me, yet live more for the world than for My work of Redemption. They do not think about their vocation. Do penance for your sins and for theirs also. I desire so much to cleanse them from their sins. If only they would come to Me! Do not spare yourself, My little one. Know no limit. Do not separate yourself from My work of Redemption for even one moment, because if you did, I should feel that the love you have for Me has lessened. I desire ardently your love. May you always feel what I feel!"

The Lord had me contact a person whom I had not seen for fifteen years. Because my personality is very reserved, the Lord gave me great confidence. I spoke to her about the state of my soul and my great darkness. After the conversation that took place in the chapel, the Sister (she was a religious Sister) said, "This might be autosuggestion." This upset me greatly. Terrible thoughts attacked me and the lack of faith darkened my understanding. I thought that all my experiences were an illusion. Perhaps the Evil One, disguised as an angel of light, wanted to disturb the peace which I had gained at such a great cost.

EVERY BEGINNING IS DIFFICULT

I spent the whole day filled with anxieties. At night, as I went to adore the Lord, I thought in the midst of my uncertainty: "My God, what is going on with me? Where have I allowed myself to be led? What is true? What is now in me or what was there before?"

Whoever has not suffered this temptation can hardly understand this uncertainty. After a long period of silence, this terrible darkness began to clear away. The Evil One was no longer confusing me and my soul was experiencing relief.

The next day, when I kneeled to receive the Lord in Holy Communion, I had totally recovered my peace. While doing my housework, I was immersed in the Lord. While doing my wash, I adored Him and thought: "How sinful I am. Why am I so powerless to help Him?" While I was lost in His eternal thoughts, the Lord began to speak in my soul.

FAST ON BREAD AND WATER FOR TWELVE PRIESTS

Jesus: "Give yourself completely to Me, My little Carmelite. Only in this way can you offer Me sacrifice. I ask something great from you. Listen and do not fear. Be humble and little, only in this way can you fulfill My task. Every Thursday and Friday, fast on bread and water and offer this for twelve priests. On both days, spend four hours in My Divine Presence and make reparation for the many offenses that I have received. On Fridays, from noon to 3:00 p.m., adore My Sacred Body and My Precious Blood that I shed for the sins of all the world. Keep the Friday fast until the hour when My Sacred Body was lowered from the Cross. Accepting this sacrifice will gain extraordinary graces. Daughter, do what I ask!"

He pleaded so much.

Jesus: "Commit yourself to this fast for twelve weeks for the twelve priests who will best carry out My plans. By special graces, I want to make them worthy. Do it, My little one, in this way you will also become the favorite of My Heart. You will know who should take My petition to these twelve priests. They must do the same thing that I asked of you, that is, to make reparation and to be immersed in My Sacred Passion. My little one, these twelve priestly souls are the best in the country."

He asked that we keep this fast for twelve weeks.

Jesus: "My little one, I am going to allow you to suffer a great spiritual dryness. Different temptations will torment you. Do not fear because My grace will always be with you. Have total confidence in Me, this is the key to My Heart. Put aside your doubts. The Holy Spirit whom you invoke frequently will take possession of your soul through Our Mother, His favorite.

I know that you share with Me a thirst for souls. My Heart rejoices when you tell Me that you have an unquenchable thirst for Me. I feel the same for you and for all the souls whom I have filled with My graces. If only they could experience My Soul's consuming thirst for them. I beg you for your love. Daughter, you, at least, do not abandon Me. With each beat of your heart, repent of your sins. Make reparation and console Me. If your love decreases, turn to our heavenly Mother and she will fill your heart with abundant love for Me. I am grateful to you because your heart suffers with Me, beats in Me. Never tire of contemplating My Sacred Wounds, from which you will always draw strength. Offer yourself to the Eternal Father. Abide within the Most Holy Trinity.[2]

In temptations, flee under the mantle of Our Mother. She will defend you from the Evil One who will continually trouble you. I will be with you if you stay close to Me. No one and nothing will snatch you from Me.

My little one, do not be overwhelmed. Live hidden in great humility. Except for a few persons, no one should know about you. You will gain merits by your sufferings. These you must offer in union with Me to the Eternal Father for the souls consecrated to Me. May your humility be so great that you radiate goodness and love to all whom you meet.

My little one, we will always be together. Always ask Our Mother to protect you in a hidden humility. Learn to speak to your neighbors so your words lead them to Me. You must seek Me and receive love from Me. Make your sacrifices without getting discouraged, because they are needed to gain the goal. The Eternal Father knows how He created you. He knows that you are intense, forceful and irritable, and you must be transformed according to My Heart. In the future, use your intensity only against evil. Do not

2. Although these words were said in the singular, they apply to all.

be dejected. Seek what is above. Look to Me with confidence and seek abundant graces. Be a burning sacrifice among your family. You must especially make the small, insignificant sacrifices. Come to Me as I am suffering, in total abandonment. Do not be upset that you can only do small things. Just continue to be the little one. Dissolve yourself in Me like a drop of water in wine."

RENOUNCE YOURSELF - INSISTENCE OF JESUS

April 8, 1962

The Lord asked me not to mix up the holy hours with His creatures.

Jesus: "Do not seek yourself! I have constantly said that I want you entirely for Myself. Renounce yourself. Nothing must exist between you and I."

"Lord," I said, "I am only a beginner."

Jesus: "Do not grow discouraged, daughter, because you must begin somewhere. Remember as a young girl, you had a great desire to study but you never had the opportunity. I am the One who did not permit this. I placed all the obstacles in your path. Because I had plans for you, I wanted you to be totally ignorant. You were to mature for My goal."

"O Lord, how many times You have sent me life-giving rays of Your graces. I avoided You and went by other paths."

Jesus: "Do you remember a few months ago? You wanted to register in the public high school. I opposed this because I wanted you in My school. Now you rejoice and are a happy student. I am the Master, learn from Me. I will spare no effort. I will dedicate Myself to you from morning until night."

"Lord," I answered, "The problem is that I understand very little."

Jesus: "That is true, daughter."

He showed me the many times that I had offended Him. For example, I was in a place where there was a chapel. I said goodbye to everyone but Him. Also, when I genuflect, I should think of Him with much more love.

Jesus: "I feel badly when you do not do these things."

Remembering these faults, my eyes filled with tears of repentance.

GO TO MY MOTHER

Jesus: "I repeat, My little one, you must change so you become like I want you to be. I will help you to follow the right road but you must understand My teachings and do the homework that I assign you. Draw close to My Mother, she will help you."

"O Lord, I love her very much. She was the one who invited me to adore her Most Holy Son and to offer Him reparation. Oh, how deeply moved my heart was when I heard her voice. Her cry awakened profound repentance in me."

Jesus: "That first meeting was the great step, My little one, when My Mother entrusted you to Me in a special way. Since then, My little one, you have been flying like an arrow towards Me. In your flight, never turn to look back at earth so that the world's noise does not bother you."

I HAVE BEEN WAITING FOR YOU

Jesus: "Since your birth I have awaited you and all the souls."

"My Lord, never let go of me!"

Jesus: "You let go of Me. I did not let go of you."

"O my Jesus, that is why I have been so unhappy and without learning. Educate me, my Master."

Jesus: "My daughter, renounce your will. I ask this so many times because you can only share in My work of Redemption if you live united with Me totally and without interruption at every moment.

My little Carmelite, remember when you became a widow and your children were growing up, you would ask each one to help you for just an hour. What a great help that would have been for you. How sad you were when they excused themselves with every kind of pretext. You did your tasks alone and abandoned.

Think of how many children I have, My daughter. How delightful it would be if each one helped Me only for one hour. In those moments, My thoughts go in a special way towards those souls consecrated to Me. Those are the chosen ones of My Heart. Even though they are chosen, they do not want to be intimately united with Me. They are distracted by their worldly concerns. Immerse yourself in Me. Take their place, not just for one hour but continuously. Do not ask Me what to do. Be creative! Take advantage of every opportunity to quench My thirst with your desire to save souls."

"O Lord, I desire You with an insatiable thirst. I want to love You with all my strength. I want to love You for all who are not close to You."

During this conversation, I received great graces from the Lord.

"O God, what have You done with me? Why do I no longer value earth? My eyes see nothing. My ears do not perceive the world's voice. My heart beats only in You and for You. My lips desire only to praise You. I want to bless You but I cannot find words worthy of You.

I look upon You with my eyes closed and my lips mute. I contemplate the incredible suffering You endured for me, poor sinner. I cannot even understand what You did for me. Why me? Are there not so many pure souls that are worthy of You?"

Jesus: "My daughter, I choose souls to bring about My work of Redemption from among the worst sinners. If they accept, I fill them with special graces.

Whoever feels with Me and lives for Me, with My boundless love, I snatch from the world just as I have done for you. My suffering is unspeakable, My little Carmelite. How good it is to feel that you are united with Me and that you feel My love."

"O Lord, my will is Yours. Do Your work in me."

BRING SINNERS TO ME

Jesus: "My daughter, be faithful with all your strength in bringing sinners to Me. Give no thought to anything else. Always look into My eyes and see My sorrow for souls.

With your entire soul, desire that My consecrated souls always look upon Me and are never distracted by worldly things. They must see My sorrowful eyes and be immersed in Me. If they look into My eyes with a repentant heart, I will make them holier with the rays of My grace. By plunging them into the love of My Heart, I will give them new birth provided they trust Me fully.

My daughter, because you have given Me refuge so I can rest in your soul, I will radiate My love to you. Accept this as a great honor, because by this means you are honoring Me. Never deprive Me of this refuge. This depends only on you. I have gone to the extreme limits of My love.

You know how pleased I am when you prostrate before Me and say that you are sorry for your sins as no sinner has ever been sorry, and that you want to love Me more than all converted sinners. By your desires, My little Carmelite, you have entered entirely into My Heart. Your simple words have moved My merciful Heart to infinite compassion.

You see, to do this, you did not need great studies! What happiness your profound and sincere repentance has also gained for the heavenly Father. Continue to repent every moment of your life. My daughter, fulfill all your responsibilities with an untiring persistence to save souls. Let this be your school. The Holy Spirit will work to correct your natural tendency to evil and lead you to salvation. Do you know that My Kingdom suffers violence? Your constant failures do not destroy your spirit; instead, they ensure your humility. Meditate frequently on this until you perfectly understand it, because today is the day of our special union by which I fill you with graces to strengthen you in an extraordinary way.

A great battle awaits you, but you will conquer in the sign of the Cross. Do not be distracted when you make the sign of the Cross. Think about the Three Divine Persons. Make public all that I tell you now: Make the sign of the Cross five times while thinking of My Sacred Wounds. Always look at My eyes bathed in blood from so many blows that I received even from you."

"O Lord, do not continue because my heart is breaking."

Jesus: "Feel sorry for Me."

PERSEVERE WITH ME

April 10, 1962

Jesus: "Do not worry, My dear little Carmelite. Do not think, 'How will I make the Cause prevail?' I work with chosen souls. Be satisfied with being good. Do you know how to be a good Carmelite? Live humbly. Live the hidden contemplative life in union with Me. Refrain your tongue and be on guard not to say unneeded words.

My love for you knows no limits, My little Carmelite. Do you know how happy I am when you accept the sacrifices I offer you? (He said this with great tenderness.) Persevere with Me! By this, you make Me happy. Desire many souls for Me so I can distribute My graces to them."

While I was prostrate before Him, He said:

Jesus: "Do you know that I was awaiting you with a sad heart? You see how lonely I am! You are the only one here. If you did not come, I would be an orphan. You were an orphan, My little one, and you know how bitter it is."

He kept talking and instructing me.

Jesus: "I always tell you not to worry that you can give Me only little things. I say again, always remain little. Do you know what we are going to do? You will give Me the little pieces of a mosaic which you collect throughout the day. I will arrange these pieces according to their color and shape. When all is finished, you will marvel to see the work of art that I created. But I cannot be an artist unless you gather the pieces. Without you, I cannot bring about My work of art."

Jesus said all of this with a pleading voice.

WEEKLY AGENDA

One day, He said:

Jesus: "My daughter, I'm now going to specify how each day of the week should be allocated. If you remember, I began to speak about this previously. However, I put this off until today to include more things in your schedule.

Come, if you have time. If you have plenty of it, tell Me. The decision is yours. I respect your free will completely. You flatter Me if you abandon it spontaneously to Me.

Monday - The Day of the Holy Souls

Let all your actions be done with the purpose of helping them. In union with Me, desire that these souls contemplate My Face as early as possible. Offer for them the strict fast as well as prayers during a part of the night.

I do not ask this strict fast and prayer just from you. Make public these requests jointly with other messages from My Heart.

Anyone fasting on bread and water on Monday will free each time the soul of a priest from the place of suffering.[3]

Whoever practices this will receive the grace of being liberated from the place of suffering within eight days after their death.

Our Mother herself is asking for this. Her appeal to her Flame of Love obliges Me to fulfill her request."

Editor's Note – This supposes that the person has died in the grace of God. In a private conversation, Elizabeth said: "In different places in the Diary it speaks of freeing the souls. Each time I would have had to write 'If they had died in the grace of God.' This fact appeared so evident to me that it seemed superfluous."

Tuesday - Offer this Day for the Family

"Make spiritual communions for each member of the family. Offer each person, one by one, to our dear Mother. She will take

3. Purgatory.

them under her protection. You will also offer that evening vigil for them."

Elizabeth: "Lord, I usually sleep deeply. What if I cannot wake up to keep watch?"

Jesus: "I will help you with that as well. If there's anything too difficult for you, confidently tell Our Mother. She also spent many nights in prayer vigils. My daughter, you must be responsible for your family leading them to Me, each in his own particular way. Ask for My graces on their behalf unceasingly. We will work together and I cannot do without your support. Your most worthy patron is Saint Joseph. Do not forget him, invoke him every day. He will gladly help making our Cause a success.

Wednesday - A Day for Priestly Vocations

Ask Me for many young men with a fervent heart. You will get as many as requested because the desire lies in the soul of many young men but there is no one helping them to realize their goal. Do not be overwhelmed. Through the prayers of the night vigil, you can obtain abundant graces for them.

Thursday - Reparation to the Blessed Sacrament

On that day, you will spend hours in My Sacred Presence. Adore Me with great fervor making reparation for the many offenses inflicted upon Me. Offer the strict fast for the twelve priestly souls. Offer also the nocturnal vigil for them. Immerse yourself into My sorrowful agony as I was sweating blood. You will draw great spiritual strength from it.

Friday - The Day of My Passion

With all the love of your heart, immerse yourself in My sorrowful Passion. When you arise in the morning, recall what was awaiting Me the entire day after the terrible torments of that night.

While at work, contemplate the Way of the Cross and consider that I did not have any moment of rest. Totally exhausted, I was forced to climb the mount of Calvary. There is much to contemplate. I went to the limit, and I tell you, you cannot go to excess in doing something for Me.

From noon until 3:00 p.m., adore My Sacred Wounds. Hopefully you can keep fasting until the time My Sacred Body was taken down from the Cross. Then, on that day, offer the night prayer for the twelve priests. If you accept to sacrifice yourself, My daughter, you will receive an even greater abundance of graces.

Saturday - The Day of Our Mother

On this day, venerate Our Mother in a special way with a very particular tenderness. As you are well aware, she is the Mother of all graces. Wish that she be venerated on earth as she is venerated in Heaven by the multitude of angels and saints. Seek for agonizing priests the grace of a holy death. Offer every moment of the day for that purpose. What a great reward you will receive! In Heaven, priestly souls will intercede for you and the Most Holy Virgin will be waiting for your soul at the hour of your death. Offer the night vigil for this intention also."

Sunday

For this day, the loveable Redeemer gives no specific directions.

(This conversation took place approximately in July, but no specific date.)

FIRST COMMUNICATION OF THE BLESSED VIRGIN

April 13, 1962 - Good Friday

On that day, according to the desire of the Lord Jesus, I adored Him and made reparation from noon until three in the afternoon. I asked the Blessed Virgin to engrave the Holy Wounds of her Divine Son in my heart and urged her to have more compassion for us. My tears flowed abundantly as I could feel the indescribable pain and the sobs of the Mother of Sorrows deep in my heart.

MESSAGE OF THE MOTHER OF GOD ABOUT THE FLAME OF LOVE

Sobbing, she said to me:

Mary: "My little Carmelite, so many sins are committed in this country. Help me. Let us save the country. I place a beam of light in your hands; it is the Flame of Love of my heart. Add your love to this Flame and pass it on to others, my little one."

"My Mother, why do you not work miracles like you did at Fatima so people may believe in you?"

Mary: "The greater the miracles, my little one, the fewer those who believed in me. I asked for the First Saturdays and they never heeded my request. I am your gentle and understanding Mother. United with you, I will save you. King Saint Stephen consecrated your country to me and I promised him that I would gather his intercession and that of the other Hungarian saints into my heart.

I would like to place in your hands a new instrument, which I want you to accept and appreciate the importance of, because my heart looks upon my country with great affliction. The twelve priests whom my Divine Son chose will be the most worthy to fulfill my petition.

Take this Flame, my daughter, you are the first one I am handing it to. It is the Flame of Love of my heart. Ignite your own heart with it and then pass it on to others."

The Blessed Virgin was sobbing so much that I could barely hear what she was saying. I asked her what I had to do. On behalf of the entire country, I promised her everything, so I could relieve her pain because my own heart was on the verge of shattering.

FAMILY HOLY HOUR

Mary: "On Thursday and Friday, I ask you, my daughter, to offer a very special reparation to my Divine Son. This will be an hour for the family to make reparation. Begin this hour with a spiritual reading, followed by the Rosary or other prayers in an atmosphere of recollection and fervor.

Let there be at least two or three, because my Divine Son is present where two or three are gathered. Start by making the sign of the Cross five times offering yourselves to the Eternal Father through the wounds of my Divine Son. Do the same at the conclusion. Sign yourselves this way when you get up and when you go to bed, and during the day. This will bring you closer to the Eternal Father through my Divine Son, filling your heart with graces."

THE MIRACLE OF THE FLAME OF LOVE

Mary: "With this Flame full of graces that I give you from my heart, ignite all the hearts in the entire country. Let this Flame go from heart to heart. This is the miracle becoming the blaze whose dazzling light will blind Satan. This is the fire of love of union which I obtained from the heavenly Father through the merits of the wounds of my Divine Son."

When I heard this, I began to make excuses, saying: "I am not worthy... how can I accomplish this?" After a few days, the Blessed Virgin promised she would help me with her maternal love to make the sacrifices which her Son wanted.

Mary: "I will be with you, my little Carmelite, and I take you into my heart."

"O my heavenly Mother, Blessed Virgin Mary, I wanted to ask you something."

She already knew my question and responded:

Mary: "Take the petition of my Divine Son to Father E."

The Blessed Virgin called him her beloved son. While she was speaking, I understood, by a marvelous grace, how the will of the Blessed Virgin is united with that of the Eternal Father, her Divine Son, and the Holy Spirit.

The Most Blessed Virgin promised that she would be with us so that the tiny flame would spread like wildfire.

A SUBLIME MISSION: TO SPREAD THE FLAME OF LOVE

April 15, 1962

Mary: "My little Carmelite, I invite those living in the house of the Carmelite Fathers. They accomplish missionary work throughout the country with great devotion and love. Let them be the first to receive the Flame of Love and spread it. Their mission is sublime and moving. Don't hesitate, start working as soon as possible.

My Flame of Love will go forth from the Carmel. They are the ones who honor me the most, or rather, they are the ones most called to honor me. Take two little candles. Light up your little candle first, and then the other one from it, then pass it on to my beloved son who will spread it among my twelve most devout souls."

(Later, I asked the Blessed Virgin whether the twelve priests were all Carmelites. She said, "No.")

Mary: "I will be with all of you and I will overwhelm you with very special graces. After the twelve priests have come together, let this devotion begin simultaneously in twelve churches dedicated to me. In this ceremony, pass the lighted candle from one to another. Take the candle home and begin the family prayer in the same way. If your fervor does not fail, I will be consoled."

ALL MUST TAKE PART

April 17, 1962 - Petition for the priests

The loving Savior told me many things. He asked that the spiritual combat not be abandoned because an endless battle increases grace.

Jesus: "Ask My sons (the priests) to direct souls towards My beloved Mother. They should never give a homily without exhorting the faithful to have a profound devotion for her. We are the land of the Great Lady of the Hungarian people. They must bring this truth continually before the eyes of the faithful for this is the wish of our Great Lady.

And you, My daughter, with all your strength and all the sacrifices of your life, ceaselessly desire the coming of My Kingdom, and that My Mother's Flame of Love be lit and spread through little sparks of love."

One time, prostrated before the Lord Jesus, I lamented how much time I had wasted in my life. He said:

Jesus: "The increase in your charity compensates for the wasted moments you let slip by. As your love increases, My graces in you will also increase in great measure."

Then He spoke at length.

Jesus: "My daughter, what I am about to say to you is not just for you. Share it with all My beloved children. Assimilate the essence of My words with the thoughts from your heart. You must shake lukewarm souls out of the indifference which drowns them. First, make them realize that they must live in intimate union with Me; especially those who despite receiving Me frequently in their souls avoid getting closer to Me. My effort to take them to a deeper spiritual level is wasted if they turn their backs on Me and abandon Me.

During your daily tasks, you do not even think of Me within your souls. This hurts Me and I suffer so much. When you say: 'Lord, I am not worthy that You enter my house…' do not turn your back on Me, make yourselves worthy and dispose your hearts for constant union with Me. Do it also during the day by means of a fervent ejaculatory prayer or a loving glance. I yearn greatly for you! Yet, so few come to Me. At least for those who do, be totally abandoned and recollected. Develop trust in your heart for Me. What hurts Me the most is that you do not trust Me. It is in vain that you have faith, without trust you cannot grow closer to Me. Ask My sons to arouse courage in the souls. Tell them how much those who fight are pleasing Me. Let them not give up the fight because My graces increase within you through a continuous fight. Direct them to My sweet Mother.

Wish Me many souls, My little one. This is the objective of your life; keep it always before your eyes. For this reason I chose you and snatched you from the world. I appreciate that you, at least, have compassion for Me, you understand Me and console Me in My immense sorrow."

While He said this, His unlimited sorrow poured into my heart. "My Lord Jesus, I am a miserable sinner." He continued:

Jesus: "My daughter, your repentance has brought you closer to Me. Seek this profound repentance for a great number of souls. I call many souls to follow Me, but few come. I am not capricious. I choose souls from many places and from diverse circumstances, but unfortunately with little result. Today, I have many complaints. I open My Heart to you with its ocean of sorrow. Why should I tolerate such an unworthy conduct from souls consecrated to Me? Come to Me sooner and console Me even more. Surpass your own limits. May your love for Me be burning and filled with fervor. Suffer with love and listen to My voice with greater love. To hear My voice, you must be very silent. Only souls plunged into My love can hear My delicate and silent voice. Keep your desire for Me alive and be a living host for love. Only the constant acceptance of sacrifices keeps the fire of love burning."

PASS ON THE FLAME OF LOVE TO SAVE YOUR COUNTRY

April 20, 1962

Jesus: "Take part unceasingly in My work of Redemption. Do not ask how. Fervently desire the coming of My Kingdom for yourself and for all the souls. When you rest at night, examine your day. What have you done for My Kingdom to arrive?"

The next day, a sharp burning pain burdened my soul. "You know that, My Jesus, because You told me, You promised to give me different sufferings. Although I suffer greatly, it is pleasant for me to suffer. I do not know to what I can compare this pain."

Jesus: "You could know. Remember when you were still a child, you lived far from your mother and your beloved country. This is the pain that tortured you for such a long time."

"Dear Jesus, is this my homesickness?"

Jesus: "You guessed right. The strong sorrow that I send you is a longing for your heavenly home. Suffer for those who have no desire for their eternal homeland."

Today, Jesus said:

Jesus: "Quickly pass on My Mother's Flame of Love so that My heavenly Father's chastising hand departs from this country."

To begin this work, I paid a great price, but the Lord gave me courage.

Jesus: "Do not hesitate any more, My little one. The Holy Virgin, under the title of the Great Lady of the Hungarian People, will confirm your work. Let our words be your prayers."

In those days, I was attracted strongly to give the messages to Father E. The following day, I went early to the Lord Jesus. He began to speak in my soul in such a mild voice that I barely heard Him. He told me many things but it was all going into my subconscious.

Although I sensed the great importance of these sweet words, I could not express them. I only remember the words telling me to take action. He also told me not to delay in giving the petitions and the instructions which He dictated to me as soon as possible to Father. I was fearful in knowing that there was no more time for delay. In my great fright, I asked the Sister sacristan to tell Father to remember me in his prayers. I said nothing more. In such a confidential matter, I could only speak with the person chosen by the Lord.

Today, the Evil One oppressed my soul ceaselessly. It ended only when, in the evening, I prostrated myself before the feet of the Lord. After a short silence, He spoke with a marvelous tenderness. An indescribable love, formerly hidden from me, came from Him into my trembling soul. For a long period, this extraordinary sensation traveled all through my body and soul. The Lord spoke in a voice more tender than ever. I sensed that He felt great sorrow in what he was going to say.

Jesus: "My little Carmelite, this is our farewell night. Your soul was the tabernacle of My peaceful words. From now on, I will cover you with silence. I will deprive you not only of My words but of the feeling of My presence."

When the Lord said these words, He permitted me to sense that the Evil One breathed a sigh of relief. Then the Evil One said, "My hour has come." I sensed that he was far away and that the Lord, with a gesture, would have annihilated him. I felt that the Lord was pained to have caused this sadness, so He filled me with His goodness.

Jesus: "I have to do this for the good of your soul."

Just as this inspiration penetrated my soul, a feeling totally unknown to me, delicate, moving and full of grace, flooded my interior. This was the Holy Spirit of Love and of Holiness.

While the Lord poured out His Spirit in my soul, I felt the Holy Spirit breathe upon me a different level of grace, so I could overcome all temptations. Peace filled me so much that the tears falling from my eyes because of the Lord's departure gave way to a silent recollection. When my heart calmed down, the Lord spoke one more time:

Jesus: "My daughter, do not misunderstand Me. I will continue to be with you in Holy Communion. There, I will await your coming as I did today. Be loyal, do not seek consolations. Renounce yourself and love only Me. Let only the Holy Spirit of Love fill your heart. Love Me as an infant wrapped up in his white swaddling clothes. Seek Me like My Mother once sought Me among the crowd with an anxious heart. And wherever you are, rejoice because of Me! Think of Me when you need a helping hand. If you think to be in need of fatherly support, look up to the Eternal Father, and with the Holy Spirit, be immersed in our love."

These were His parting words. Although they were kind, they left me sorrowful. Previously, the Lord Jesus always awakened me for the nightly prayer. From now on, my Guardian Angel awakened me. Oh, what a difference between the former and the latter!

AT THE SCHOOL OF HUMILITY

April 27, 1962 - Friday

After Holy Mass, I went to Father E well determined to give him the Blessed Virgin's message. "I have a letter for you, Father." In the letter, was the message of the Blessed Virgin. My whole body shook but the Holy Spirit was helping me. I waited until he finished reading. He looked surprised and answered with evasive words. "I cannot reply to this." I was not looking for a reply. I am a sinner and I have already suffered much because of this Cause. Feeling deeply humiliated, I left with a downcast spirit.

Afterward, I spent a long time in church, deep in thought. I complained to the Blessed Virgin: "Whom did you send me to, dear Mother? He refused me and did not say a helpful word." I left the church with sorrow and shame because of the humiliation. However, Father E did tell me something. He said I should go to Father X. I did not know him; I never heard of him. The following day, I went to see him, but since I did not find him, I returned the next day to meet him. In his confessional, I exposed before him the special condition of my soul. A flow of words suffused with tears sprang from me. Even though I had never met him, I opened my soul completely and asked him to direct me in this unique state of my soul. With great humility, I asked him to tell me if I am in error. His kind and sweet words gave me peace. He found nothing abnormal. It is from my humility that he drew this conclusion. His words consoled me and I returned home very calm. The next time, I was to bring the written messages of the Blessed Virgin and he would discuss them with other priests that trust him.

THOSE WITH RESPONSIBILITY

April 30, 1962

The Blessed Virgin encouraged me again.

Mary: "Tell those who have responsibility not to be afraid and to trust me. I will protect them under my motherly mantle. Let the eight best attended sanctuaries in the country and four churches dedicated to me in the capital city begin simultaneously this devotion, the handing over of my Flame of Love. Ardently long to make sacrifices, my little Carmelite. Constantly feed the Flame of my Love by your sufferings."

THE COUNTRY'S BEGGAR

May 2, 1962

I took the written messages to Father X. They told me that Father was sick, he had to undergo a serious operation and I could not speak with him. My heart was filled with sorrow and I thought that the Flame of Love would suffer a new setback.

The Lord Jesus said:

Jesus: "Have no fear, My little Carmelite. My Sacred Heart will be your permanent refuge. Don't you feel it is so, and consequently, feel instantly relaxed? The compassion of love is forever enduring among those who love one another. Stay in My love and draw others to Me as well. You know, there are so few of us that a quick look captures the entire encampment. My eyes always watch over you and My Heart suffers greatly from those who are absent. Stay at My side in perseverance so I do not undergo a bitter disappointment."

His plaintive voice caused my soul to burn for Him. The next day, I felt such anguish that all my physical strength was weakened. The Lord told me:

Jesus: "Suffer with Me, My daughter."

Another time, I was walking on the street at noontime. Unexpectedly, the Lord began speaking. He was grieving quite sadly and He asked that I put His words in writing.

Jesus: "My little one, I am the country's beggar. They refuse to give Me work. All forms of begging are forbidden in this country. I alone keep on begging. I wander without eating or drinking, from street to street, from house to house and from village to village, in the cold winter and in the heat, in the howling wind or in the heavy rain. No one asks where I am going in such a lamentable condition. My hair is soaked in blood, My feet are chapped from having followed you. I constantly stretch out My hand asking for help. I go from heart to heart and I receive only a small donation. Then they quickly close the door of their heart and I can hardly cast a glance inside. I have to withdraw quietly and My graces remain accumulated in My Heart. My little one, keep asking for many graces, also on behalf of others. Truly I am indebted towards you and grateful for your fidelity. Does that surprise you? Do not be amazed. Even the slightest sacrifice soothes My infinite, harrowing thirst. Do not live even for one instant without sacrifice!"

SACRIFICE AND PRAYER

Jesus: "I must tell you that, recently, I have called many souls to follow Me in this special way. However, very few understood what I wanted from them. Include them unceasingly in your prayers and make sacrifices for them, so that the army of souls who make reparation that I am thus trying to gather may provide a counterbalance to My just wrath.

My dear Mother pleads with Me. She is the one who has kept back My just wrath until now. Her Flame of Love obliges even Me."

While I was adoring Him, the Lord Jesus said:

Jesus: "Let there be repentance in every beat of your heart. With every breath, take in My love, and when you exhale, pass it to your neighbor."

On May 2, 1962, the Sister assigned to accompany me asked: "What difference did you experience when your Guardian Angel woke you up instead of the Lord?" I could not answer. Since the Lord no longer speaks, my prayer has become a monologue.

LITTLE FLASHES, CREATURES OF GOD

"O good Jesus, You have made me understand many things. Thanks to Your inspirations, I can express them. But when this happened, You had already covered my soul in silence. Now I understand but cannot express the experiences in words."

As I was kneeling silently before the Lord, a great brightness shone before my spiritual eyes, but I could not see it clearly. It was like a living light which sparkled and sent out small flashing particles in every direction. These particles were smaller than a grain of dust. Nevertheless, even the smallest particle shone with a great flash.

While contemplating this, the Lord allowed me to understand why I could not find adequate words to express it. These tiny particles of marvelous brightness had awakened in me the sensation that they were God's creatures.

This was a Tuesday, when I usually made spiritual communions for my children. I commended them to the Virgin's care. However, I had not been able to make these communions. Now, since the Lord Jesus deprived me of both His words and His presence, a great dryness was consuming my soul. As I knelt speechless, I remembered the Lord's words:

Jesus: "One Our Father or one Hail Mary prayed in the midst of spiritual dryness is much more fruitful than exuberant prayers of someone who abounds in spiritual favors."

COMMUNITY PRAYER

As I recalled these words, I felt a great calm in my spiritual dryness. As I was kneeling there on this May afternoon, I heard the chanting of the Litany of the Blessed Virgin. I never experienced before the power to raise up my soul to such great fervor that came from this community prayer.

THE TEMPTATION OF THE EVIL ONE

Remaining in devout silence, I intended to pray, but could not. Instead, the Evil One began to torture my soul. I was totally unable to free my thoughts from his influence. First, a great fear arose, a terrible feeling, as if he wanted to take possession of me but something blocked him.

While I knelt there, with my mind darkened, I thought I should run to the priest and ask him to pray for me before the Evil One would possess me. I saw Father E leave the church but I had no strength to follow him. After he left, I couldn't move because the thought that I was possessed and that I had no reason to be in the church weighed me down. The demon ordered me to leave the church but I stayed there a long time. I did not know how to be freed from the Evil One.

When I did leave the church, the Evil One accompanied me. He began to speak with me in a quite human manner. "Go back to your family! Don't stand out from the others! Do you not see that what you are doing exhausts you and drains your life? All your life has been a battle; now you should rest. Life is so short. Why do you pressure yourself so much? Why do you want to give your foolish thoughts to others? Do not think that you will call attention to yourself. This attention would flatter you. Stop and reflect and you will see that I am right. When you finally understand, you will thank me for sparing you the trouble."

I was happy when I arrived home because my grandchildren were waiting there and they paid me many compliments. This ended the devil's attacks.

After lunch, I went to my new home. Even there, the Evil One did not leave me alone, and he continued to bother me. Again, he hurled himself at me. I tried to reject him with all my strength. I started to meditate with great fervor but such disturbance forced me to think. I examined my conscience but found no reason for this... Before giving myself to this Cause, I would have to think it over. When the Evil One reminded me of my pride, I had to stop... It is amid these great worries that I went to rest. All of Heaven's help was gone and only the restlessness of the night came upon me. How good it would be to hear the Lord's sweet voice! What would He say about these events? In these days, I had so many serious temptations... The Evil One wanted to strip me of my human dignity.

SUFFERING TO RECEIVE GREAT GRACES

May 4, 1962

The Blessed Virgin began to speak.

Mary: "My daughter, now that you are over this great temptation, I will reward you. You have overcome a great trial. We wanted to increase your humility. This is why my Divine Son let Satan get so near to you, to make you more able to propagate the Flame of Love.

To receive great graces, your soul must be prepared by greater sufferings. This is the only way to increase grace in your soul. Now, following your victory, I press you to my heart. When I speak to you, you will take up my Cause with greater fervor. This test was an opportunity to gain merits for others. Make constant sacrifices for the twelve priests because they, too, will suffer. Be happy that you can suffer with them.

Your merits, no matter how small they seem, will increase your graces. I entrust my Cause to just a few. After they are won over, a multitude will follow. Rejoice that you are one of the few. Unfortunately, even among the few, some reject me and cause pain to my motherly heart.

And now, you must spread my Cause. Those I have chosen must have total confidence in me. As a watchful Mother, I lead all their steps. I ask only that they make their souls ready and prepare with great fervor for the work of reparation. I am hurt to see the fear that my Flame of Love awakens in you.

Why are your hearts fearful? How could I, your loving Mother, abandon you? Come together and prepare your souls to welcome the Sacred Flame. The faithful in the sanctuaries will be ready to accept it. I, the Mother of Grace, always ask my Divine Son to take your smallest effort and join it with His merits.

Do not be afraid of the Flame that will light up imperceptibly. As a soft light, it will arouse no suspicions. This is the miracle that will come forth in your hearts."

THE FEAST OF CANDLEMAS

Mary: "On the feast of Candlemas,[4] my beloved sons will introduce the Flame of Love of my heart in procession, so that, in such fashion, it becomes a living fire in the hearts, in the souls. Everything must be prepared in such a way that it spreads like wildfire.

---

4. February 2nd.

Let those souls whom I have chosen do everything to prepare for the great mission ahead."

"My Mother, Our Lord Jesus Christ promised me that you would confirm me." Then, within my soul, I heard the gentle reply of the Blessed Virgin that fully quieted me.

Mary: "Go to my beloved son, Father X. He will do everything as I myself would. He will be my messenger to my sanctuaries to confirm the Flame of Love. Do not fear, he will not be opposed to the Cause, nor will he excuse himself. Just live in hidden humility and be consumed in suffering. I, the Mother of Sorrows, feel as if, with each of your sufferings, you pour medicinal balm upon the wounds of my Divine Son.

Be a soul which cannot live without sufferings. By their union with the sufferings of my Divine Son, these souls increasingly feel His closeness. Desire with all your heart that my Flame of Love be lit quickly and blind Satan."

Between May 3 and 11, 1962, the Blessed Virgin told me four times not to neglect her command.

ANNOUNCE MY MERCY - SACRIFICE YOURSELF

The Savior said:

Jesus: "I choose you, My little one, to be the bearer of My Divine Mercy. Fill yourself with the abundance of My Divine Mercy and when you open your mouth to speak, proclaim the mercy of My Heart burning of desire for sinners. Let your whole life be a burning desire to take part in My work of Redemption through prayer, sacrifice and desire."

"How many times, good Jesus, I have written down Your sad complaints, but I can do very little."

Jesus: "Let your heart burn with desire, My little one. Just with that, you lessen the burning sorrow of My Heart. If all the souls consecrated to My Heart yearned just as I would, the number of those making reparation would increase. You know, they form a large group. If all took part with their heart and soul, by prayers and sacrifices, in My work of Redemption, I would not complain so much. Love Me more, My little one, and serve Me with greater surrender. Do not let the power of routine take control.

Let your sacrifices always be fervent. I would like to increase My graces in you. However, to do that, I need a greater acceptance of sacrifices. Accept My plea, be very humble and renounce every pleasure which does not serve Me. Renounce the reading of frivolous books, the hearing of your favorite music, and your seeking to be among others. On your walks, think only of My Sacred Passion.

I want you to increase your fasts if you accept. Do not give yourself to any pleasure. Let your breakfast and your afternoon meal be bread and water. You can have other foods only at your principal meal, but make them tasteless. Do not eat to please your taste but only to nourish your body. Anyway, the body will demand what it needs. You must renounce more of your sleep. I ask you for two hours of prayer, so that you have to get up twice every night for one hour. My beloved, can I count on you? I, the Man-God, ask this of you."

"My Lord and my God, without You, I am nothing. My soul is willing but my body, You know, My Lord, is weak. Here on earth, there are two 'I' within me like two eternal and inseparable enemies. My soul and my heart accept it, but they get irritated against the darkened side of my weak will and mind. I renew my offering, sweet Jesus. I am Yours, dispose of me as You wish. In no way, do I want to oppose You because I love You ardently. Clothe me in Your power, so I can fulfill Your request."

OFFER YOUR NIGHT VIGILS FOR YOUNG PEOPLE AND CHILDREN

I found the nightly vigil very difficult. To rise from sleep cost me much. I asked the Blessed Virgin: "My Mother, I beg you, wake me up. When my guardian angel wakes me up it is not effective enough."

The next night, the Blessed Virgin awakened me. I wanted to get dressed because I did not think it was respectful to speak with the Blessed Virgin while I lay in bed. But the time for the vigil had not yet arrived; it was just midnight, not 2:00 a.m. The Blessed Virgin said:

Mary: "Stay in bed, my little one. This is no lack of respect. A mother can speak to her daughter any place and any time.

Listen to me, I beg you, do not let your mind be distracted during the night vigil... as it is an extremely useful exercise for the soul, elevating it to God. Make the required physical effort. I also did many vigils myself. I was the one who stayed up nights while Jesus was a little baby. Saint Joseph worked very hard so we would have enough to live on. You should also be doing it that way. Even on Sunday, your day of rest, you will do vigils and attend as many Masses as possible. Offer them for the youth. Think of the many children guided every year to my Divine Son. How many souls are lost, not taking root because no one is concerned about their spiritual progress. Let your soul be filled with prayers of sacrifice, even on your days of rest. Offer these days especially for the young. Even when my Most Holy Son was tired, He wanted the children to come to Him. That is why you also must never be tired. You know, it is Him who asked you to continually share in His work of Redemption."

Jesus spoke to me again today.

Jesus: "My little Carmelite, you have accepted all the sacrifices that I have asked for lately. Perhaps you are surprised, but I must thank you. Do you see how your Master is so condescending? Yet, I will go still further. Unite your sufferings totally with Mine. Then your merits will grow greatly and they will move My redemptive work ahead. Keep this great grace you received from Me in the depth of your soul. It is a special gift of God. He honors you, poor little soul. Can He give you anything more sublime? Learn from Me. I chose you because you are small and miserable. Never tire of suffering for Me. With the help of My grace, dedicate yourself even more."

Then the sweet Redeemer asked me to pray with Him the prayer that expresses His deepest desires:

May our feet journey together,
May our hands gather in unity,
May our hearts beat to the same rhythm,
May our souls be in harmony,
May our thoughts be in unison,
May our ears listen to the silence together,
May our glances melt in one another,
and may our lips beg our heavenly Father,
together, to obtain Mercy.

I made this prayer completely mine. The Lord meditated on it many times with me, asserting that these are His eternal longings. He taught me this prayer, so I would in turn teach it to others. With all our strength and mind, let us make our own His eternal thoughts and burning desires.

Afterward, the Savior added this:

Jesus: "This prayer is an instrument in your hands. By collaborating with Me, Satan will be blinded by it; and because of his blindness, souls will not be led into sin."

HELP! I NEED YOUR STRENGTH

May 14, 1962

Again, the Blessed Virgin awakened me. This time, I stayed in bed.

Mary: "My little Carmelite, in the silence of the night, I want to speak with you. Pay attention to what I say, but continue to rest. You know how my heart is immensely in pain. Satan is sweeping souls away in a terrifying way. Why do you not all try your best to stop him and do it as soon as possible? I need your help. My heart is burning with sorrow because I see how many souls are being damned. Many are dragged away in spite of their good will.[5] With a sarcastic smile, the Evil One extends his arms, and with terrible

5. Many souls begin with good will but the stream carries them away because they do not see the temptations that Satan puts in their path.

malice, he drags away those for whom my Divine Son suffered unspeakable torments and death. Please, help!"

SPEAK TO MY SONS

May 17, 1962

During morning prayers, the Blessed Virgin spoke to me. Also during Holy Mass, she complained in a sad tone of voice. She was suffering, as if she was wringing her hands. She begged:

Mary: "Satan's wild rage is growing steadily, he wants to dominate even persevering souls. Do not let him do this. Help me!"

She continued imploring me. The sorrow in her soul poured into mine. I struggled as my prayer was drowned in tears. Now, as I write these words, the sorrow divides my heart and I have to stop writing because of my tears. "O my Mother, what can I do?"

Mary: "Go, speak to my sons. They will be my messengers."

"My Mother, you must speak in my favor because I am miserable and a nobody. They do not pay attention to me even though I bring your words. What can I do? O Mother, again I ask that you be the one who speak. Your Divine Son promised that you would confirm what I do. I beg you, Most Holy Mother, act so that they pay attention to your constant pleas. Also, Mother, I am being consumed and I suffer because the priest you sent me to has not accepted your request."

That same day, the Lord Jesus also spoke in the great silence of my soul. His voice was like a whisper:

Jesus: "Be careful, My little one. Renounce yourself entirely. Give yourself totally to Me. You know that I want no evil to enter your heart. With My sufferings, I paid a great price for you, for your soul. Let nothing make you lose the graces which I am constantly giving you. Be careful. The Evil One wants to enter without notice and, as a ravaging animal, destroy the powers of your soul."

"Beloved Jesus, how can this happen? As soon as I wake up, at my first heartbeat, I offer myself to You forgetting and despising myself, so that the demon finds no place in my soul when I awake. Receive me, my Lord and my good God."

Jesus: "Tell me this all during the day, not just when you wake up."

Then, with just a gentle sigh, He said:

Jesus: "My little daughter!"

THE DREAM

May 23, 1962

In the morning, I thanked the Lord for the strength He gave me for the night prayer. He was deeply moved and I could hardly withstand the beating of His Heart. This resonated in my heart with a sweetness I had never experienced. "O Lord, I am not worthy of what You are doing in me, but I will use all my strength to thank You for Your goodness." He continued having me experience His extraordinary love. I was not going to write down my dream, but Jesus said:

Jesus: "Write this down, also."

On the night of May 16-17, I had this dream. Usually, I do not dream or I forget my dreams, but this dream was even clearer after I awoke.

I saw a large black disk with grey clouds gathered around. Next to the disk, I saw strange-looking men. They were thin, as if not having bodies, and dressed in grey suits. I saw only the back of their heads. Suddenly, I felt that they were devils, the worst ones. At that moment, they were finishing a sheet of iron to cover the disk which until now was fully visible. When they covered the disk with the sheet of iron, by another mocking grin, they expressed their satisfaction for the work done.

On the right, there were white clouds and I felt that someone was watching them. I did not know who it was but I had the feeling they did not have bad intentions. I saw three young men with him. I felt that they were enemies of the Evil One, because in contemplating the black disk, they discussed among themselves on the means to remove it. Meanwhile, one of those on the left side, the closest to those on the right, turned towards one of them. He was absolutely sure of his work, so he said with great sarcasm: "You can look at it. We have made it very well. It will cause you many headaches."

I observed the disk and I wondered how it could be dislodged from the dark cover. To my great satisfaction, I saw a small opening in which the light was coming through. I do not know if the good persons on the right realized this. On seeing this opening, I felt relief and decided to tell the others that all was not lost. If we started to remove the dark cover, I felt we could succeed. At this point, I woke up.

Reflecting later on the dream, I could not understand it, but I had the impression that if we work hard, we can find a way to make the dark disk transparent again.

SWEET COMPANY AND WISE ADVICE

May 1962

Since the Lord Jesus no longer addresses me with His kind and sweet words, there is a silence between us, or rather, the conversation is but a monologue. One day, I had to go shopping for my children. After lunch, as I left the house, I reviewed what I needed to buy. At that moment, He said:

Jesus: "Do I bother you?"

He drew near with such a delicate attention that I could not contain my tears. I whispered those words which He loved to hear, "With insatiable thirst, I desire You." Then we went on without any words. Moved by His unlimited thoughtfulness, I said: "My adored Jesus, I hope I can draw near to You as You draw near to me." With that longing, I arrived at the store and He left me. This caused so much pain. He, the Man-God, acts with such tenderness and understanding towards me. As I returned home, He said:

Jesus: "Do you not want to tell Me more?"

"My sweet Jesus, I return to You Your own words as prayer: You are the apple of my eyes."

Now that He spoke to me after a long time, a great joy filled my soul. The spiritual dryness had lasted for so long and my misery had kept me tied to the ground. I accepted this willingly because it was for the good of my soul.

One day, very early in the morning, the Lord Jesus started to complain with great sadness.

Jesus: "My daughter, I ask for many mortifications so I can give you many graces in return. Let the spirit of sacrifice, of prayer and of mortification always burn within you. Remain always silent because only in this way God's voice will continue to speak within you. Be silent and do not praise yourself. Your spiritual life must take root in silence.

By your silence, make reparation for many who speak empty and senseless words. Make reparation for those who hold back because they lack confidence. Above all, let your fidelity and confidence in Me increase. If only you knew the sorrow of My Divine Heart when they pay no attention to Me or they exclude Me totally from their heart.

Each morning, present to Me the offering of your sacrifices; place it at the door of My tabernacle, it will ignite at the fire of My love. During the day, let not the flame of your sacrifices fade away. See to it that the love of many victim souls rise up to Me, and through My intercession, obtain the mercy of the heavenly Father."

He filled me with His infinite love and continued:

Jesus: "My little one, do you know My love for souls? I would speak to every soul in this way if only they would receive Me and give Me shelter."

"O Lord, You are the One who gave me my first shelter. I owe You an eternal gratitude that I can never give You."

Jesus: "I do not demand this from you nor from anyone else. However, if you tried it, it would please Me exceedingly."

INTERPRETATION OF THE DREAM

This morning, the Lord told me many things and asked me some questions. I was surprised because He asked me about my dream and said:

Jesus: "Do you know what that black disk is? It represents the country of the Great Lady of the Hungarian people. In the white cloud is My Mother, and the person next to her is My beloved son whose heart is tied to Mine and is ready to do everything for Me." (He was speaking of a priest.)

He did not say who he was and it did not occur to me to ask. In the meantime, the Lord turned the word over to the Blessed Virgin. He did it with so much respect and devotion that my heart began to beat strongly as I heard Him. Then the Blessed Virgin repeated the same words the Lord had just said. Then the Lord Jesus began to speak.

Jesus: "Do you know the meaning of the disk's dense blackness? It represents the seven capital sins. This iron is composed of seven sheets which seem to be of one piece but are really separate. The top sheet is lust. It is a very thin and resistant layer. To remove it, it must be bent by much prayer and sacrifices. The second is negligence in doing good. This one cannot be bent. It is made of an unbreakable black color. Only with great effort can small particles, like little grains of dust, be taken out. Do not fear. I will be with you in this great work. But, be careful, because the Evil One is active. Only unceasing labor can remove this negligence in doing good, this hard disk."

DO NOT FEAR THE EVIL ONE

Thereupon, Jesus once again turned the word over to the Blessed Virgin. She began to speak in an encouraging and pleading voice.

Mary: "All of you, look at me and take advantage of my intercession. I want to help you and I have the power to do so. If only I could sense your goodwill and your readiness to take the first energetic step. Do not delay any longer. You have already wasted too much time. The Evil One is working with greater success and determination than everyone. That hurts me so much!

My little Carmelite, I bend over you, and with maternal tenderness, I protect you from all spiritual danger. Do not fear the devil who is always lurking around you. I have crushed him. You do not have to fear. Hide beneath my mantle and frequently kiss my holy garment (the scapular) that you wear."

TAKE CARE OF THE MOST BEAUTIFUL DRESS OF SANCTIFYING GRACE

After this, the Lord Jesus said many things but I could not write them down. After Holy Communion, I thanked Him for His abundant graces and asked pardon for receiving Him unworthily so often in my heart. I made reparation for those who would receive Him unworthily today. Seeing my affliction, the Lord's complaints flowed like a torrent.

Jesus: "My little one, when a father buys a new suit for his son, he makes him give thanks and he teaches him to take good care of the suit because he sacrificed much to buy it.

In Baptism, My heavenly Father gave all of you the most beautiful robe of sanctifying grace. In spite of this, you do not take care of it. Is there any father who has suffered more than I so that this robe of sanctifying grace can regain its whiteness? I instituted the Sacrament of Penance, yet you make no use of it. For this, I have sweated blood. For this, I was crowned with thorns. I let Myself be nailed to the wood of the Cross. I endured unspeakable suffering. Then I humbly hid Myself under a common appearance so as to be more accessible to you, so that you would not fear Me. I hid Myself in the white Host like a child wrapped up in swaddling clothes. When I enter your heart, make sure that the robe of your soul is free from any stain or tear, because no father has made greater sacrifices to acquire a suit for his child.

Many do not thank Me even a little bit. Every day you repeat the same prayers with passivity and coldness, without feeling, without paying attention, with your thoughts elsewhere. This happens day after day, year after year. You do not realize that I, also, am a Man and that you do not have to distance yourselves from Me since you have received Me in your heart. You should speak to Me in simple words. Do not leave Me alone. My Heart yearns for love and confidence. I want you to speak with Me so I can respond with the fullness of My grace.

Daughter, wherever you can, draw souls closer to Me."

MAKE REPARATION FOR CONSECRATED SOULS

May 24, 1962

This moves me to tears every time I think of Him as a little Child, and I prostrate before Him. In spirit, He extended his two little hands toward me and said:

Jesus: "Kiss them for those to whom I have extended them in vain."

I gave Jesus every longing of my soul and asked: "Are there persons to whom You extend Your hands and they pay no attention?"

Jesus: "Unfortunately, there are. It saddens Me that I will have to act as a severe Judge and raise My hand against them."

Today, He said:

Jesus: "Make reparation for those souls who, although consecrated to Me, have no interest in Me. I have sheltered them in My Heart and have showered them with My precious treasures. However, they leave their treasures to gather dust in the depth of their souls. If they used the Sacrament of Penance to polish these treasures, they would shine again with the light of My graces. But they have no interest and are distracted by the world's glitter. Whoever does not gather with Me, scatters."

The sweet Savior asked me to meditate with Him upon His eternal longings. This took a long time. He meditated the prayer with me. I feel badly that I cannot describe this because His words went right to my consciousness. They penetrated my interior so much and were so merged with Him, that I am incapable of expressing them in words.

I had to do some work, so I left hurriedly. Still, He told me:

Jesus: "Is it true that we will always be united?"

"We will never be separated since we cannot live without each other." We both spoke these words simultaneously, so I do not know who pronounced them first, He or I.

THANKING JESUS BY REPENTING FOR SIN

June 2, 1962 - Saturday

At Holy Mass, there was exposition of the Blessed Sacrament. I took my prayer book (the Little Psalter), when the sweet Savior said:

Jesus: "Keep your prayer book and let us talk."

His words filled my soul with graces and great emotion overwhelmed me. I turned to the Blessed Virgin.

"O Mother, come and help me to thank your Divine Son. I can hardly stand His overwhelming graces. I cannot pronounce the words. How can I thank Him?"

Mary: "Respond to my Divine Son with a deep sorrow for your sins."

Her words brought about a deep repentance in my soul and my eyes filled with tears. This is how I spent the time before Holy Communion. The choir sang 'In the deep silence of the temple.' This is my favorite hymn and these words increased the tenderness I felt for Him. For months, I had not heard this hymn. Now, it has been sung for four successive days. Never had it touched me so much as today. The tears ran down my face, I could not stop them even when I was receiving Communion. When I knelt down, I wanted to thank Him for this union but He did not stop talking. He began to praise me.

Jesus: "My little sister! How happy I feel to enter your heart which tries to love Me with all of its strength."

He filled my soul and took away several days of spiritual aridity. With His fruitful graces, I felt overwhelmed by the knowledge of my misery. He kept speaking.

Jesus: "Did you enjoy the hymn? I was the One who touched you by the melody. This is the hymn which we like the most. I use it to praise you because you so much love the silence of the church where I dwell."

On June 2, the sweet Savior awakened me for the nightly prayer with these words:

"IN THE QUIET OF THE NIGHT, I SEEK SOULS"

Let whoever might one day read these lines not take it badly that once more I have to indicate that I was in tears. His tenderness and attention filled my eyes with tears. Then, He said:

Jesus: "Since this so pleases you, from now on, when I awaken you, these will be My words: In the quiet of the night, I seek souls."

From these words, I knew that His eternal thought is to seek souls.

SUFFER WITH ME

June 3, 1962

Early this morning, when I finished my second hour of night prayer, the Savior said in a pleading voice:

Jesus: "My little one, suffer with Me. Feel what I feel! Relieve My sorrow."

The eyes of my soul saw a vision which broke my heart. This terrible vision not only caused me spiritual sorrow, but for a few minutes, I was suffocating.

I HAVE PITY ON THE CROWD

June 4, 1962

During the Forty Hours Devotion, I went to the Máriaremete Sanctuary to prepare my soul for the nocturnal adoration. The crowd's fervor had a wonderful effect on my soul. After an hour, my soul recovered its peace after the interior disturbances in the morning. I rejoiced to see a large crowd offering reparation and adoration. The Lord Jesus said:

Jesus: "I have pity on the crowd."

About two hundred persons attended the nocturnal adoration. They persevered in prayer until 2:00 a.m. and all were trying to stay awake. I left to get some fresh air and to get rid of my tiredness. When I returned, only a few were still awake. I was not able to conquer the sleep that came upon me. I asked the sweet Savior to accept my constant battle against sleep as if I was adoring Him, and to accept it also for those who forgot to ask His pardon.

COMPLAINT OF THE SACRED HEART OF JESUS

July 2, 1962

When I visited the Blessed Sacrament on this feast of Our Lady of the Snows, the Lord Jesus flooded me again with His sorrowful requests.

Jesus: "Tomorrow is the Friday of the Sacred Heart. How I want to pour out My abundant graces on all of you! Ask much for everyone, not just for yourself.

Love Me even more and with greater fidelity. Do not tire of hearing My continual complaints. I complain much, My little one, because so few listen to Me. I complain in vain to My consecrated souls. They do not enter into the intimacy of their own heart. If so, they would hear My laments. How greatly I need to tell them how to promote the coming of My Kingdom."

STIR UP THE FIRE

July 12, 1962

Jesus: "You see that almost no one is doing anything. The Flame of Love of My Mother is not yet going forward. You, My little one, must stir up the fire because you have been chosen for this. This is a great privilege. Never interrupt your desires and sacrifices because this would cause My Mother great sorrow."

"O Jesus, You know the burning desire of my heart. How much I also suffer because nothing has been done. All day I have fought my pride." He spoke sadly.

Jesus: "Your pride distracts you, My little one. I observe you with sadness. How long will this last? This causes Me so much sorrow."

SO MUCH SORROW

July 14, 1962

Jesus: "Do you remember what you spoke about with your relative? You said that the greatest happiness is making others happy. Yet, how much more I would like to make all of you happy! However, you seek happiness in other things, not in Me. You turn your back on My graces when it is precisely these graces that would make you happy. I repeat My words: This causes Me so much sorrow, so much sorrow..."

DEFICIENCIES AND PARDON

July 15, 1962

Jesus: "My little one, how long will you make Me wait? When will I be able to embrace all of you in My Heart? My patience has no limits. I have promised so much good to draw you to Myself, and yet, you are so indifferent to Me."

On that day, I had finished nine days of a strict fast. He said:

Jesus: "Invite Me as a guest to the table of your little breakfast. Do not be indifferent to Me and do not make a boring face. If not, I will have to believe that you are doing it reluctantly for Me. Bring your frailties to Me, do not think that this has no merit. I know you very well. The most hidden corner of your soul is an open book for Me. I hope that you can recognize your deficiencies. In this way they become meritorious."

"O Jesus, I want to repent of my sins as no one has ever repented before. All the beatings of my heart are nothing. How many grains of dust are in the world? In every one, I place the sorrow of my heart so that the wind takes them to you in reparation for my innumerable sins." When I was sorry in this way, Jesus was very touched, and with a sweet voice, He said:

Jesus: "I place the smallest part of a single drop of My Blood over your great sorrow. I forgive your sins fully and I forget them. Offer this profound repentance for all the sinners."

In my joy, I did not know how to speak to Him.

> Sweet Jesus, I come to You in the morning covered with dew, flowery and fresh in a summer day when hearts are still sleeping in the hiding place of sleep, to be the first one to greet You.
>
> The time I spend with You is always short. It goes like the light that swims over the clouds. I come in suffocating heat, beneath scorching sun, because I love You so much.
>
> I come to You in the humid shade of evening, the lamp of the Eucharist calls me. I sense that no one is with You. I love you and bring souls to You.
>
> I come across deep ditches covered with snow. My eyes see only the falling snowflakes. I come in the torrential rain, in mud so deep, because my heart beats for You, O my God.
>
> Elizabeth Szántö Kindelmann

(The Sister who was assigned to accompany me knew every vibration of my heart. When she read this, she asked me where I had copied these verses. I told her: "The grace of God brought them forth in my soul.")

CHOSEN SOUL

July 16, 1962

I went to the church and knelt before the altar of Our Lady of Sorrows. A great sadness came over me. I thought about Father X who was still sick. Because of this burden, I complained to the Blessed Virgin. She said:

Mary: "Offer your sorrow for his healing."

I asked the Blessed Virgin if he would be healed. She consoled me with loving words.

Mary: "Yes, in a short while, but not for long."

The Blessed Virgin continued to speak of Father X.

Mary: "He will come to me soon, he is already on the road. He is my beloved son whom I hold so deeply in my heart."

I WILL BE YOUR GUEST

July 20, 1962

The Lord Jesus asked me:

Jesus: "My little one, get rid of anything that gives taste to your meals. Only in this way, will I be your guest. What is tasty for you is tasteless for Me. I ask you, therefore, that if you invite Me, seek what pleases Me."

Today, the Blessed Virgin asked me to place our parish community under her patronage and that of Saint Joseph. Also, I should seek every day the grace of a happy death for souls.

THE FEAST OF CORPUS CHRISTI

The sweet Savior filled my soul with such an attraction for His Sacred Body and Precious Blood that for weeks I could only meditate on the Eucharist. It was His desire that He and I penetrate deeply into these inexhaustibly profound words: "He who eats My Body and drinks My Blood remains in Me and I in him." I cannot describe what I experienced in my soul while I meditated. This went on for weeks without being tired of it. I have no words to express it.

The Evil One envied this strengthening grace. He came to my side with his constant vexations and wanted me to stop thinking of the Holy Eucharist. "Why are you so in love with this thought? I can do even greater miracles." To such infamous words, I answered: "You could only do miracles that God permitted but you cannot save anyone." With that, he went blank.

Even I could not conceive that these words would leave him so disarmed. In great shame, he stopped bothering me.

THE LOVE OVERFLOWING MY HEART

July 30, 1962

Jesus: "My little Carmelite, I complain because seeing so many indifferent souls grieves My Heart. Now, as First Friday again approaches, thinking of them fills Me with sadness. The love overflowing from My Heart receives no response from these souls. You, My daughter, must love Me even more. Embrace Me ever more closely in your heart. Offer your soul and serve Me with profound submission. Do this in place of those who do not, even though they are consecrated to Me."

I had to stop writing because He again poured the sorrow of His Heart into my soul. Oh, that sorrow of His Heart, how it breaks my soul! Leaving aside the writing, I prostrated and adored Him and said to His Heart with a tiny voice: "I want to love You as no converted sinner has ever loved You." He often overwhelms me with the sorrow of His Heart and I have to stop writing.

Jesus: "You know that I complain to you because you have given Me refuge in your heart. I know that you can feel My pain. Suffer with Me, My little one."

Also that same day, the Blessed Virgin told me in a pleading voice:

Mary: "My little Carmelite, intensify your desire so that my Flame of Love will be put into action. Make even greater sacrifices."

It is with these very words that she spoke to me. She also repeated them on the feast of her Visitation.

Mary: "Offer me greater sacrifices. Do not ask how, just improvise!"

Because of her request, I ate only bread and water and a little fruit for nine days. When she asked a second time, I deprived myself of water on various days. This was difficult because of the terrible heat, but my heart feels the great longings of the Blessed Virgin and this gives me extraordinary strength during the fast. I said to the Blessed Virgin: "O heavenly Mother, I desire so much that your Flame of Love burns that I feel a great sadness and affliction because it is being delayed. O Mother, smooth out the road of those called to promote your Cause."

IN THE LONELINESS OF THE NIGHT

August 1, 1962

I was sick. For days, I could not pray because I was so weak. The great heat of this summer contributed to my fatigue. I could hardly walk. When I felt a little stronger, I firmly resolved to return to prayer at night. I asked Jesus, "My adored Jesus, give me strength." At 3:00 a.m., the Lord awakened me by His presence and His words.

Jesus: "In the loneliness of the night, I seek hearts."

Then He left me. After He departed, I wondered about the intention for which I would offer this night's prayer. I saw clearly that I should offer it so the Flame of Love of the Virgin would be ignited. As soon as I made this intention, the devil's presence filled me with anguish. "O heavenly Mother, I am praying for this with all my strength and all my longings. But, I am nobody. What can I do?"

While I was immersed in the Flame of Love, I realized to my surprise that the anguish caused by the devil's presence had disappeared. It had left imperceptibly. I felt as if a blind man had left my side. I was very surprised. My soul felt so light, like nothing I had ever felt in my life.

When this happened, I felt as if my body had been left behind, leaving only my soul. I was knocked to my knees, completely astonished. I felt that my soul was like covered rags crudely sown, such as the beggars wear. I was overwhelmed by a very depressing sensation.

MY MATERNAL MANTLE

"You see, my Jesus, how I am." When I said this in a pleading voice, the Blessed Virgin covered my sorrowful rags with her mantle (scapular) and said:

Mary: "My little one, there are many souls like this in my country (Hungary). But together with you, I cover them with my motherly mantle and I hide their mendicant soul from the eyes of my Divine Son, so He will not be sad because of all of you."

The Most Holy Virgin continued speaking.

Mary: "The past days have brought you many sufferings, is this not true? You have many doubts whether making so many sacrifices that demand such efforts is useful. I gazed at you with joy. So you could gain more strength and make even greater sacrifices, I did not want to console you amid your doubts. I will obtain a great grace for you."

By saying this, she permitted me to feel in a wonderful way the effects of grace of her Flame of Love which, at that moment, were felt not just by me, but by all the souls in the country. Then she began to speak.

SATAN BLINDED FOR A FEW HOURS

Mary: "Now, Satan has been blinded for some hours and has ceased dominating souls. Lust is the sin making so many victims. Because Satan is now powerless and blind, the evil spirits are set and inert, as if they have fallen into lethargy. They do not understand what is happening. Satan has stopped giving them orders. Consequently, souls are freed from the domination of the Evil One and are making sound resolutions. Once those millions of souls emerge from this event, they will be much stronger in their resolve to stay firm."

As the Blessed Virgin spoke, she allowed me to experience what was happening in these souls under the power of grace.

THE TIME IS CLOSE

Feeling this grace, I went to church early in the morning. "O most powerful Virgin, I hail you. From what sorrow you have saved me! Why do you give me so many graces?" The Blessed Virgin said:

Mary: "Gather strength from so many graces, my little one. I gratified you so that if new doubts should enter, the inextinguishable fire of my Flame of Love will already be burning in your soul. Already you see how sublime this is."

Today, the Blessed Virgin told me many things.

Mary: "I assure you, my little one, that I have never before given into your hands such a powerful force of grace, the burning flame of the love of my heart. Ever since the Word became Flesh, I have not undertaken a greater movement than the Flame of Love of my heart who rushes to you. Until now, nothing could blind Satan as much. And it is up to you not to reject it, for this rejection would simply spell disaster."

"My heavenly Mother, you're entrusting me with this great Cause, me the most miserable in the world? Me, a beggar clothed in rags. I am worth nothing in human terms and much less in your sight."

Mary: "My Flame of Love will first flare up at the Carmel, my little one, for is there any place where I am more venerated? They are the ones who are called to venerate me the most. Also the Daughters of the Holy Spirit, together with those devoted to me, must collaborate in spreading the Flame of Love.

Hurry, my little one. The moment is near when my Flame of Love will ignite. At that moment, Satan will be blinded. I want all to feel it in order to increase your trust. This will give you great strength. All those whom this force will reach will feel it. The Flame will ignite and will reach the whole world, not only in the nations consecrated to me, but all over the earth. It will spread out even in the most inaccessible places, because there is no place inaccessible to Satan. From it, draw strength and confidence. I will support your work with miracles as never seen before, and that the reparation to my Divine Son will accomplish imperceptibly, gently and silently."

FEAST OF THE FLAME OF LOVE

Mary: "I ask the Holy Father to make the feast of the Flame of Love on February 2, the feast of Candlemas. I do not want a special feast."

BRING ME YOUR CONCERNS

One time, I was so preoccupied that I did not think of the Lord Jesus from the morning until late in the afternoon. (This is the first time that this happened since I entered my new state.)

When I was alone, Jesus spoke:

Jesus: "Do you see how you act? Again, you are busy with your concerns. Why do you not bring them to Me? You act as if you can do something. Learn now. With My help you can accomplish everything for others too. Bring Me the problems of your neighbor and the difficulties in your family. I will set everything right. How can I set everything in order if you do not trust Me with your concerns? Trust in My power. I want your unconditional trust."

JESUS DISTRIBUTES HIS GRACES

August 3, 1962

In the morning, the family again discussed the house. This depressed me. At the Lord's request, I went for adoration from noon to 3:00 p.m. I was so upset that I could hardly walk. This family disagreement keeps getting repeated and it disturbs my soul.

It was difficult to settle myself, so I used the first hour of prayer to order my thoughts. My distractions discouraged me so much that I was even incapable of vocal prayer. I thought of the priest souls who were forgotten in Purgatory and I wanted to make the Stations of the Cross for them. I was so tired and wanted to stop many times. Then the Redeemer spoke in a sad tone of voice.

Jesus: "I never abandoned or interrupted my way of sorrows! Come, let us go together, it will be easier this way for you and for Me. Shared pain is half pain. You know, I pulled myself along with great difficulty. It is not without reason they made Simon of Cyrene help Me. Now, you also help Me."

As I was immersed in Him, He said:

Jesus: "I feel compassion for you, My little one. I see your great efforts. Do not think they are in vain. I bless your family greatly. I free them from the Evil One who disturbs the family peace. Just trust in Me."

"O Lord, the family discord is so great that only a miracle will help."

Jesus: "Cannot I work a miracle?"

"But I am not worthy, Lord."

Jesus: "Nevertheless, I will work a miracle. I will so bless the problem which seems impossible that all will be straightened out."

I asked the Blessed Virgin to intercede with her Most Holy Son for that. When I finished the Stations of the Cross, the Savior promised me four times:

Jesus: "My little one, I will smooth out all the difficulties. Our dear Mother again has appealed to her Flame of Love. I cannot deny her anything. She asked Me to deny nothing to the one to whom she entrusted her Flame of Love, but that I distribute My graces to whomever wishes that she be the one who asks Me for them."

I cannot describe the strength and confidence that I received from these words.

INCREASED DESIRE TO SAVE SOULS

August 6, 1962

From the morning until the time of Communion, or a little while before, the Lord again overwhelmed my soul with complaints.

Jesus: "No soul I have entrusted to the care of My priests ought to be damned. This word, damnation, causes a terrible pain in My Heart. I would suffer death on the Cross again for each soul, even suffering a thousand times more since there is no hope for the damned. Prevent this! With your burning desires, save souls.

You know, just as there are three forms of Baptism: Baptism of water, of blood and of desire, it is such for the salvation of souls. From My Sacred Heart, came blood and water flowing over you, and the strong desire with which I did it for you.

Do you really know what desire is? It is a marvelous and delicate instrument that even the most helpless man can use as a miraculous instrument to save souls. The key point is that he should unite his desire with My Precious Blood exuding from My side. Increase your desire with all your might, My little one, to save as many souls as possible."

Expressing that the loss of souls through damnation was extremely painful for Him, the sweet Savior allowed me to share His pain in my heart. Because the pain was so sharp, I almost collapsed. O Lord Jesus, I will make every effort that the souls entrusted to me are not damned.

PUT OUT THE FIRE OF SATAN

August 7, 1962

I complained, "O Jesus, I am so abandoned."

Jesus: "What shall I say? Has there been anyone more abandoned, more despised, or more forgotten than I? If all of you knew the longing I feel for you. In My continual loneliness, I call out to you with great love and patience, but you treat Me like someone who has no feelings. If you just drew close to Me with trust, you would feel the love which My Sacred Heart has for you.

If a fire breaks out in a place, people come from everywhere so there is as little damage as possible. Then why do you not put out Satan's fire? You let the flame of hell carry out its destruction. Woe to you who look with cowardice, because you are responsible. You close your eyes and let souls be damned."

DO NOT LET LAXITY GAIN POWER OVER YOU

Jesus: "Oh, chosen souls, you know Me. You also know that My patience and My goodness have no limits. You also know the severe words which might be said to you: 'Depart from Me into the eternal fire. Your hands do not gather with Me, they only scatter.' Oh, you unhappy consecrated souls, enter your own hearts and be converted to Me. There is still time. Don't let laziness have power over you. This sin is the root of every evil that enters your soul. You at least, get rid of this horrible sin that leads to despair and which you do not even want to hear about. Satan raises obstacles that block the Divine Light in your souls. Without the brightness of this life-giving light, you suffer and torture yourselves beneath the dark burden of laziness.

Come to Me, you who are overwhelmed by laziness and I will take it off your shoulders and lighten your burden. The Evil One has been carefully piling this problem upon you. Only the reception of My Body can help you out of it. Give yourselves to Me. I walk behind you. Are My warnings in vain? Realize that Satan causes these disorders. This is his work and it will continue as long as I permit. Do not tear yourselves from My arms which embrace you. Turn to Me and be sacrificed on the sacred altar of inner recollection and martyrdom.

You want to see for yourselves that this is My Will. Satan cannot stop this inner martyrdom. This battle in the depth of your souls brings about abundant fruit, just as does martyrdom. Watch and pray. As two or three gather, they take up the battle against the Prince of Darkness and his devastating power. Do not be idle! You act as though you did not have a heavenly Father who takes care of you. Set the earth ablaze with your burning desires. Use your sacrifice made from pure love to burn away all sin. Do you not believe this is possible? Just trust Me. Your faith and trust will give strength to a million souls to persevere. My daughter, you must never be half-hearted. Unite yourself to those souls that are consecrated to Me. I call you, also. Do not make decisions based upon the feeling of that moment. Have a firm and persevering acceptance of sacrifices. This is what produces abundant fruit in the souls."

A DESIRE UNITES HEAVEN TO EARTH

August 8, 1962

On returning home after adoration of the Most Blessed Sacrament, we were speaking on the way. Rather, it was Him who was speaking. I listened, astonished... He recalled the early moments of my marriage, the ejaculatory prayer that we added to the family prayer at night: "O my sweet Jesus, make sinners and pagans also know You. Let them be converted and love You very much."

Jesus: "My little one, with those longings, you wanted many souls for Me. Do you know that I listened to you? Thanks to your desires, souls came to know Me. Many were converted and many love Me deeply. Do you know why I mention this again? Because I see the doubts that continually disturb you. What is the value of your desires? They are of great value. Just intensify them, and also your mortifications.

Again, My little Carmelite, I must use an example from your own life. Not long ago, after you had raised your children, you desired to have time to prepare for a good death. You see, I also fulfilled this desire. Understand in your heart that a desire is a wonderful instrument that unites Heaven to earth. From the first moment of My human existence, I wanted to bring about My redeeming work. An uninterrupted desire for the salvation of souls always filled My Heart.

Let this desire for souls burn in all of you. Be not of little faith. Remember what I told you: If you need strong support, say 'Father, I need Your strong, fatherly support.' He will extend His strong, fatherly arm. Take courage and grab His arm, not only you, but all those souls that I entrust to you."

AN INCREASE OF DESIRE

That same day, the Blessed Virgin also spoke to me.

Mary: "My little Carmelite, I ask you to continually increase your desire for my Flame of Love. You know the great sorrow I have for my country. Hungarian families are torn apart and live as if the soul were not immortal. With my Flame of Love, I want to make the home come alive again with love. I want to unite families that are scattered. I want you to be numerous so that many, many souls are united to my Flame of Love. Help Me! My Flame being lit depends upon you. Let the families of Hungary plead fervently so that we can hold back the chastising hand of my Divine Son."

THE COMING OF GOD'S KINGDOM

One day in August, the Lord Jesus spoke:

Jesus: "You know, do you not, that I invited you to My private war camp? Do not be attracted by the passing comfort of this world. The coming of My Kingdom must be your only purpose in life. My words will reach a multitude of souls consecrated to Me. Trust! My grace will be with you and I will help all of you in a miraculous way."

(The Lord's words sounded very harsh in my soul. I was very surprised as I never heard but sweet words from Him.)

Jesus: "Do not be surprised, My little Carmelite, if you hear My severe voice in the depth of your soul. I do this with love. Do not be lovers of comfort or cowards. Do not allow yourselves to be convinced and do not make others believe that everything is meaningless. Everything has meaning! It is easier to wait for the end of a storm rather than to confront the tempest and to save souls. You do not need more examples or more explanations. Give yourselves to the work. If you do nothing, you abandon the earth to Satan and to sin. How can I wake you up? Open your eyes and see the deadly danger that claims victims all around you and which threatens even your own souls."

Afterward, He asked me to take these words to the competent persons. He will help me in this. I did not want to keep recording Our Lord's complaints, but He asked me to keep writing them down. We had just come to a park. I would have liked to kneel before Him, but due to circumstances, I just sat on the grass. I got out my notebook to take notes. He flooded me with a wonderful feeling of His presence. He said:

Jesus: "I make you feel this way to prove to you that it is I who speak. Do not discard My request with a scorn. This disrespectful attitude causes indescribable sorrow. Take to heart My anguished and important desire, and that each one enters into himself and begins a new life. Draw from Me the strength to do that.

I know this is not new for you. You speak enough about this. What upsets Me is that you only speak about it, and you do not strive to establish the Kingdom of God among you. You know better than anyone that great efforts are needed for My Kingdom to come. Do not live as hypocrites. You offer the Holy Sacrifice for the faithful but you do this superficially. How many of you act this way!"

COMPLAINTS ABOUT CONSECRATED SOULS

August 16, 1962

Again, the Lord Jesus complained.

Jesus: "You see, My little one, how many consecrated souls live a carefree life. They waste their time in great idleness and on their own desires. From their table, they throw Me little crumbs, as if I am a beggar. And how long I let this go on! And for how much longer? Woe to you should the patience of the heavenly Father wear out. There will be no one to hold back His chastising hand. To you also, I will have to say: Depart from Me, you accursed, you did not defend the Cause of My Kingdom, you gave no value to the call I bestowed upon you. I have walked with you for so long. How many times I have reprimanded you! And you responded with a gesture of the hand that would have offended even a beggar." (His words caused great sadness in my soul.)

Again this same day, the Blessed Virgin spoke of the same topic.

Mary: "I am the one giving you the strength to begin. In spite of many objections and bad intentions, my Cause will succeed.

Accept the sufferings I will send to you: bodily sorrows, spiritual torments and great dryness of soul. In exchange, I will keep you safe from all sin. We will not allow you to be separated from us. You are here at our feet and we will fill you with innumerable graces. We will even make your faults and sins serve the good of your soul. These will always keep you humble. Always be concerned about humility. Only a very humble soul can fulfill our Cause.

Do not fear. You do not suffer alone but with me, with us. You will suffer much because consecrated souls will have many objections against our Holy Cause. We know that you will accept them with love. We see both your internal and external sufferings. You have thought about my Flame of Love for months. You yourself can see the need for persevering strength."

"Heavenly Mother, my feeble strength also takes nourishment from you."

Jesus: "Trust, My little one. No one can destroy God's plan. It is true however that I need your effort for My work of Redemption. I do not want to lose any of you. Satan is undertaking a battle against the human race like there has never been before."

A CHEERFUL SPIRIT

Today, the Lord Jesus instructed me.

Jesus: "Be My servant! Be always joyful! Every day that you serve Me must be a feast. Do not let anyone or anything that disturbs your cheerful spirit come near your soul. Take good care of your nuptial garment and let it radiate happiness. Wherever you go, let it be felt that you partake every day in the heavenly banquet. Desire that everyone have this same yearning. Let the coming of My Kingdom be the only object of prime importance in your life.

Be valiant! Testify to Me before men. How numerous are those whose lack of courage prevents them from getting closer to Me. Do nothing without Me. Have no thought without introducing Me into it. Am I not the One who gave you understanding? Sadly, there is hardly anyone grateful to Me for that. You, also, have not thanked Me yet. Without understanding, you would be no different from other creatures. Whatever the human understanding creates proceeds entirely from My own understanding. Be grateful for this gift on behalf of those who are not."

Unfortunately, I do not have a spiritual director to whom I can recount the constant changes that happen in my soul. I need advice in many things. The Lord Jesus unexpectedly answered my words.

Jesus: "I see that you have little faith. Why are you impatient? It is My responsibility to give you a spiritual director. Do not fear. I will give you a director according to My Heart. Do not fear, I will never abandon you."

These words coming from Him were so encouraging that they gave me great peace.

CONSECRATE OUR HOMES TO HIS DIVINE HEART

On a certain occasion, I complained to the Lord Jesus: "My Lord, I suffer because my meal has no taste." He was touched and spoke with me for a long time. It is unfortunate that I have not written these words, even if He often asks me to do it. But frequently His words are so jumbled within me that I cannot put them into words.

The Lord Jesus promised to give me a special strength for the nightly prayer because I am already exerting all possible effort. He promised that He would wake me up. What happiness fills my soul to experience His presence when He awakens me. The night prayer goes so quickly in His presence. While I was joined in union with

Him, something special happened. I will describe these things with the greatest humility.

While we were talking in the silence of a summer night, the conversation suddenly ended. Before He left, He stayed a long time in front of our house and made me sense that He was thinking about our house. He began to list the merits of our family, those virtues which I made the children practice when they were small. He emphasized how meritorious were the fervent night prayers. He said how much He appreciated the small ejaculations that we added to those prayers. He also noted that our family was consecrated to His Sacred Heart. I experienced His blessed presence and was deeply moved. We constantly hurt Him by our many sins. He, in spite of everything, is always kind. He said:

I BLESS THIS HOUSE

Jesus: "I bless this house that is consecrated to My Sacred Heart."

What a sublime experience was this blessing He gave to our family when He stayed for a long time before our house. Yet, even afterwards, He did not move. For a long time, He allowed me to feel His presence filled with goodness and majesty. As an insignificant person, really less than nothing, I felt great emotion. I could only babble: "Depart from me, O Lord, I am a great sinner." He replied:

Jesus: "The debt that I owe to My Mother obliges Me. The abundant graces and My blessing which I gave to your family, I gave at her request because you live in this house and you desire to spread the Flame of Love of her heart with every longing of your heart."

UNITE YOUR SUFFERINGS

Later, the Blessed Virgin spoke to me, asking that I pray for a soul that refused her.

Mary: "I know that you suffered much when he who rejected you did not judge my Holy Cause worthy of attention, even though you had enlightened him concerning your own person. My Divine Son unites your humiliations to His sufferings, which are of eternal value. And now, prepare your soul and body for still greater sufferings, in whatever way and measure they come upon you. Do not retreat, be humble, patient and persevering."

When the Blessed Virgin said this, a great anguish oppressed my heart. She had announced at other times that I would suffer. However, this time I trembled within...

All seems dark and insecure. The difficulties which do not allow the Cause to move forward were coming against me. I said:

"My beloved Jesus and loving Mother, I have great fear concerning the sufferings and humiliations that you warn me about. Without you, I am nothing. Hold me tightly."

BE MORE PATIENT

While I was at adoration in the church, someone began to play the organ. Suddenly, I heard the voice of the Lord Jesus in my soul.

Jesus: "I see how much it costs you to concentrate, My little one. Off key notes irritate you. The words through which you address yourselves to Me are heedless and insincere. I wait with patience and love that your words and your voice become clear and vibrant. Be more patient with yourself and others."

Once, I wanted to leave after the 7:00 a.m. Holy Mass, but Jesus' sweet voice tried to hold me back.

Jesus: "Why do you want to leave Me? Can we not walk together? Do not go. Why are you in such a hurry?"

I wanted to weed my garden because the weather was favorable.

Jesus: "Don't you want to attend the following Holy Mass? You know, do you not, why I called you to remain so close to Me? What you can do for Me, give it precedence over all other things! What did I tell you? Your great merit is suffering in whatever form it takes. Cover My holy hands with kisses. Have you forgotten that I chained you to My feet at your own request?

Why do you prefer some passing goal? Do you not trust the value of sufferings? I give value to your sufferings and it causes Me sorrow if you do not appreciate them. I would think that you are not accepting them with love. Without love, even great things have no value."

THE GIFT OF SILENCE

On another occasion, the Lord instructed me.

Jesus: "Remain silent, My little Carmelite. Do not be surprised if I say this often. Do you know who is truly wise? The one who says very little. True wisdom matures in the soil of silence, and only in silence can it take root. I am your Master and I instruct you. I prepared Myself for three years of activity by thirty years of silence. Being your Master, and united with Me, you will also find wisdom. Speak only when I give you the signal, expressing yourself only in the way you have learned from Me, or in the manner I would say it Myself. In a word, imitate Me. You will see that just a few words can produce good abundant fruits in souls."

August 20, 1962

Such great silence reigned in my soul. The Lord had not yet overwhelmed me with His kind words, but He had filled my soul with His Divine Presence in a marvelous way. I experienced this in my veins and in my bones. Although this feeling penetrated my entire body for only a short time, it caused me to tremble. I experienced this at other times, sometimes intermittently for weeks. Until now, nothing had been this intense. My body had become almost useless; I only felt my soul filled with Divine Grace.

SMALL SPARKS: GREAT SAINTS

August 21, 1962

The next day, I woke up thinking of how the saints give praise and adoration to God. Their homage and adoration filled my soul, I felt so small and miserable compared to them. I said to the Blessed Virgin: "My Mother, share with me your Flame of Love so I can continue to adore the Divinity in the company of the saints and Seraphims." Meanwhile, the Lord spoke in my soul. I found this marvelous because He had never spoken to me in that tone of voice.

Jesus: "You, little spark, no matter how small you are, were created by Me and from Me. Draw close to Me without fear. I give you My brilliance, and by enlightening one another, you will no longer notice the lackluster of your soul. Even great saints were My small sparks. I made each one great to the degree that they tried to come close to Me. Those souls which used great effort received the brightness of My light. For Me, time does not exist. Some souls can run a long race in a short time, and I call them quickly to Myself. Others start late. Nevertheless, they make more progress than those who walk slowly and cautiously. Do you remember what I told you one time? 'You fly like an arrow toward Heaven, but do not turn to look toward the earth lest the clamor of the world makes you dizzy.'

Now I say to you: 'Give yourself to Me with confidence and go beyond all that would keep you from coming to Me.'"

August 25, 1962

A face appeared before the eyes of my soul. I do not know why I contemplated it with my eyes opened or closed. I understood that it was the face of a priest, and I tried to remember where and when I had seen him. However, I couldn't remember. Then I put it aside. A few days later, while I was resting one afternoon, my daughter was with me, putting books in order. Suddenly, she put a photo in front of me. It was the face I had seen in the spiritual vision a few days earlier. I read his name beneath the picture, Father Biro, a Jesuit priest. I had never seen him or known him, or heard his name. Nevertheless, he was a great soul. I knew this from reading the page my daughter showed me. Besides his photo, were his famous words: "Even if I have to suffer until I die, what have I lost if I become a saint?"

This produced a great explosion in my soul. In those days, the Evil One had besieged me with many difficult temptations.

REPRESENT THE SOULS OF THE PARISH

August 28, 1962

Jesus began to speak.

Jesus: "Do nothing from your own will. Tell your spiritual director all that Our Mother and I ask of you. His direction will always show you the road. Leave the rest to him.

Accept with humility his words which are also from Me. Let your fervent desire to share in My work of Salvation continue to burn in your soul with great humility. You will not lose your reward, everlasting happiness. Just serve Me with all your strength."

On one occasion, a great yearning overwhelmed me and I desired many souls for Him. The Lord Jesus told me with kindness:

Jesus: "My little Carmelite, now I see that I can trust you with a great missionary work. I give you a new task, take it into your heart.

From now on, you will be the representative of the souls of our parish community. This is a great task. Every day, you will recite the morning prayers in the name of the parish community; in the name of the fathers, the mothers, the young people, the indifferent children and the foolish elderly who, even now, do not even think about the end of their life. Ask for the gift of the Holy Spirit for them. I will answer your prayer. Ask the Father in My Name and pray for the parish community. Ask His mercy by My Holy Wounds. During the day, offer Me reparation for the unfaithful souls in the parish. You see, for this you must renounce yourself entirely. I have chosen you to be the intercessor of the city. Do you know what this means? It is almost a priestly dignity. Make many spiritual communions for them. Also, do not forget the sick. Take care that not even one soul be damned."

"Adorable Jesus, I will ask that Your Kingdom come to them." He continued talking.

THE WOMB OF THE FAMILY

Jesus: "With this task, My little Carmelite, I fulfill all the dreams of your youth. You always wanted to go to the missions. Do you know why this was impossible until now? For this great task, you had to mature first in the womb of your family. Don't forget, your principal missionary work will always be your own family. I could not entrust you with that before because I did not want you to stop halfway. Your family is the point of departure for your mission. This work is not yet finished. Be interested principally in priestly vocations.

Remember what I told you. Whatever you ask, you will receive. Pray and do much penance. This is the goal of the life of a true Carmelite."

"Help me, O Lord, to renounce my own will, to obey only You and to seek only what pleases You. Let Your light enlighten me and all that You have entrusted me with."

This teaching and conversation were very long and the Lord Jesus was not yet finished.

SEEK AND LOVE HUMILIATIONS

Jesus: "Each night, My little one, ask yourself what you have done for the coming of My Kingdom. Never be content with yourself. There is no room on earth for self-satisfaction. The reward of your labors is not a worldly reward. Work as hard as possible. See humiliation as a great instrument that guarantees abundant fruit for your work. Seek and love humiliation. I did this during My lifetime. If this is difficult for you, seek out Our Mother. She is the true teacher of humility and she will help you. Seek all her virtues. You will find in My Person a powerful strength to do this. Do not think about rest; you will receive from Me an abundant reward for your tiredness."

August 31, 1962

The Blessed Virgin said a few words:

Mary: "My Flame of Love must be carried across to the other side of the ocean."

I do not know how I will fulfill this because the Blessed Virgin did not explain. She just asked me to be cautious.

Editor's Note – The spark has skipped over to America; it first arrived to Ecuador and, next, to Mexico and to the entire South America. This same spark continued its journey towards the north up to Canada, and from that country, towards the United States and many others, including Africa.

MEDITATING ON THE PASSION

I went to the church for the three hours of adoration. When I came to the altar, the devil began to tempt me, disturbing me with his disgusting thoughts. Later, during the holy hours, he tried to come close to me with his flatteries. He said that I am unique, that the life I lead is not for any human being, and that he does not wish me any harm. He just wants me to live a normal life. People are going to think that I am an eccentric bigot; that I am foolish because my dress, my food, my enjoyments, and the way I treat others is not like other people.

When I forced myself to be immersed in the sufferings of Jesus, the Evil One became very angry. In his useless rage, he shouted his words in the silence of my soul, which was already filled with the Lord's presence, "I am waiting, that's all." My heart was shaken. "O adorable Jesus, free me from the Evil One."

On innumerable occasions, he comes suddenly and threatens me. However, he knows very well that they (Jesus and Mary) use me to blind him and I give myself to them.

The frequent temptations exhaust me very much and I undergo many battles because of the Flame of Love of the Blessed Virgin. When I realize clearly that I suffer for the Flame of Love, all becomes easy. The greatest suffering is when my soul is in total darkness and the awful torment of doubts weigh upon me. This suffering, produced by internal anguish, invades me so greatly that I hardly have the strength to walk.

The following day, the Evil One used his tortures to disturb my peace. When I implored the Lord to give me understanding so I could see His Holy Will, the fury of Satan increased to such a degree that I was horrified. It was daytime and his terrifying presence, while I was kneeling at the altar, produced an overwhelming shaking in me. A new thought pierced me: "Do you know that this is pure imagination? When someone, in their life, has never been able to do something that is worthwhile, they try to get attention. Look at the great artists, the wise men, the inventors of technology. See all that man has produced by his own strength. You see, you are incapable of doing these things; that is what provoked your thoughts, these awkward confusions."

These terrible torments! Taking the Elect of the Holy Spirit as an intermediary, I implored the Lord Jesus not to let me perish even though I am a great sinner.

I do not want to sin. Then how have I gotten involved in this terrible sin? It is cruel suffering when I have to suffer from my own pride. "Adorable Jesus and Most Holy Mother, I offer you my sinfulness, restore me from my sins."

With great torment, I made the Stations of the Cross and after finishing the three holy hours, I knelt at the altar. "Adorable Jesus, I am very fearful."

A terrible anguish continued to torment me. However, the confused thoughts of my spirit began to calm down. A gentle peacefulness came from the Lord; it was like a calming breath upon my soul, and He let me hear His voice.

Jesus: "Do not fear. I will not allow anyone to harm you. If he were able, together with his henchmen, he would have crushed you like dust. Be strong. The Holy Spirit will strengthen you."

On hearing those words, I received an inner illumination. I recalled what the Blessed Virgin told me a few days ago.

Mary: "Now we set out, my little Carmelite, together with Saint Joseph. You must walk with us along Bethlehem's dark roads covered with mist. You have to seek a refuge for my Flame of Love, which is Jesus Christ himself. Do you want to come with us? Because it is now that we are leaving to carry on my Flame of Love. You will receive strength and grace from us."

After this, I was in such a state of mind that I almost did not have strength to walk. I felt that physical strength was no longer needed; only the strength of my soul carried me with the Blessed Virgin to travel the dark paved roads of Bethlehem.

We were looking for a refuge, but everybody turned us away.

GIVE YOURSELF TO JESUS WITHOUT RESERVE

September 1, 1962

In this extraordinary mental state, the Lord spoke to me day after day. Today, He said:

Jesus: "Do you want to give yourself to Me entirely and without reserve? I, the Man-God, ask this of you. I need you for My work of Salvation. What I am asking you now is a total abandonment. Therefore renounce yourself completely with all your strength and all your will. You must serve only Me. No one else and nothing else now exists for you. Only I."

"O Lord Jesus, my adorable Christ, you ask me to serve only You. Can I do anything else? As You ask, I give myself totally and without reserve. Sweet Jesus, I live for You and I die for You. I am Yours for all eternity. To whom else can I belong? Who else would accept me with all my sins, failings and defects? With the greatest pleasure, Lord, I sacrifice my little life for souls. My only desire is that Your eternal Will, the salvation of souls, is brought about. Divine Sculptor, form me in Your image and likeness, so that at the hour of my death You recognize the work of Your holy hands. O blessed Divine Hand that carves and caresses at the same time. My soul burns with desires when You say that You need my sacrifice. What a great distinction! I bless You, beloved Jesus, and exalt You without end."

BRING TO THE POPE

September 3, 1962

Mary: "I want to speak to you as a mother speaks to her daughter. I know that you struggle greatly for the Cause of the Flame of Love of my heart. My little Carmelite, I am happy that you have so much taken it into your heart. Listen. Soon, the day will come when the first official step will be taken. This should have happened already. The many humiliations which you experienced for my Flame of Love and the many sacrifices that you make are powerful means to arrive at this first step.

Tell your spiritual director of my desire. In turn, he must bring my Cause to the Primate Bishop of your country, and then to the Roman Pontiff, Vicar of my Divine Son on earth. There has never been a time of grace like this since the Word became Flesh. Blinding Satan will shake the world."

EFFECT OF GRACE FOR THE DYING

September 7-8, 1962

While praying before dawn, the Blessed Virgin spoke with me about the effect of grace of her Flame of Love.

Mary: "From today on, when you, together with the person designated to you as companion, are in vigil, to you who already know my Flame of Love, I will grant the following grace: as long as your night vigil will last, my Flame of Love will act upon those who are dying throughout the whole world. I will blind Satan so that my Flame, gentle and full of grace, will save them from eternal damnation."

I was filled with joy when I heard the Blessed Virgin say this. But later, a terrible doubt assaulted me. Did I correctly understand what the Blessed Virgin said in the early morning?

This is an immense grace. How can I receive it? The grave doubt concerning this grace granted to me and my companion weighs upon my soul. Is this coming from my pride? At other times, it seems that the Blessed Virgin said nothing at all. In one word, I really do not understand. Maybe I doubt because my pride does not allow me to believe. "There is no need to believe everything." The Evil One has me so confused that I say the Rosary with my lips, but not as I usually do. Instead, I keep repeating, "I believe in you, O miraculous Virgin." I only say this with my lips, but my mind and my heart refuse to accept it. I want to cry for not being able to believe. The Evil One insists that this is my interpretation. With all my strength, I resist his intrusions. "O Blessed Virgin, dispel my doubts." It upsets me that my nighttime prayer would be so meritorious. Is it possible and permissible to believe this? In the darkness of my soul, the Blessed Virgin gave no reply. Therefore, I asked the Lord Jesus. He said:

Jesus: "Only through the medium of My Mother."

These words confused me even more. In vain did I go to His holy feet. Now, even this security has ended for me. In my powerlessness, I kept asking, "Lord, will You abandon me?" Again, I heard His voice:

Jesus: "You should accept this miraculous power of the Flame of Love of My Mother not just with your lips but with your mind as well."

In spite of all my efforts, my mind refuses to accept these words. Satan has so confused the light of my vision that I have no conclusion.

I would like to know, if I refuse to accept this immense miracle regarding my miserable self, will I sin against the Blessed Virgin? What should I do, adorable Jesus? Come and help me to escape from the Evil One. Without a spiritual guide, I have no one to help me through these terrible temptations. I spent the whole day in these torments. For hours, I could only repeat: "I believe in you, O miraculous Holy Virgin."

That same night, I went to the religious Sister who was assigned to accompany me. I told her the most recent message of the Blessed Virgin and my doubts that lasted all day. We were talking in the chapel, before the Lord Jesus. When she heard these messages, she did not doubt. She accepted what I told her with simple faith and holy admiration. A child's smile, so characteristic of her, came across her face. Her faith dispelled my doubts.

While we were talking about the great grace that had touched us, she turned to the tabernacle and said, speaking to the Blessed Virgin: "O Most Holy Virgin, you are all powerful and yet men want to act against you." In admiration of the Flame of Love of the Most Holy Virgin, we both were overwhelmed and we resolved to pray for the greatest number of souls to be saved from eternal damnation. My Sister companion gave me a lot of advice which I accepted with a humble heart. When we said goodbye before the altar of the Lord, she did not know what strength and tranquility the Lord Jesus poured into me through her.

CONTINUAL HUMILIATIONS

September 15, 1962

During the morning, the Blessed Virgin lamented with heart breaking grief that many souls were being lost due to the lack of understanding caused by superficiality.

She does and grants everything she can; however, the consecrated souls reject everything. She asked me to accept the sacrifices and humiliations whose merits make it possible to save souls.

"My Mother, I ask you humbly to forgive me. I do not waver, not even in the midst of my terrible temptations. You know that I am only an insignificant speck of dust. I can do nothing without the two of you."

She replied:

Mary: "It is precisely because of your littleness, incapacity and humility, that my Flame of Love will move ahead gently and without disturbance. Therefore, be careful and remain hidden in humility. You will be continually subjected to humiliations, both internal and external. It is only thus that I can guard you so to pass on my Flame of Love."

At another time, the Virgin gave me her kindest words.

Mary: "Come with me. We are going to walk the dark and misty streets of Bethlehem with my Flame of Love. Do not fear. Saint Joseph and I will be with you. Before others join us, there will be just the three of us."

Many times, the Blessed Virgin makes me feel her sorrow. Some days, I suffer so much with her that I can hardly walk. All morning, she poured into me, to a great degree, this grace of suffering. Because of my tearful eyes, I tried to avoid everyone, so they would not notice my great affliction. I have only one thought - to fulfill all that she asks of me.

The anguish of my soul is brought about by sufferings and doubts, but it is increased even more by Satan. In his cruel hatred, he stirs up terrible doubts in me. "In every way, you are so useless. Why do they not entrust these matters to the bishops? Why to a creature as foolish as you? Because they do not believe such gossip! An intelligent person would not even have time to talk with you. Even those to whom they have sent you did not accept your message. Seeing that such a thing is impossible, they rejected you. Do not keep trying, be reasonable. Anyway, it is useless."

Satan even bothered me at the sublime moment of Holy Communion. I tried to keep him far away.

SUFFER WITH ME

One day, on my way to be with the Lord Jesus, I did not intend to stay a long time because I was very tired. I recited my office and I wanted to take leave of Him. He asked me:

Jesus: "Why are you leaving so quickly? Is there anything more important for you than I? Perhaps your knees hurt. Think of Me when I fell on My knees, nevertheless I did not abandon the Way of the Cross. Remain with Me. Do you not see how lonely I am? Do you have nothing to say to Me? This also has no importance. Listen to the silence. Our hearts beat to the same rhythm. May our glances melt in one another. Just tell Me that you love Me and adore Me, also on behalf of others.

You know that you must always gather with Me. Now, here in this silence, you can gather with Me; also, in the quiet of the night, while you are watching. I teach you so you learn and teach others how to gather souls. The will of the soul is love, and love can do everything. You must just desire with all your strength. May our thoughts be always in unison – to save souls from eternal damnation. Only in this way can you lessen My cruel sorrow. Let that not be boring to you. I have repeated it to you over and over: Suffer with Me."

At this time, He shared with me the precious sorrow of His Soul as a precious gift of His grace.

On another occasion, He said:

Jesus: "Do you know how much My Soul suffers because souls are lost? May our hands gather in unity."

"Lord, I am only able to gather so few."

Jesus: "Make up for this by your desires and your ardent yearnings, My little one, and take refuge in Me with all trust."

FAST FOR SOULS OF PRIESTS

September 28, 1962

This is a day of fast I am offering for the souls in Purgatory, especially the souls of priests. The Lord Jesus said that He could not resist the pleas of the Blessed Virgin. He flooded my mind with the following words:

Jesus: "Because you are appeasing My intense desire for souls, My little one, I will tell you about your reward. Thanks to your fast, from now on the soul of a priest will be freed from Purgatory within eight days of his death. And anyone who observes this fast will obtain this grace for a suffering soul."

(Note: If that soul died in a state of grace.)

These words were filled with such mercy and majesty that I cried because we can so effectively help the souls suffering in Purgatory. My heart rejoiced when He told me of this new and great grace. When I left Holy Mass to go home, He whispered in my heart:

Jesus: "I will walk with you and stay with you all day. May our lips beg our heavenly Father, together, to obtain mercy."

With profound adoration, I said: "My most adorable Jesus, to live this grace with You in my soul, and through Your lips, petition the Eternal Father together!" On my way home, my soul was consumed in adoration. Under the effect of grace, my heart beat so much that I almost fainted. I then begged Him: "My adored Jesus, I desire so much that your great grace become known publicly and that more people come to profoundly experience your intimate yearnings."

The Lord Jesus asked me to write especially about how we can help souls.

Jesus: "By observing the fast I ask for, priests will be freed from Purgatory on the eighth day after their death."

(The strict fast: for one day, just take bread and water.)

THURSDAYS AND FRIDAYS ~ DAYS OF GRACE

September 29, 1962

My soul is continually filled with the Blessed Virgin's Flame of Love. Even in the night hours when I stay awake for a while, I ask ceaselessly that her silent miracle be enkindled over the whole world the soonest possible.

I arrived at the church early in the morning. The Blessed Virgin waited for this moment to speak to me in the silence of the church.

Mary: "My little one, Thursdays and Fridays should be considered as great days of grace. Those who offer reparation to my Divine Son on these days will receive a great grace. During the hours of reparation, the power of Satan will weaken to the degree that those making reparation pray for sinners. Nothing flashy is required, no boasting about love is necessary. It is burning in the depth of the hearts and spreads to the others.

I want you not just to know my name, but to know also the Flame of Love of my maternal heart beating for you. I entrusted you with the task of making known this burning love. That is why you must be very humble. Such a grace as this has only been granted to only very few. Hold such great grace in high esteem. What you must love and seek the most in it are the internal and external humiliations. Never believe that you are important. Your principal task is to consider yourself as nothing; never stop doing this. Even after your death, this should be happening. It is for that reason also that you receive the graces of internal and external humiliations. In this way, you can remain faithful in spreading my Flame of Love. Take advantage of every opportunity; seek these external and internal humiliations with your own effort, because what you seek for yourself increases your humility even more."

When the Blessed Virgin finished these maternal instructions, my heart was filled with profound humility. The Blessed Virgin allowed me to feel how powerful she is. Yet, in her earthly life, she was humble and modest.

The Blessed Virgin commanded me to write her words in a detailed form because this request, which she gives through me, is a 'message' for all her children who will be the first to spread her Flame of Love.

That same day, I went to the hospital to visit Father X. The Sister nurse gave me five minutes for my visit. These were serious moments. I asked her if she could leave us alone for a while. When she left, I asked Father if he knew who I was. He recognized me only after I began to speak about the Cause. I mentioned the Flame of Love of the Blessed Virgin which he already knew. I asked him to read it, if possible. He said: "My daughter, I cannot even read the Breviary or the mail that I receive."

After a few moments of silence, he looked at me with his eyes half opened. I understood that his eyes shone with a light that is not of this world. I felt that he was already contemplating God. In a low voice, he said: "I am a victim, my daughter. I gave myself over fully to the Lord Jesus and the Blessed Virgin. I choose nothing. They do with me as they see best." I revealed to him what the

Blessed Virgin told me about those instances when the doctors have given up hope.

Mary: "I will restore him quickly but not for a long time."

I asked Father: "What should I do with the Flame of Love of the Blessed Virgin?" – "I can do nothing. If the Blessed Virgin had entrusted this to me, it would be different. But I can do nothing." He added: "Have confidence, the Blessed Virgin will arrange everything." For his part, he will pray and offer his sufferings for the Cause.

I began to collapse from the many spiritual sufferings that have consumed my soul for the past months. I told Father: "I, too, undergo many sufferings, like the living dead."

At this point, the Sister came in and Father obediently said, "I bless you, my daughter." At the moment he raised his hand to bless me, I took it to my lips spontaneously and with great veneration, perhaps for the last time. I thought that even if he gets better, I might not see him again. At this point, the nurse said, "Please end the visit."

As I left and went to the Church of Perpetual Adoration, a great darkness weighed upon my soul. On the way, Satan again threw in my face his insulting words. Filled with evil, he rejoiced. I prostrated myself before the Blessed Sacrament: "O Jesus, I have come to complain to You, even though You know all that I will tell You. Do You know what Father told me? You know, do You not? My Jesus, I beg You unceasingly. How sinful I am, and still, You entrust me with this matter that concerns the whole world. I am weak and useless. How I would rejoice if You would entrust this to a worthy and pure soul. My Lord, I am not worthy of this." It is thus that I begged the Lord Jesus.

Meanwhile, Satan wanted to overpower my soul with all of his forces. He said: "At last, I am about to conquer you. Did I not tell you that only you would be so foolish to accept this and spread your impious and inhumane thoughts to others. Why do you not pay attention? I always told you that only I want your good, but you are committed to follow your foolish ideas. I hope that you will start being reasonable. Finally, this lesson has torn away the veil over your foolish thoughts. Tell me. Why do you want, at a total sacrifice, to be superior to the rest of mortals?" My soul was unaware of anything else except the voice of the Evil One. I remained in a darkness that I could not bear with human strength. Prostrate before the Blessed Sacrament, I battled within myself: "What should I do? O Lord, do not abandon me. Purify my thoughts and put them in order."

MATURE BY SUFFERINGS

October 1, 1962

Today, the Lord Jesus spoke again.

Jesus: "You suffer, do you not? Suffer for Me. This is My gift. You can only receive suffering like this from Me. Whether the suffering is spiritual or bodily, accept it from pure love for Me. You know what I told you: We must go up to Calvary. May our feet journey together. And if you are feeling alone, I permit it only so that you receive merits that you can offer for your faults and for souls consecrated to Me.

Do not be impatient because you have no spiritual director. Now, I am in charge of directing you. Just pay attention to Me. Even when I keep you in the darkness of your doubts, I am with you. Do not forget that when I was asleep in the boat, I chided My apostles for their lack of faith. It takes only one word from Me to bring about silence and light in your soul. Sometimes, I will send it through other people; accept it, even if it is through the most insignificant person. I repeat: I do this to increase your humility.

Do not be concerned about your spiritual father. Trust in Me and abandon yourself to Me. This is the important thing. My little sunflower, turn to Me! I, the Divine Sun, am nurturing you through sufferings and sorrows. Do not be frightened by the suffering that frequently comes upon your soul. I do this to get you accustomed to sufferings. By these, we walk together and gather together."

October 2, 1962

Jesus: "My little Carmelite, your continual sacrifices give witness to your continual fidelity to Me and to My work of Salvation. These make you walk on the path of martyrdom. Do not fear, our feet journey together, and even though you grieve, let us continue walking together. I am giving you abundant graces, My little one, because My Heart overflows with love and prompts Me to be lavish. I fill each of your efforts with graces that are a thousand times greater. Would that many souls loved Me as you do. What great joy I would experience if I could give to many souls the abundant graces which I give to you."

"Accept, dear Jesus, the prayer that I say with all my heart, 'I love You very, very much.'"

October 3, 1962

After lunch, I stayed in the silence of the dining room, meditating. The Lord Jesus surprised me with His consoling and revitalizing words:

Jesus: "Let the light shine in your soul! Be humble and fulfill My will with all your mind. When what I say arouses resistance in your soul, then you know that this is My Will."

For two days, the Lord Jesus has been saying that I must try again to put in action the Flame of Love of the Blessed Virgin. I must act precisely where I was once rejected. My heart was shaken by these words. The previous embarrassment, the rigid refusal, and the humiliation penetrated like a sharp sorrow into every part of my body. Meanwhile, I thought again: "Is this truly the Lord Jesus who speaks in my soul?" While I was going back and forth, the Lord Jesus made me hear His voice in the depth of my soul.

Jesus: "You have to humble yourself in every way and in every form that it happens."

HAVE RECOURSE TO SAINT JOSEPH

October 4, 1962

Today, the Blessed Virgin spoke again.

Mary: "Remember what I told you. You must set out on the dark, muddy, noisy and distressing road to Bethlehem to seek a refuge for my Flame of Love. You are coming with Saint Joseph and me, my little Carmelite. The Flame of Love needs a refuge. Take all the anguish and love of my maternal heart, and also those with which, humiliated and in dark insecurity, I sought a refuge with Saint Joseph. Now, you also must set out along this road silently, without a single word of complaint or moaning, humiliated, misunderstood and exhausted. I know that this is difficult, but your Redeemer is with you; that also gave me strength. Saint Joseph will accompany you. Turn to him for help. He is kind. Ask him for his active protection."

REMAIN IN MY WORK OF REDEMPTION

While I was praying the litanies with exposition of the Blessed Sacrament, the Lord Jesus surprised me with His words.

Jesus: "Today you are very distracted and have hardly lifted your soul to Me. Why do you abandon Me? I long for your words and for each vibration of your soul."

"Pardon me, my beloved Jesus." As I was repentant and immersed in Him, the litanies began. When I lifted up my eyes towards the monstrance where He rested in His immaculate light, I looked at Him with deep homage. At that moment, it seemed like the monstrance moved and turned slightly toward me.

The Lord's unlimited love poured out into my heart. With my eyes closed, in deep humility and conscious of my misery, I offered myself to Him. I gave Him all my weakness because I had nothing else to offer Him. Moved, He told me:

Jesus: "You see, the Divine Sun turned toward you because you did not turn to Him. You have wasted your word on trifles. Therefore, I speak to you to regain what you did not accomplish. Now, give Me your thoughts. Let us harvest together. We need each drop of oil. Your oil bearing seeds can only mature and produce abundant fruit in the rays of the Divine Sun. Try to serve Me even better. Do not forget. There should not be even one hair between us. There is much to do and few laborers. With all your strength, remain continually in My redeeming work. You will not be paid less because you came later than those who arrived early. But, naturally, from you I require surrender and faithfulness that must last unto death, because it is the only way you can help from up there also. There, our hands will gather in unity."

The next day in the church, He began to complain.

Jesus: "The affliction of My Heart is so great because of many souls consecrated to Me. How I walk with them! I follow them step by step with My graces. In spite of that, they do not recognize Me nor do they ask where I am going. They are bored. They live in wasteful laziness, seeking only their own comfort. They exclude Me from their lives, taking every opportunity to hide like cowards and to deceive themselves. They act as if they were not My workers. O unhappy ones, how can you give an account of your wasted time?

Do not force Me to raise My Sacred Hands to curse you. I am love, patience, kindness, understanding, pardon, sacrifice, salvation and eternal life. Do you not desire this? Was My Sacred Body crucified, covered with blood, and raised on high in vain? O you blind and heartless, do you not see what I have done for you? Is not your heart moved? Do you not want to walk with Me, and harvest with Me? To have your hearts beat in union with Me? Are not our souls in harmony? Did I open My Heart to you in vain? Would you let My flow of graces be wasted? Do you not want to share My feelings? Do you not want to hear the beating of My humble and kind Heart? Or do you prefer that I shout at you with My voice of thunder: 'Why are you standing here doing nothing?' Don't be delicate and scrupulous. You should stand where I put you, firm and full of the spirit of sacrifice. I arranged everything so I could suffer for you, but you, comfort lovers, show no initiative. You only excuse yourselves and spend your whole life like this. Take upon yourself the Cross that I also have embraced and thus offer yourselves as victims as I have done. Otherwise, you will not have eternal life.

My little sunflower, I know that you listen to My many complaints. In the warmth of your heart, I experience warmth. I am so lonely."

OUR HEARTS BEAT TO THE SAME RHYTHM

Jesus: "Let this sublime feeling be a reward for your fidelity. May our souls be in harmony. What happiness this is for Me. Immerse yourself in the ocean of My graces.

I give you this grace because you asked to be immersed in Me. Always ask, My little Carmelite! I am happy to distribute My treasures. You can cash them in at the hour of your death. You might believe that your reward will be as great as your sufferings. Not at all! Human words cannot express what I have prepared for all of you. I await your arrival with a rich gift. My Heart will rejoice at your arrival. Many souls whom you helped to set free from Purgatory through your sacrifices will welcome you. They will overflow with joy. Like good friends, they will wait to meet you. Understand that this joy will never end, and let nothing that you must do for My work of Salvation seem tiring to you.

May our glances melt in one another. In My eyes bathed with tears and blood, you will see the longing of My Heart for souls. Gather with Me, My little one! I placed in your heart that desire for souls and I will continually increase it, but you must take advantage of every opportunity."

LIGHT FOR MY CHURCH

October 5, 1962 - First Friday

Jesus: "Today, My Heart joyfully awaits all the souls. I will pour out upon all of you My extraordinary graces. Take advantage of this moment in which I distribute such richness.

My daughter, be the window of the Church which My Divine Grace makes bright and shining. To make this a reality, you must continually work so that through you, the Divine Sun can shine upon all those in My Holy Church who are close to your soul. Your window receives the brightness of My splendor and transmits its light. Those who are close to you will feel the Divine Sun shining upon them through you. This will make the fruit of My work of Salvation more abundant in souls."

The Lord Jesus told me this after Holy Communion. At the same time, the Blessed Virgin began to speak with maternal goodness.

Mary: "My little one, I unite you firmly with me. The Flame of my heart, that I entrusted you, will project onto you its rays of abundant graces. This will continue even in Heaven. With my maternal hand, I bless your drops of oil which you collect so zealously.

With motherly love, I will await your arrival in Heaven. The drops of oil resulting from your sufferings will fall on the earth into the lamps that are either extinguished or barely flickering in the souls, and they will ignite at my Flame of Love. You, therefore, can take your place beside me until the end of the world."

ASK FOR MANY SPIRITUAL GUIDES

October 6, 1962

At Communion, the lack of a spiritual guide weighed again on my soul. The Lord Jesus reprimanded me lovingly.

Jesus: "Be patient, and let the value of your suffering be well obvious to your eyes. I tell you why I leave you without a spiritual guide. Offer this suffering so there will be many true spiritual guides. I allow you to experience this suffering on behalf of many others. Ask for abundant graces so that there will be many holy confessors. How many souls would come closer to Me if spiritual directors guided souls with more understanding and patience. Let that also be part of your missionary work. Sacrifice much for this. May our hands gather in unity." (His voice was gracefully entreating.)

THE GRACES RECEIVED BY MOTHERS

October 9, 1962

Today, while I was with the Savior, He infused the joy of His Heart into my soul.

Jesus: "How wonderful that you have come. How I awaited you! At other times, I told you to be immersed in Me like a drop of water in wine. I am the wine, you are the water. Just be united with Me and you will be astonished. Only I will reign in you. My Body and Blood give strength and life to all of you. How happy you will be to receive more of My life-giving strength. Gather with Me."

With sadness, I complained to the Lord Jesus that the Evil One seeks to destroy the peace of our family. "Oh, give us peace!" I asked for abundant graces that My children live in God's grace. He allowed me to hear His consoling voice.

Jesus: "When you are in Heaven and from up there you contemplate the death of one of your children, you will be by his bed. Your drop of oil will fall on the empty lamp and the Flame of Love of the Blessed Virgin will be lit. This great outpouring of graces will save souls from damnation. They will experience your motherly hand caressing them. Also, you will feel the great power which your many sufferings possess. These souls will also experience your hand which will help them at the moment of death. They will see your meritorious life on earth which they do not now appreciate."

SATAN TEMPTED ME

On another occasion, Satan tempted me terribly. I could hardly keep my thoughts on God. He argued: "Do not try so hard. You will gain nothing that way. You see that you have no protector. You continue to foolishly make efforts only because of your stubbornness."

In the middle of these terrible vexations, I asked the Holy Spirit: "Spirit of Understanding, of Strength, of Wisdom, descend upon me and take possession of me." The Evil One shouted in the depth of my soul: "Your strength, wisdom and understanding are only in your freedom. Why do you not use your human rights? You are not bad. You are only terribly stubborn. Be strong and aim to free yourself from this foolishness. Be convinced that you will never attain your end. All will end in unending shame. After so many failures, be reasonable. Live a quiet, tranquil life. Why be a martyr? You will receive no reward."

MESSAGE TO DISPERSED RELIGIOUS

October 11, 1962

Jesus: "My little Carmelite, I want you to write down what I tell you and send it to all those who have a great need to think about their vocation. Let them offer the real situation – where they are not allowed to engage freely in any apostolic activity – in reparation and for the benefit of souls. For them, this causes great suffering. Tell all those who consecrated their lives to Me, and now, due to the present situation, cannot engage in external activity, to give themselves to a deep spiritual life that will produce great fruits for themselves and for souls.

Today also, I count on their love. I desire it so ardently. Hopefully, they will take notice and listen to My sighs. Help Me to carry My Cross, it is so heavy. Do not leave Me alone. I call you because I need you. Even more, the time and the opportunity have arrived for you to give testimony on My behalf. Do not be lovers of comfort! Look at Me and look at My Cross. What comfort did I permit Myself? Does this not stir you? Or, have you become so accustomed to My goodness that you no longer esteem it? O you who are lukewarm, how can I gain your attention if you have no sensitivity to My immeasurable suffering? You, also, I have nourished in the warmth of My Heart. In spite of your great infidelity, I call to you with love. You no longer come with confidence. I redeemed you from eternal death. Now, you do not want to live with Me? You are content with the passing things of the earth. Oh, take account of the pain of My Heart which longs for you. You have free will and I want you to come to Me of your own will.

Write, My little Carmelite, write about My dissatisfied sigh! Perhaps when they read it, their hard hearts will soften. And if they were just a few, you would have done a good job. May our lips beg together the Eternal Father."

THE SUFFERING SOULS SHOULD FEEL THE EFFECT OF GRACE

October 13, 1962

Jesus spoke to me for many months but I did not record all the words because I did not always have the means to do it. Today, I was in the quiet of the church. I was praying for dying priests. Moved, the Lord Jesus whispered in my ear.

Jesus: "May our hands gather in unity."

NOVEMBER - MONTH OF THE EFFECT OF GRACE

I asked for the effusion of the graces of the Flame of Love of the Most Holy Virgin on the suffering souls. The Lord Jesus allowed me to sense that, in that moment, a soul was freed from Purgatory. I felt in my soul an indescribable relief. At that moment, by a pure grace of God, my soul was plunged into the immeasurable bliss of a soul that comes into God's presence. Then, I prayed with all the strength of my soul for the dying priests. Meanwhile, a great feeling of anguish filled my inner being, which is the suffering the Lord gives in order for me to reap souls along with Him. During my deep meditation, a delicate sigh, like a breath of the Blessed Virgin, surprised my soul.

Mary: "My little one, your compassion for the poor souls has so moved my motherly heart that I grant the grace that you sought. If at any moment, while invoking my Flame of Love, any of you pray in my honor three Hail Mary's, a soul is released from Purgatory. During November, the month of the deceased, ten souls will be released from Purgatory for each Hail Mary recited. The suffering souls must also feel the effect of grace of the Flame of Love of my maternal heart."

Editor's Note – The Bible proves that God has a right to express the conditions that He demands in order to grant a grace.

For Naaman the Syrian (2 Kings 5:1-14), the condition specified for his being healed is expressed in numbers even if its realization does not depend on the number. Why did the Prophet Elijah impose the condition to wash precisely seven times in the murky waters of the Jordan? Would not five or even three times be enough? Or maybe one immersion would have been enough! It was not the seven times, but the submission of his humble faith with which, at the request of his servants, he overcame his resistance and submitted to the desire of the Prophet.

It is certain that numbers often have a different meaning in the supernatural realm than the one we give them here on earth. The reason is that we often fall into the error of transposing our so mercantile way of thinking to the supernatural life, while Heaven has a very different intention with numbers.

The essence and the deeper meaning of this "heavenly mathematics" is neither the number nor the result, but love. This means that we should burn continually with the desire to liberate the suffering souls. How many useless thoughts, how many unnecessary concerns swirl around our own "I" we do meet in one single day! We should be thinking and acting out of love for those suffering souls. They will thank us and help us in our work to save souls.

If the Blessed Virgin expresses this in numbers, she does so only to adapt to our poor way of understanding ideas, and to stimulate and encourage us, as if to say: Listen, even if all of your contribution is quite insignificant, it can get a suffering soul to see God face to face! (The corresponding Diary annotation of July 17, 1964 confirms this interpretation. – The Publisher)

THE WORD BECAME FLESH

October 15, 1962

The Lord Jesus appealed to me with such sadness... and words that were nearly entreating.

Jesus: "Come, My little one, bow your head towards Me and let us talk about something that is difficult for you. Will the sufferings you do for Me be many?"

He mentioned one by one all the difficulties I am battling and said:

Jesus: "Do you want to give them up? Do not let the temptations which cause you so much suffering take you away from Me. We suffer together. I, also, was tempted by Satan. You can never be greater than your Master. In your life, you have not yet completed your task."

His words penetrated my soul deeply. He promised to give me special strength for every trial and told me to keep trying.

Jesus: "The main thing is to fight continually."

Although He spoke of many things, I could not record them all. Experiencing such goodness, my heart was moved. I said to the Lord Jesus: "My Jesus, You know that my soul is ready, but my flesh is weak." He filled my soul with the strength of His grace. Then He spoke to me, just as we humans speak to each other.

Jesus: "You see My riches. I need you and I enrich you. Therefore, may our hands gather in unity since our thoughts are one and our souls are in harmony.

You can see how intimate our prayer is. My little one, when I will be able to speak with many, My complaining words will be less frequent. I ask you to take advantage of every opportunity to ask our heavenly Father that more would know Me. For many, this is not easy, but they will experience difficulty only until they get very close to Me. Once they are beside Me, all will be easy because love makes sacrifices easy to bear."

One time, He overwhelmed my soul with His Divine Splendor. He said many things but I could not record them, except for this:

Jesus: "And the Word became Flesh. Penetrate and live in this sublime mystery, which signifies the Redemption of the world."

Even though I meditated on these words, I am incapable of expressing them. For months, I meditated only on this mystery, which is an inexhaustible miracle.

DESTROYED FAMILIES

October 18, 1962

Jesus: "My little one, did I send you many sufferings in these past few days? I implore you, do not grow weary of these great pains. Endure them for your family and those of the whole country. You know that Satan, foaming with rage, wants to destroy families. Let us suffer together. I suffer united to you and you to Me. I love you very much and I will not leave you without sufferings. Embrace suffering. Love only Me, serve Me with fidelity, and do not be surprised that I always manifest My love through sufferings.

The excessive love of My Heart makes Me consider you worthy of sufferings. This is the only way you can save many souls. You are a mother of a family and you are aware of the several forms of family disintegration. To save families, throw yourself into the furnace of suffering. Oh, how much sinning is done against Me by destroyed families! Make reparation and suffer for them. Do not lose the least opportunity. May our thoughts be in unison. Consider clearly the value of your sufferings. The number of those reaping with Me is so small. Do you know why? Because there are no souls willing to bear sufferings, especially those who would do it steadily. Without it, they cannot merit that I shower My graces on them continuously."

While He was speaking to me, I got out my little lunch. On Thursday and Friday, at the Lord's request, I eat only bread and water, and I offer it for the twelve priests and to make reparation to the Lord. Meanwhile, the Lord sat – in a spiritual way – next to me and said:

Jesus: "Oh, how this pleases Me! So few times have I enjoyed participating in such an intimate banquet. The souls that make reparation and faithfully follow My desires are so few."

While we were eating our bread, He allowed me to feel His inner emotions and He breathed His words full of grace into my soul.

Jesus: "May our souls be in harmony. In this way, our hands will gather in unity."

We continued to eat our bread and were taken up in our thoughts. He said:

Jesus: "What would I not give to you? Ask! Just ask! I will make up royally for your lunch. I offer the stream of My Heart's love to all who discover My hand asking for help. (He confided so much about what concerned me.) Now I fill your heart with the feeling of My Divinity. Oh, that we might gather together as much as possible!"

TO BLIND SATAN

October 19, 1962

The Blessed Virgin continued this conversation in the church.

Mary: "My little one, my Flame of Love has become so incandescent that I want to spread on you not only its light, but also its warmth with all its power. My Flame of Love is so great that I can no longer keep it within me; it leaps out at you with explosive force. My love that is spreading will overcome the satanic hatred that contaminates the world so that the greatest number of souls is saved from damnation. I am confirming there has never been anything like this before. This is my greatest miracle ever I am accomplishing for all. (She begged me not to misunderstand her.) My words are clear as crystal and easy to understand, hence do not create confusion with misinterpretations. Your responsibility then would be great if you ever did this. Get to work, do not be lazy. I will help you in an almost miraculous way, and my help will always continue. Trust me. Act quickly. Do not put off my Cause to another day.

Satan does not look on with his arms folded, he is making enormous efforts. He already feels that my Flame of Love is lighting. This provoked his terrible fury.

Enter into battle, we will be the conquerors. My Flame of Love will blind Satan to the same extent that all of you spread it around the world. Just as the whole world knows my name, so I want the Flame of Love of my heart performing miracles in the depths of the hearts to also be known. There will be no need to investigate this miracle. All will feel its authenticity within their hearts. Whoever has felt it once will communicate it to others because my grace will be active in them. There is no need for authentication. I will authenticate it myself in every soul so that all recognize the effusion of grace of my Flame of Love."

While the Blessed Virgin was saying these things, she kept my soul immersed in the thick darkness of the cave at Bethlehem. By the clarity of her Divine Motherhood, she enlightened me about the great and admirable mystery of the Word became Flesh: how the

Son of God, from the moment of His birth, came to be in our midst with the greatest poverty and humility. The Blessed Virgin strengthened me again in humility and said:

Mary: "Seek humility always and everywhere. Distance yourself from those who honor you, who love you. Seek only to be despised. Love those who speak evil of you and misunderstand you."

When she finished saying this, her voice became one with Jesus' words. He said:

Jesus: "This is My teaching, do it. I give you the time and the opportunity to practice this lesson. To participate in My work of Salvation, you must attract those souls who despise Me and do not understand Me. This is not easy but our hands will gather in unity. Whoever gathers with Me is assured of the results. Although the fruit may not be apparent, you can be sure of it. Ask the Father in My Name and He will grant you whatever you ask for on My behalf. Have confidence and always refer to the Flame of Love of My Holy Mother because the Three Divine Persons are obligated to her. Through her, you can receive the graces you ask for. She is the Spouse of the Holy Spirit and her love warms up the hearts and souls which have grown cold in the world. Then, waking up with renewed energies, you will be able to rise towards God."

THE SMALL SACRIFICES

October 25, 1962

While traveling, immersed in Jesus, I was thinking of what I should do to draw closer to His love. The Lord Jesus said:

Jesus: "Do you know how much you please Me? Just embrace My teaching. My insistence has not been in vain. I am truly happy. I just do not understand why you are so ambitious. Why are you not satisfied with the little sacrifices? Why do you not remain small? Do not believe that if you had powers to do great things, you would be a saint sooner. You are mistaken. Great things carry in themselves their own glory and receive their reward right here on earth. May our hands gather in unity. All that we gather together will be of great value, even the smallest things. For Me, nothing is insignificant. I hold in high esteem all that you do for Me."

AN IMPORTANT EJACULATORY PRAYER

October 1962 - A later note

I am going to record what the Blessed Virgin told me in this year, 1962. I kept it inside for a long time without daring to write it down. It is a petition of the Blessed Virgin:

Mary: "When you say the prayer that honors me, the Hail Mary, include this petition in the following manner:

'Hail Mary, full of grace… Pray for us sinners, spread the effect of grace of thy Flame of Love over all of humanity, now and at the hour of our death. Amen.'"

Note: The competent bishop asked Elizabeth: "Why the very old Hail Mary should be recited differently?" – On February 2, 1982, the Lord answered:

Jesus: "It is exclusively thanks to the efficacious pleas of the Most Holy Virgin that the Most Holy Trinity granted the effusion of the Flame of Love. By it, ask in the prayer with which you greet My Most Holy Mother:

'Spread the effect of grace of thy Flame of Love over all of humanity, now and at the hour of our death. Amen.'

So that, by its effect, humanity is converted."

The Most Holy Virgin added:

Mary: "I do not want to change the prayer by which you honor me;[6] by this petition, I want rather to shake humanity. This is not a new prayer formula; it must be a constant supplication."[7]

November 2, 1962

The Blessed Virgin told me various things about the Flame of Love.

---

6. The Hail Mary.
7. Let us pray the usual Rosary adding this supplication to each Hail Mary.

Mary: "Truly, my little one, this is our common thought, our common Cause. I must praise you. You make me very happy when I see your heart always busy with my Flame of Love. I will say it again: You make me very happy."

I cannot describe how I felt after these words of praise of the Blessed Virgin. I wanted to humble myself.

HISTORY OF HUNGARY

November 4, 1962

Bending over me, the Blessed Virgin began to speak:

Mary: "My little one, with great joy, the Hungarian saints are asking that my Flame of Love be lit as soon as possible in this country."

The Blessed Virgin allowed me also to feel this joy. I was united in spirit with the grateful homage of these saints, while the Blessed Virgin caressed my soul and continued speaking.

Mary: "The most powerful prayer of all the Hungarian saints is Saint Emeric's intercession for youth."[8]

She allowed me to feel in my soul the wonderful union of the saints. I was filled with an indescribable joy.

THE EFFECT OF PRAYER OF REPARATION

November 6-7, 1962

I was kneeling in silence. He did not cease to praise me. Meanwhile, the devil tried to torture me. To my great surprise, his presence stirred up in me a peculiar sensation, but it was not fear. He could not harm me even though he called for attention. I was struggling to listen to the Lord's words. The devil, however, was powerless and said: "Now, it will be easy for you. You have slipped away from my claws." I was stunned and could not understand what was

8. Saint Emeric was the son of Saint Stephen, the first king of Hungary. Educated with great care in the Christian faith, he died as a youth in 1031. His feast is celebrated on November 5.

going on. It never happened before that I would kneel in silence for hours and meditate deeply, while the devil was so exasperated. Then I perceived the voice of the Blessed Virgin in my heart.

Mary: "My little one, you are the first one showered by the effect of my Flame of Love full of grace, and in union with you, I am extending it to all the souls. Whenever someone does adoration in a spirit of atonement or visits the Blessed Sacrament, as long as it lasts, Satan loses his dominion on the parish souls. Blinded, he ceases to reign on souls."

How can I describe the weight that I felt in my soul when the Blessed Virgin told me these things? During my meditation, I heard:

Mary: "My little one, your acceptance of sacrifices and your faithfulness stir me to pour out upon all in a greater measure the effect of my Flame of Love, but first of all and in a greater measure on you, because you are the first to receive it."

After this, the Blessed Virgin prepared me for even greater sufferings. This caused me no fear because I possessed the Flame of Love of the Blessed Virgin. I knew I was clothed with a great power which gave me almost superhuman strength and consolation.

BE MY LITTLE SUNFLOWER

November 10, 1962

Today, the Lord spoke at length. He told me to what extent He was so pleased with each soul which, in its powerlessness, surrenders to Him.

Jesus: "Again, I will speak of something from your past. Remember when you were still working in the factory. Besides your work, which you did with great fidelity and responsibility, you took a course on quality control. You were very tired when you studied, so you thought and knew that you would not pass the exam.

As a working mother with six children, burdened with a thousand preoccupations, you needed enormous effort to study. You surprised yourself by becoming the top student. Although you did not think of Me, My hand was upon you.

Because there were four reels, the machine produced abundant material in just a few minutes. You had to be attentive so there would be no waste. The supervisor continually oversaw the good functioning of these machines and was ready to stop them immediately. He did not want a hundredth of a millimeter of error.

I remind you of these facts so you see that you gained success from your application and your conscientious work, not from your knowledge. I am with you as the supervisor of the machine. I walk here, I walk there, I am near you so you do not produce anything wasted. Not even an error of one hundredth of a millimeter is admissible. As I told you, not even a hair should separate us."

Later, He spoke about another place of work.

Jesus: "When you handled the hardening material, you had to do your work with great circumspection. You had to set aside the material that was harder than permitted. It was returned to the furnace and melted again. Many times, My little one, I have to melt again those hardened souls in the furnace of My love. I do not want them to be wasted material. My little one, accept that I also meld you within the flame of My love. I do this to form you according to the demands of My Heart. Only in this way, was your later formation possible."

On one occasion, the Lord Jesus said:

Jesus: "look at the great pear tree that extends its branches over the cultivated lands and offers both shade and exquisite fruit to poor, tired people. You, of course, cannot change yourself into such a great tree. Do you know what? Be My little sunflower and turn toward Me your oily seeds which mature in the rays of the Divine Sun. Do you want your oily seeds to be greater each time? Then accept every sacrifice I offer you. Only in this way can your oily seeds be useful. Do you want Me to squeeze your seeds so the oil comes out? We can do this only through sacrifices.

These drops of oil squeezed by your sufferings will fall in the empty lamps of souls, and the fire will be lit in them by the Flame of Love of My Mother. By its light, they will find the road that leads to Me. This drop of oil squeezed out by your sufferings, when united to My merits, will fall on those souls who still do not have a lamp. They will be astounded and will seek its cause, and they will find the road that leads to salvation."

Editor's Note – Those without lamps are pagans who do not yet have light of true faith.

HOLY PURITY

November 17, 1962

I woke up early that morning when I heard my guardian angel saying: "The angels and the saints are looking at you with great admiration." He asked me to increase my profound adoration and praise for the Divine Majesty, "Because rare are those chosen to receive graces to that extent." Upon hearing those admonitions, the burden of my sins weighed upon me. I felt so unworthy of this abundance of grace that the effect of grace of the Flame of Love of the Blessed Virgin pours out over me.

On that day, the Blessed Virgin spoke with me at length. I cannot describe everything, only what happened during the morning hours. My misery was so deep and I was greatly depressed. I was listening to her words with even more respect than I had until now. I had the feeling that she was about to communicate some extraordinary things to me. During Holy Mass, the Blessed Virgin infused into my consciousness what I am feeling now. This has caused my soul to be light and lifted up to a sublime state.

Mary: "This great grace, my little one, is holy purity."

I was astounded at these words, and following a brief pause the Blessed Virgin added:

Mary: "Now you have been purified of every stain, any trace of sin against purity. From now on, wherever you go, it will be granted to many to perceive the particular purity of your soul that the effect of grace of my Flame of Love has shed over you, and will distribute to all who will believe and trust in me."

WHY I CHOSE YOU

November 19, 1962

The Blessed Virgin:

Mary: "In the course of your long struggles, I am now going to tell you why I chose you the first to be handed the Flame of Love. You have yourself recognized that you are not worthy of this. This is the pure truth. There are many souls more worthy than you. However, the graces I have bestowed upon you and the sufferings you endure with such great fidelity have made you the chosen one. I see your perseverance and I am rewarding you in advance for that. Just so you not be distressed, I will mention a little detail which pleases me and is for your merit. Many people in your neighborhood have known you for years. You have fought your great battles before their eyes. Many admire you and even your enemies speak of you with respect. I am pleased to hear that. A mother is pleased to hear one of her children is recognized as being good. And you are my daughter, twice over.

I know you are refuting this, my little Carmelite, and you have reason enough to do so. I rejoice because you are not pretentious. This is why I came towards you. I, the Mother of Mercy, entrusted you with the most excellent of my graces: to make my Flame of Love known to others. Why precisely you? I will tell you. Listen, my daughter, you are also the mother of a large family. Through your children you know all the pains and problems of a family. Many times you were close to falling beneath the cross of difficult trials, and you still experience many sorrows over your children. Bearing such ordeal is meritorious for you and for any mother. By Divine Will, these experiences that affected your life have not been in vain. I have taken them all into consideration. I know you understand me, and this is why I shared with you how I feel in my motherly heart. My sorrow is just like your sorrow.

There are many cold families like yours in my country. I want the Flame of Love of my heart to warm them up and others just as well. I can see that you understand this well since you are living the same reality. This is why you have compassion for me. As a result,

I first entrusted to you the abundance of my graces. Only a mother can truly share my sorrows. I am the Mother of Sorrows, I suffer greatly because of the souls being lost. I am tortured in pain as I grieve for the suffering of my Divine Son. Never despise any tiredness, be my eternal companion helping me bear my sufferings. This is what I ask of you."

VEXATIONS OF THE EVIL ONE

November 22, 1962

After entrusting the Flame of Love of the Blessed Virgin to Father D, I thought that I would find a little relief for my soul. However, the overwhelming sorrow of my sufferings began. The Evil One began to humiliate me in a horrible way, something that had never happened to me before… I went to the Sanctuary of Máriaremete, where I am quickly immersed in the Flame of Love. The Blessed Virgin said:

Mary: "Your longing is great, but remember what I told you: We must look for a refuge for my Flame of Love. Let's take action!"

My heart shriveled up. The sufferings and humiliations that I must experience in spreading the Flame of Love signify a new and greater battle. With my head bowed, I listened in silence to the Blessed Virgin. She told me to whom I had to go.

Mary: "Right here, in this sanctuary, you will spread this devotion."

Directed by the Blessed Virgin, I went to the other side. First, I went to Confession. After that, I told the priest why I had to meet with him. My heart was in my throat. I did not know this priest at all. I only half-finished when he asked why I had to tell him all that and why I was so restless. He reproved me, saying that I could have told him everything in five minutes. He then continually hurried me. Unfortunately, I couldn't breathe right and this slowed down my talking. I do not want to give any more details of the terrible torment, humiliation and shame that I experienced.

He then began to speak of the cardinal virtues and highlighted prudence as the most important. He cited Saint Paul's words, "Discern the spirits..." After a long conversation, we agreed I would bring him the Blessed Virgin's messages next Sunday. In an indifferent tone, he added: "If you want, bring it to me. I will read it. However, this does not mean anything." At the end, he asked me to pray to the Spirit of Love. I also asked if he would pray for me and bless me.

When I left the confessional, I thought about what I heard. I also asked the Holy Spirit to enkindle light in the souls who already know something of the Flame of Love of the Blessed Virgin, and that an outpouring of graces of the Flame of Love penetrate to their interior. Then I thought about the cardinal virtues. Would prudence be the most important? "My adorable Jesus, I attend Your school, and if there is something that I do not know, it is up to You to decide if I should know it or not. It isn't necessary to have the cardinal virtues to spread the Flame of Love. Otherwise, You would have instructed me." With that, I grew calm.

Each time, the Evil One burst in with greater force. For weeks, he tortured me at the thought that all of this comes from myself. I think that I am trying to deceive myself, that all that I do is just vanity, that I am full of pride and self-sufficiency. Because of my pride, I will be damned. It would be prudent to stop occupying myself in this matter. "The one that they sent you to was content to tell you that he would read it but this doesn't mean anything." I thought I should admit my error to Father D. I should go back to him and to the Sister assigned to accompany me, and I should confess humbly to them that everything is a lie springing from my pride which caused me to deceive them. If I do that, I will recover my peace of soul and be pure and sincere in my own eyes.

When the time came to receive Communion, I was still fighting within myself. Should I dare receive the Lord? My pain was so great that my soul was trembling. I said: "My adored Jesus, I do not wish to offend You. How did I ever fall into this great sin? If I do not want it, how have I been able to commit it?" I recalled the answer from my childhood catechism: "Someone commits a sin who, knowingly and willingly, disobeys the commandment of God." I examined my conscience. I do not desire this sin. Therefore, I have not sinned. I thought that something tried to keep me back from going to the altar of the Lord. This battle was discouraging. "O Lord, be merciful to me."

When it was my turn to receive Communion, the priest stopped in front of me. With open lips, I was trembling as I awaited the Savior. Perhaps the priest considered me unworthy of Communion. Really, he was just trying to separate Hosts that were stuck together. When the priest placed the Sacred Host on my lips, I received two, not one. While placing them on my tongue, he grazed my teeth. They separated and appeared like two wings that the Lord used to fly into my soul. This brought a limitless relief to my soul. I broke into a shout, "How good of You to come!" I even used His own words: "Truly, You do not despise me. O Lord, because I am a sinner, You double Your strength in me." What goodness, what limitless compassion You have for a repentant sinner. For a long time, I gave thanks for His infinite mercy.

Afterwards, I went into another chapel where a late Mass was celebrated. There, I continued my thanksgiving, reflecting for a long time on my misery and my sinful condition. The idea that I would have invented the Flame of Love of the Blessed Virgin was not at all apparent.

I thought: "O adored Jesus, I give myself entirely to You. It has been a while since I renounced myself and my own will... And then, there is nothing which comes from me. Once again, I give myself to You. Accept me, I beg You..."

The Lord Jesus did not speak, but He inundated my soul with the sublime feeling of His presence. Without any words, He poured into my consciousness a feeling of peace: it has been a long time since I surrendered completely to Him. I ought to be at peace. Nothing comes from me. He poured out His grace and permitted me to understand clearly the reasons of these great disturbances and sufferings.

MASS AND THE BLINDING OF SATAN

On one occasion, the Blessed Virgin spoke:

Mary: "If you attend Holy Mass while under no obligation to do so and you are in a state of grace before God, during that time I will pour out the Flame of Love of my heart and blind Satan.

My graces will flow abundantly to the souls for whom you offer the Holy Mass, because when Satan is blinded and devoid of his power, he is unable to do anything. The participation in the Holy Mass is what helps the most to blind Satan. Tormented and breathing out terrible vengeance, he wages a ferocious battle for souls since he feels the impending coming of his blindness."

DISPERSED RELIGIOUS

November 23, 1962

Jesus: "Come, My little one, let us gather the scattered grains of wheat."

At first, I did not know what the loving Savior wanted of me. I waited in silence until He made known the meaning of His words. With His pleading voice, He said:

Jesus: "Forgive Me if I now expose before you the well-known pain of My Heart. You know, many souls consecrated to Me have fallen on good soil and produced abundant fruit. Now they are dispersed. They have no greater dream than to give themselves as fodder to the animals. They do not allow themselves to be plucked or ground, but without this, they will never be useful creatures. Oh, how My Heart sorrows for these scattered grains of wheat. My little one, feel the sorrow from which My complaining words spring up. May our souls be in harmony."

(Explanation – The scattered grains are the religious who produced good fruit but now are scattered due to Communism. Many no longer let themselves be guided by Divine Grace to live a life of victim and apostle.)

SKEPTICAL WORDS OF A PRIEST

November 29, 1962

Today, I went to confession to Father D to whom I had given the messages of the Blessed Virgin. Because he only read a few lines, he spoke about different topics before getting to the messages. I gave them to him a week ago. Distressed, I listened. "O my good and Holy Virgin, you see for yourself. What can I do? Nothing! You act through me, but it is not my fault that nothing has happened so far." Father D talked about everything except the Flame of Love of the Blessed Virgin. He talked about how the soul has various experiences that might not come from God. I was very upset to hear this. Although preferring to speak, I did not.

I practiced patience, humility and control of my tongue. I listened to his digressions. He pondered the admirable Providence which helped me to educate my six children by myself. He admitted that what I say is true. His skeptical words led me to say, "God sees my soul." His lack of confidence in me was painful. I thought: "God is working through me, I am nothing. To Him be the glory." I felt happy to place these humiliations at the feet of the Lord Jesus. The Blessed Virgin had assured me that it is only through humiliations that I would be ready to spread her Flame of Love.

On one occasion, the Lord Jesus asked me:

Jesus: "Don't be impatient. You know how to be indulgent and patient with others, but you are impatient with yourself. You also have obligations towards yourself. Turn to Me. Receive My light and give it to others. Live a hidden life. Look at the violet in the woods, is it not touching? It is just a little glimmer upon the earth yet people want its perfume. The violet also receives its perfume from Me. May your life also be hidden. May it exude its nice fragrance and the evil ones will pursue it. Release some of it yourself willingly and I will compensate you with My graces because you keep giving off My sweet perfume. I ask you to love your neighbor. When you hear anyone pronounce My Name with a sigh, let this ring unceasingly in your ears. Help that soul to come close to Me."

Friday is always a day of suffering and of a generous acceptance of sacrifices. Because of wariness, I had to drag myself to the Lord's feet.

During the three holy hours, I wanted to be immersed in His sufferings. Gathering all my strength, I tried to dispose my soul for prayer. The sweet Savior took compassion on my weakness, and in the solitude of my soul, He spoke to me.

Jesus: "Look where I walk. Abandoned in towns and in cities, wherever you look, you see Me, poorly dressed. Sadness and failure fills My sublime Being."

His words moved my soul and I sobbed abundantly. He continued:

Jesus: "You see how much I walk with souls but they do not want to perceive Me. They look at Me for a moment. Then, when they see My sad look, they quickly turn their head. Some tell Me: 'We have compassion for You, but it will wait for another day.' The vast majority do not even notice." And, broken with grief, He shouted in my soul: "Oh, boundless indifference! My daughter, My Heart stays here with you. Rest a little. You understand Me and try to please Me with all your strength. I plead with you, stay with Me. Oh, this abandonment, and being despised. Relieve My sufferings with your frequent presence."

"O adored Jesus, I am fragile. My soul desires You much but my body's tiredness obliges me to leave You." I looked at my watch, the three hours were coming to an end. The Lord Jesus said:

Jesus: "I grasp your hands. I will go with you. May our feet journey together."

We did not stop our conversation. He continued to complain about His abandonment and again pleaded:

Jesus: "Do not leave Me alone, My little one. Through My sufferings, I bind you now more tightly to Myself."

OFFER YOUR WORK

November 30, 1962

When I rang the bell at six this morning, the Blessed Virgin said:

Mary: "Throughout the day, you should offer me your daily chores for the glory of God. Such offering, made in a state of grace, also contributes to blind Satan. Live in accordance with my graces so that Satan will be blinded even more and in an increasingly large range of action. Take advantage of the abundant graces to make a multitude of souls live a holier life."

NEW TRIALS

December 1, 1962

Mary: "My little one, I see your great anguish. You fear the long road and the new trials demanded of you by my Flame of Love. Be humble, valiant and decisive. I will accompany you. You possess the Spirit of Love; His strength accompanies you and enlightens the souls to whom you are sent."

The Blessed Virgin also showed me the disposition of those souls who will receive her Flame of Love. As she spoke, her words filled me with strength.

Mary: "On this road, you must accept generously the many painful misunderstandings and humiliations. The one to whom I send you is also suffering. He is tormented by sorrow and doubt, even more than you are. My little one, you and those to whom I send you must suffer, pray and fast much, so that one way or another you can gain merits so as to reveal my Flame of Love that is proceeding with great hindrance. I deliberately send it to souls that struggle with doubts. I do this so they feel the effusion of the effect of grace of my Flame of Love. Then they will believe and trust in me."

When I heard the Virgin's kind words, I was astounded. After the sufferings and temptations of the previous day, the Lord Jesus said:

Jesus: "Suffer with Me. I will increase the suffering of your soul and will deprive you of My word."

Whenever I hear this, I shake from sorrow. The Savior consoled me.

Jesus: "I will leave you with the feeling of My presence. In the great sufferings that I will pour out on you now, the Flame of Love of Our Mother will give you great strength. She is the one who forces Me not to deprive you of the feeling of My presence. Be also grateful to her for that."

The Blessed Virgin explained many things. She instructed me like a little child.

Mary: "Tell me, why are you afraid?"

I was thinking that I had to go to the bishop. Every time I thought of this, my heart shriveled up.

Mary: "You have no reason to fear. Although we prepared your soul, you must unceasingly feel that you are an instrument in our hands. Attribute nothing to yourself. Fear is inevitable, it is a reflection of your pride. Do you think you are capable of anything? Devote yourself fully, my little one. Recognize your nothingness. We will lead you."

TO THE BISHOP

December 12, 1962

In the Máriaremete Sanctuary, I gave the messages of the Blessed Virgin to the priest whom the Blessed Virgin had pointed out. That same day, we went to Székesfehervar. We left by train at 2:00 p.m., taking with us the messages for the bishop. When we arrived, twilight had come upon the city covered with snow. I thought of the Virgin's words: "We must find a refuge for my Flame of Love." Devotion filled me. Will this be the place where the Flame of Love of the Blessed Virgin finds a refuge? The Blessed Virgin said only:

Mary: "Let us set out."

I traveled with the Sister who had been assigned as my companion. As we got off the train, the first road took us to the tomb of the young Jesuit, Esteban Kaszap. After seeking his intercession, we entered the church to visit the tomb of the saintly bishop, Ottokar Prohászka. For a long time, I prayed, meditating on his words: "O Lord, what do You want of me, who depends on You and lives for You and in You?" While kneeling at his tomb, I was very touched. Only with difficulty did I leave. I wanted to say much, the many requests that are the common cause of souls. "Help me and bless me, O holy bishop Ottokar."

The Blessed Virgin arranged everything for the good of the Cause. That night, I assisted at the bishop's Holy Mass. Our accommodations were better than expected. The following day, at the Mass of dawn, the Blessed Virgin got my attention.

Mary: "Look at the two little children sitting in front of you."

I looked up and saw two thin children. Since the Blessed Virgin called my attention, I looked at them for a while. They were well behaved. Their clothing was poor but arranged with care. The Blessed Virgin continued.

Mary: "My little one, because of your desires, I breathed the grace of my Flame of Love over these two children. Look at them. Pray for them. They are favored in a special way by my Flame of Love. Help them also financially."

When I heard that the Blessed Virgin, through my intercession, breathed the Flame of Love of her heart on these children, I began to sob, "My Mother, how kind you are!" I kept sobbing during the whole Holy Mass. How many graces she is pouring out on us! After Holy Mass, I kept looking at the children. When they left, I followed them to get their names and address. I found that they came from a large family.

At 9:50 a.m., we were taken to the episcopal palace. We did not go through the main entrance but through the kitchen where a religious was mixing dough. She interrupted her work and signaled for us to follow. We came to a dark corridor that went through the basement. Finally, we arrived at the bishop's waiting room. After a brief wait, they took us to the bishop's secretary, who led us to the chapel. There, I was immersed in fervent prayer, "My adored Jesus, finally we are here."

After a few minutes, someone came in and began to pray aloud the Veni Creator Spiritus. At first, I did not look. However, as the prayer kept going on, I looked and saw the bishop. I stood up while he placed the kneeler. I knelt before him to make my confession, which was scheduled in advance. This lasted a long time. I admired his holy peace and the self-control that he showed throughout the meeting. He did not interrupt me even once. When I finished, he asked if I had anything else to add. "No," I said. He responded point by point. I admired his extraordinary mental capacity in responding to my questions. After giving me absolution, he blessed me at length. His words calmed my soul and scattered my cruel doubts. While I gave thanks to the Lord, the bishop prayed some ejaculatory prayers.

When I finished, he came close to me and, with a paternal hand, he traced a cross on my forehead. I was not expecting this. I quickly kissed the hand that was blessing me. This touched me deeply. When he left, I stayed there and pondered how I should make known the Blessed Virgin's messages. With kindness and sweetness, she said:

Mary: "This tremendous relief which you now feel is my gift. Now, let us rest a little while so that you have strength to continue the battle that awaits you."

These words, spoken with a mother's goodness, calmed my soul. While I was spiritually resting, I thought about the bishop's blessing, because through it, the peace of the Lord inundated my soul more wonderfully than ever after a blessing. Remembering this, even days later, filled my heart with great happiness.

THE GRACE OF ABANDONMENT

December 15, 1962

Today, I woke up with this blessing that had a wonderful and peaceful effect on me. My heart was shaking from joy as I thought about the Flame of Love of the Blessed Virgin. Then she spoke as we went to Holy Mass.

Mary: "Calm down, my little one. Let's walk together... I was tired with you, but now we will take a good rest."

While we were talking, I rang the bell. Then I prostrated myself before the Lord Jesus. "My adorable Jesus, how much I have to tell You." So I began to tell Him about what appeased me so much. I thanked Him for his abundant graces. After I adored Him, I remained in silence. With gentle words, He said:

Jesus: "We have to prepare for great sufferings. However, I will not leave you alone. If necessary, I will work a miracle. Your sufferings will be extraordinarily great. Now comes the persecution, just as Herod tried to kill Me when I was an infant. Just as My Mother and I abandoned ourselves to the heavenly Father, you also abandon yourself to us."

Meanwhile, He filled me with a new and wonderful grace. I cannot describe the grace that poured over me while He said:

Jesus: "What I give you now is the grace of full abandonment to Me. All during your life, it will totally control your being, and from your soul, it will radiate to others."

An incomparable and sublime feeling came from this grace of abandonment to God. I could not have endured it without a special grace. Meanwhile, the Lord Jesus continued to speak.

Jesus: "Were you not deeply touched by the bishop's blessing? I was there when he traced the cross on your forehead. I did this for two reasons: to give you a reward for your numerous sufferings; and so that the bishop would know My Divine Will concerning you."

THE PRIEST DOES NOT UNDERSTAND

December 16, 1962

I returned to the Máriaremete Sanctuary where I gave the message of the Blessed Virgin to the priest a week before. I said just a few words and he recognized me. He asked me a few questions. I told him I had gone to see the bishop and that I gave him the messages. I also spoke of the bishop's answers. "I would have said the same thing," he replied. Then he began to speak of the Blessed Virgin's messages. He had read them twice but did not understand them. I was somewhat amazed and wanted to say some eloquent words about the Flame of Love of the Blessed Virgin, but I tried in vain. No thought came to my mind and no word to my lips. I thought: "How can it be that he does not understand?" Among other things, he said that the First Fridays and the First Saturdays were also days of reparation. He seemed to think that these other days of grace were superfluous.

When I left the confessional, I was hurt most by the fact that he did not understand. I begged the Blessed Virgin: "The one you sent me to does not understand your Flame of Love." I asked the Holy Spirit to enlighten him so that the Flame of Love would penetrate him as it penetrated me. During my meditation, terrible spiritual torments began to torture me.

As I left the church and walked along, my sorrow grew greater. The Evil One raised new doubts in my soul. "You see, this priest cannot understand your confused thoughts. He is very intelligent. Nevertheless, he cannot grasp your tangled explanations. Are you still forcing yourself to suffer because of them? Only a disturbed person can believe this. Why do you keep trying?"

With all my strength, I tried to order my thoughts. These sufferings caused such terrible torments that I wanted to tell people on the road how terribly I was suffering.

My own thoughts became confused. I again remembered how I was not able to speak of the Flame of Love of the Blessed Virgin. I thought that I did not understand anything. When I got home, I hid my great suffering by singing happy songs, so my children would not notice the depression caused by my sufferings. What a terrible spiritual torture, who can free me from it? No one understands me. It is in vain that I would tell this to someone…

YOU ARE AN INSTRUMENT

December 17, 1962

The words of the Blessed Virgin penetrated my soul with kindness.

Mary: "My little one, why did you try so hard? Why did you want to speak eloquent words on behalf of my Flame of Love? Keep before your eyes that you are destined for suffering. Remember also the words my Divine Son told you: 'Give yourself to suffering and sacrifice yourself ceaselessly.' Your sufferings are not in vain, but it is not for you to worry about who understands my Flame of Love.

Do not be surprised, my little instrument, that you cannot speak eloquent words. I am the one who acts and who enkindles the Flame of Love in the depth of hearts. I am the one who confused your words and darkened your mind. I did not want any pride in your soul. That would be a great fault. You, little instrument, be reasonable and totally humble. You are an instrument in our hands. We care for you and allow no sin to come close to you. Be careful in all your temptations. The Evil One takes advantage of every situation to shake your humility."

THE DEVIL STRUCK ME...

December 18, 1962

Settling in my new dwelling, a small room two meters by two meters (less than seven feet) at the back of the garden would be my new place where atonement for sins would be carried out. This was the first day that I slept there. Although I was tired, I did not sleep. Even by midnight, I had not fallen asleep. I was thinking that if I did not fall asleep, when the time came for my vigil, I would not be able to wake up. Being awake, I thought about the Flame of Love of the Blessed Virgin – since I offer one hour of my night prayer vigil that the Flame of Love be enkindled – when, suddenly, I felt a blow on my body; then a second one, and a third, and a fourth blow with lesser intensity. I had a horrible night, but fear was not part of it. After these punches, tiredness and sorrow overwhelmed me and sleep conquered me.

I woke up past two in the morning, but I was unable to do even one hour of vigil. I felt as if I had been beaten with a stick. I know that it was the devil who struck me because I sensed his presence. The fourth blow did not cause much pain, as if two hands were holding him back. After I prayed for forty-five minutes, I went back to bed and slept soundly, something rather rare with me.

I woke up before seven. I was supposed to ring the bell at our church because the Sister sacristan was ill. You can imagine my disappointment. When I got to the church, the early morning Mass of Advent (Rorate) was already over. I was sad about this situation and I complained to the Blessed Virgin that the devil struck me and I was not able to get up on time. What I will now write is astonishing. The Blessed Virgin said:

Mary: "My Divine Son and I were also present. We permitted him to strike you, but I promptly stopped him because it was enough."

The Blessed Virgin never referred to that event again. I was ashamed. For some days, redness covered my face. During the day, the Evil One laughed mockingly: "Listen, listen, I wanted to open your eyes to make you set aside your foolishness. Enough of this fasting and nighttime vigils! Leave it all behind. It makes no sense at all."

The Blessed Virgin interrupted him and promised not to allow the Evil One to strike me again. This time, however, it was necessary. The Blessed Virgin went on to say:

Mary: "Make sacrifices, my little one, and immerse yourself into the profound annihilation of humility. You are my little and beloved instrument and your relentless efforts to attain such humility please me. It is the effect of grace of the effusion of my Flame of Love that is giving you such constancy in your perseverance."

Those words of the Blessed Virgin motivated me strongly for a long time.

AGAIN, THE PRIEST DOES NOT UNDERSTAND

Since Father X was sick for a long time, I went back to confession to Father D. He was very surprised and delighted. He asked, "Why did you not come?" He was waiting for me. I told him that I was with Father X, but this priest turned me away. Because of my extraordinary spiritual state, I could not go to confession without speaking of these things. Therefore, I told him that I had returned to him at the advice of the Sister under whose care they placed me, and not from my own will.

I began to speak of the Holy Cause, but Father D had already forgotten many parts. He ordered me to be patient: "God's Cause needs time to show its worth." From the writings he had received from me earlier, he was able to be certain that the Lord has a great predilection for me. I should be very grateful for this extraordinary love which I am receiving. He said that he does not understand these things. I said, "This does not surprise me." I told him how, at the Sanctuary of the Blessed Virgin, when I went to confession to a priest entirely unknown to me, according to his instructions, I had to give him the messages. That priest also had to read them twice and he admitted also not to understand them. Nevertheless, I understand them. I frequently pray, using the Blessed Virgin's words, and I ask the Holy Spirit to enkindle His light in those who had heard the message.

Father D responded that, in his opinion, I was pushing things too far and told me not to do that, because it is up to God for that to happen. I told him that I see clearly that this Cause does not depend on me. However, I have a strong inner drive to spread the Cause. Father X also noted that I was urging and pushing. He said that I should be patient. The Will of God will get clearer in every way. This violence exhausts my body and soul. I am incapable of doing this by my own strength because it involves great humiliation. If it depended on me, I would not open my mouth to say one word. The voice that moves me to speak belongs to the Blessed Virgin. Her voice speaks without interruption in my soul and I cannot resist the Blessed Virgin's urgency.

Father told me to stay at peace and to guard my heart in the Lord's peace. Then a major discussion began and I could not keep quiet. I felt that what I said did not come from my natural powers. In the end, he told me that he would refer this matter to another reverend priest for him to be acquainted with it, and to trust him because he leads a very profound spiritual life.

THE DEVIL'S TEMPTATIONS

December 27, 1962

In the morning, while kneeling before the tabernacle, torments afflicted my soul. Crying and sobbing, I called out to the Lord: "Where are You, adorable Jesus? Why must I live without You? Give me the grace of conversion…" In all my life, I have never cried as now. "You, O heavenly Mother, where are you? When I think of your Flame of Love, shame burns my face. Why is that?"

"As it was said of Judas, it would have been better if he had never been born... Return to your senses." Now the voice began to give off shrieks, excited by a tremendous rage. Then I understood that the Evil One had gotten furious and wanted to force me to admit that he is right. Then a gentle feeling came over me, "Is this the Will of God?"

However, in the next moment, the depressing torment of having lied weighed more heavily upon me; one cannot escape damnation. It made me dizzy to think that I prefer to damn myself rather than acknowledge and recant the lies that I had previously believed to be heavenly voices speaking to me. Because of these lies, I will be damned.

"O little Jesus of Christmas, I am not among the souls that You redeemed." Whoever lies in the name of my Mother will be damned. Now, at this summit of spiritual anguish, I no longer find words…

After this, my beloved little Sister, I do not know how you will speak to me again. Perhaps out of kindness, you will not despise me as Father X did. Let it be said in my defense that I recognize my mistaken lies. Unfortunately, this brings no relief to my soul… I ask repeatedly: "Help me, pray for me, and if it is possible, visit me."

December 30, 1962

Slowly the torments of these temptations grew less in my soul. One day, I was repairing the rug in our parish church, which was cold and without heat. My hands were swollen from the cold and I was hardly able to hold the needle. I thought: "I am almost finished. I will go home to get warm." I was repairing the rug at the altar, in the presence of Jesus in the Blessed Sacrament. Suddenly and unexpectedly, the Lord's presence filled my soul, and He began to speak in my soul.

Jesus: "Why are you hurrying to leave Me? Is it not good to be near Me? Stay with Me! No one comes to speak with Me."

When I finished my work, I prostrated before Him and in silence awaited His word.

Jesus: "Your great and violent sufferings have exhausted you. Why are you surprised? Did I not prepare you for this? Beforehand, I gave you great graces. These gave you strength for the great sufferings, and now, because you have endured these great sufferings, I can fill you with a greater abundance of grace. Each time, I multiply and intensify these great sufferings in your soul. Then I strengthen you with the grace of perfect abandonment so we both have success. The rage of Satan is savage. I permit him to be unchained against you so he can see how great is the power of My grace in a soul that is abandoned to Me."

I stayed a long time with Him: "Lord, it is good for me to be here." My soul has been freed completely from the terrible and disturbing influence of the evil spirit. The new sufferings have not yet assaulted me. I do not know in what form they will come. The good Savior has told me that my merit will be in suffering… Up to now, I did not know the cruelty of Satan. Now, my soul reposes in the Lord's peace and I remember Sister's words as we returned from

Father X: "For this rejection, you should sing a Te Deum[9] as did your holy patron, Saint Elizabeth."

The Lord Jesus told me to esteem this grace of abandonment which He gave me through the prayers of the Blessed Virgin. She again spoke of her Flame of Love which obliges Him to act.

9. A Latin prayer of praise.

Chapter 3

1963

MY ADORABLE JESUS

January 2, 1963

I was at the Máriaremete Sanctuary (Hermitage of Mary) for the hour of adoration of the Blessed Sacrament. I was plunged into silent prayer when the Lord Jesus spoke these words with gratitude:

Jesus: "Say and constantly repeat, 'My adored Jesus.' I have told you before how pleasant it is to Me, and even if you say nothing else for a whole hour, repeat it with repentance for your sins. This obtains many graces, forgiveness for sins, and provides peace for souls."

Those words were uttered in the plural and He asked that I pass this on at every opportunity.

GRACE OF ABANDONMENT

January 4, 1963

During my evening meal, a great restlessness came over me. My thoughts were filled with self-reproaches that I had permitted myself too much comfort. Whoever receives such great graces should seek zealously the occasions to acquire merits. Frequently, I shorten my night prayer. I feared that this would cause me to distance myself from God and I would completely lose my life of grace.

I felt a great restlessness. I am not capable of any more, I cannot make more sacrifices. Even those I make, I do only by God's special grace. By my own strength, I would not be capable even of this. "My adored Jesus, how silent You are in my soul. I have only a one-way conversation with You. You know that I am weak and sinful. Without You, I am a miserable nothing. I live by the grace of abandonment to You."

I AM BEGGING FOR YOUR LOVE

January 6, 1963

We were expecting a visit. My daughter-in-law, who had a child a short time ago, was still very weak. So, I had to take care of her house. This increased work was very distracting. After lunch, I wanted to go to my little dwelling, when the Lord Jesus said:

Jesus: "All morning you did not say a word to Me. Do you not feel the need of speaking with Me? I need to speak with you."

Oh, what great sadness overwhelmed me. "My adorable Jesus, infinite goodness." I prostrated myself and sought pardon for not paying attention to Him. In the silence of my little dwelling, I was immersed in adoration. Meanwhile, He flooded my soul with the grace of His presence and began to complain bitterly.

Jesus: "Do you know that in the whole parish, not one soul is adoring Me right now or saying one word to Me? Their souls are so far from Me! I am rich, but I beg for their love. Having begged in vain, I come to you. Is it true that you already know Me well and will not reject Me? Why do those to whom I offer My graces have such great fear as if I would bring them something evil, or some failure. My little one! (and His voice was full of sorrow). Accept the abundance of My graces. Adore Me and make reparation on behalf of others also. Seek many graces for them."

His words led my soul to a great repentance. The Lord Jesus said:

Jesus: "Repent on behalf of others also."

HOW MANY SOULS ARE DAMNED

January 8, 1963

I was precisely coloring decorative cushions when the Blessed Virgin began to speak.

Mary: "You are a mother also. With you, I share the immense pains and sufferings of my maternal heart. I know very well that you share in my motherly sorrow. Just think if your six children were condemned to hell. What sorrow you would experience! And Me? Oh, what torment to have to see so many souls damning themselves and going to hell. Help me, my daughter, my little one."

Hearing these words, I suffered with her in my heart. My heart cringed from sorrow. The Blessed Virgin allowed me to feel the torments that pierced her soul.

SATAN ATTACKS AGAIN

January 9, 1963

Satan again troubled my soul. In every way, he wanted me to abandon the way of life that I began when the Flame of Love of the Blessed Virgin spread the effect of its grace over me. This outpouring gives so much strength that I can constantly keep my spiritual balance in spite of my superhuman struggles. Now, Satan used another strategy against me. He brought out my weaknesses and with his smooth talk he tried to confuse me. "Whoever has received such a great mission cannot be idle. Go and give your message everywhere. Only in that way, will it spread. Do not keep it for yourself because you would be committing a sin. Why do you not believe? Why do you have no confidence and act like a coward? Spread this message! Announce it everywhere so people find out about it and believe in it."

This terribly agitated my thoughts, and in this long struggle, I remembered the Lord's words.

Jesus: "Pay no attention to his flatteries."

With all my strength, I wanted to control myself and, with the Lord's help, to reject these flattering temptations of the Evil One.

Later, Satan again made me conscious of my failures. "You are incredulous and suspicious. Why do you go backwards? Why not give yourself to spreading the petition? You, coward, are worthy of nothing!"

To reject his impertinent remarks, I repeated the prayer of praise to the Virgin Mary, the Hail Mary. This repelled his attacks.

WE SUFFER TOGETHER

Starting on Christmas night, I began to experience terrible torments. Because I could not get rid of them, I wrote to the Sister who was assigned as my companion.

My dear and good little Sister,

On Christmas night, when I returned from the chapel after early morning prayer, I asked you if it was a sin to believe in what is happening in me. Although doubting a little, you said, "No." For a moment, I regained my peace. Previously, during the night prayer that followed midnight Mass, I had suffered terribly. I suffered atrocious torments because no one believes me and I believe in vain. I try to reject this insecurity and not be taken up with this matter. However, I continue to suffer. On Christmas night, I sighed to myself, "My Jesus, I suffer so much."

Jesus: "I also suffer being abandoned. You know what? Let us suffer together. This will be easier for you and Me."

After these words, a profound silence and darkness covered my soul. Sufferings assaulted my soul and I began to sob. In the silence of the holy night, the people in the house slept peacefully, but I suffered with Jesus. A great insecurity settled in my thoughts, oppressing my heart. The next day, this increased and has continued ever since, torturing me night and day.

My dear and good little Sister! I do not want to bother you, but I ask you, in God's Holy Name, to pray for me. I suffer infernal torments and I cannot free myself from the misery of my guilt.

I sob for hours. Some unknown power wants me to abandon my continual lies and to stop deceiving others. I can see that they do not believe a single word. They fear me and hate me because they see my wickedness. They abandon me... The absolution I received from Father X is not valid because I do not have the desire to change my life. Without desire, absolution is worthless… I ask you to forgive me for having exploited your good faith and for having abused your goodness. Do not believe what I told you before, everything is a lie. I deceived both you and myself. However, this darkness still holds me captive. Even now, my stubbornness does not allow me to humble myself before others. I cannot regain my peace until I withdraw all my terrible lies. Yet, I am incapable of this because I am walking the road of pride.

Every word that I said or wrote until now accuses me. I cannot retract them, I am deprived of my will. I am going to incur damnation; there is no mercy for me. That is why they fear me. Father X also repented of taking the time to speak with me. You, too, do not waste time on me! I feel that I am going to lose your friendship, but I will have to continue with my retraction. I ask you to help me to be freed of my infernal torments. I feel that I always make sacrilegious Communions. For days, no prayer comes to my lips. My pride does not allow me to do good and find comfort… Devastated and shattered, I am struggling in doubt. Everything accuses me…

I cannot lift my gaze to the face of the suffering Christ. The voice inside me is so strong: "Do not look at Me until you have stripped away your sins. Because of pride, you do not want to renounce your lies. I, too, abandon you. I do not need you. Depart from Me… Mercy is only for the repentant sinner. Repentance for past sins is worthless without withdrawing from present lies. You must do this first. Until you do this, you are a liar… I draw to Myself only the repentant sinner. You must see that you are obstinate and without humility. You make no reparation for your sins which cry to Heaven."

I try in vain. I cannot bend my will. I cannot force myself into humble repentance… All around me, a multitude of damned souls cry out in a sorrowful voice. They were damned because they could not free themselves from their obstinate pride. I, also, find myself at the edge of damnation and I ought to save myself.

It was as if prayer had been erased from my mind. For hours, I could not pronounce the Holy Name of Jesus... I tried to pronounce it silently, even saying it letter by letter. But even pronouncing the letters incriminated me: "Do not dare to take this Name on your lips. Only a repentant soul can do that..."

Thinking that I should take the message to the principal bishop of the country, I felt a burning sorrow in my soul. "You will go there in vain. There too, you cannot receive absolution."

I could not decide if I should retract what I brought to the bishop... Also, Father D said my pride is wrapped in humility. Because of this, I want him to believe my lie. I must go and say, "You are right!" He uncovered my lying deceit...

I am sorry, Sister, that you trusted me. Did the power of a lie put these graces in my soul? I do not know how this is possible. How could I place myself so deeply in sin? When I go to Communion, I am fearful and experience the most terrible sufferings. I am sacrilegious, therefore, for me, everything ends up in the same place...

I recall what Father X said, "Suffer gently." However, my sins discourage me. Whenever I think about the Flame of Love of the Blessed Virgin, hell's torments flood over me. I am suffering because of this devotion. My lie will not go away. The Mother of Mercy is not with me because now I cannot be sincere with her. I beg her to greet me again this time... "Heavenly Mother, help me to change." I am possessed by the devil and I cannot renounce this lie...

Help me, my dear and good little Sister, to free myself. Tell me to whom and where should I go? I beg you to help me. The inner voice continues to accuse me. "...You should have been interested in your own soul first. You want to save others when you cannot even free yourself from sin." The voice admonishes me and shouts at me. This is an infernal torment. I beg you, my little Sister, help me.

BE VERY HUMBLE

January 14, 1963

The Lord Jesus spoke to me.

Jesus: "Although I will intensify and increase your sufferings, I will also add a grace to strengthen you and give you courage. I see that you make good use of the grace of abandonment. Try never to lose this wonderful grace which completely dominates your soul. Make every effort to use it in all that follows. Satan knows it very well, and he wholeheartedly wants to divest you of this grace. It is I who permitted this for him to see what surrendering to Me can produce in the soul."

During these days, the Blessed Virgin asked me:

Mary: "Be very humble, my little one."

With these loving words, grace penetrated my soul and strengthened me in humility. During these days, Satan tried to inject thoughts of pride into my soul. This was a terrible battle. Because of it, I had no peace, day or night.

MAY OUR GLANCES MELT IN ONE ANOTHER

Earlier, the Lord Jesus again strengthened me with an amazing grace. He does not make me feel His presence, but He looks at me and accompanies me with the penetrating gaze of His eyes. He said:

Jesus: "My little one, take courage and gaze at Me. May our eyes look at each other and our glances melt in one another."

I had never experienced this wonderful glance which now accompanies my soul. It helped me to win a great victory over the terrible temptations of the Evil One. The Lord Jesus said:

Jesus: "Take courage. Look at Me. Always look into My eyes because in this new battle that Satan wants to wage against you, the look of My eyes will blind him. This will not happen quickly because I allow you to be tempted. May our glances melt in one another."

When these things happened, I was crying and sobbing for my sins. Meanwhile, my soul became light and pure. I asked the Lord: "Adorable Jesus, what do You sense now?" In response to my question, He made me feel that He welcomes everyone in this way so they repent of their sins.

Jesus: "My little one, work hard so that many sinners come to Me. Cry and repent for their sins also."

SUFFER GENTLY

The words of Father X came frequently to my mind, "Suffer gently." Whenever I think of those words, I receive new strength. Oh, how wonderful is that one word he said to me, it is filled with Divine Strength. I keep on suffering in a gentle way and with renewed strength. Many times, I thought of Our Lord's words.

Jesus: "The words of your spiritual father are Mine. Receive them with the greatest veneration and follow them in holy obedience."

When I pray to the Lord and use His words, I feel some relief but not enough to dispel my soul's blindness. The torments are so painful! I can hardly think of the Flame of Love of the Blessed Virgin. I fear and feel that the Cause is not entrusted to me, as if the Blessed Virgin had entrusted its propagation to another person. Perhaps I offended her with my pride, or else I lack expediency in fulfilling her request. What is happening to me? I ask myself that many times. Did the Evil One take possession of me? Am I surrounded by evil spirits? Spiritual blindness keeps me in complete darkness. Jesus said again:

Jesus: "I will multiply and intensify your sufferings."

After that, many difficult hours followed. The battle that I was undergoing greatly affected my bodily strength. Sometimes I collapsed from tiredness.

SMALLNESS AND HUMILITY

Here, I do not write any dates. I am so confused that I do not know what day or date it is. At this very moment, Satan tempts me with my pride and I do not know what to do. While I was racking my brain about it, the Blessed Virgin said:

Mary: "You are the smallest, the most ignorant and the least meritorious soul that I ever found so as to bring these graces. In spite of that, through your littleness and humility, I want to send forth my messages."

I meditated deeply on the Blessed Virgin's words. She knows who and what I am. This calmed me down and enlightened my spirit. "The least meritorious soul I ever found..." O dear Mother, how good of you to say this. This is what I continually feel...

SORROWFUL MOTHER

While doing my work, the Blessed Virgin said:

Mary: "Many are those who often utter these words: 'Mother of Sorrows', and do not think that I am still suffering today, and not strictly back on the Way of the Cross suffered by my Divine Son."

Frequently, the sorrow of the Blessed Virgin floods my soul and I feel a burning desire to spread her Flame of Love.

A PENETRATING GLANCE

At the dawn prayer, while I was meditating, I saw again the penetrating glance of the Lord's eyes. The desire of His Heart that He shared with me a while ago, He now asked me for it and not through words, but through the penetrating gaze of His eyes. Oh, these eyes! My bodily eyes cannot withstand His glance. I shut my eyes tightly. Trembling, I could hardly look. The look of His eyes is like a flash of lightning which lights up everything. It penetrated my whole being and I saw all my hidden sins. I cried for hours without stopping. "My sins! Oh, my sins!" I whispered while moaning. While this was happening, the sorrow in my heart for my sins was greater than I had ever experienced it. Meanwhile, the penetrating glance of His eyes rested upon me. This is an unbearable brightness. The Lord said:

Jesus: "May our glances melt in one another."

"I, a sinner, a very great sinner! Yet, the glance of my sinful eyes will be one with the glance of Your Divine Eyes? Not just my eyes, but according to Your desire, the eyes of everyone." The Lord Jesus said:

Jesus: "May the gaze of he who walks and harvests with Me meld into mine."

SATAN'S WORDS

When I arrived at morning Mass, this state of extraordinary courage that had controlled my soul was totally gone. I lived through dark and difficult hours. While I attended Holy Mass, Satan burst suddenly into my soul. He confused my thoughts first with his flattering talk, and then with his cruelties. At the elevation of the most Holy Body and Blood of the Lord, he was terribly enraged and attacked with force: "Be a martyr and sacrifice your life like your Beloved! He took His life, why do you not do the same? Throw your life away. You will be a martyr, and losing your life will once and for all end all your atrocious torments. You have to sacrifice your life somehow. Sacrifice it willingly."

With all my strength, I tried to fight his temptations which cry to Heaven. I directed my thoughts to the heavenly Father: "Kind heavenly Father, I am a little spark whom You included in your plan. You created me and determined the hour of my death. Who would dare to speak against what You have determined by Your infinite goodness and power? Free me from the Evil One who dares to tempt Your Divine Majesty. O kind heavenly Father, I need the strong support of Your hand. Your Divine Son taught me to be very small. What else can I be, compared to Your greatness and glory? I am just a little spark who receives its sparkling splendor and brilliance from Your radiant light. O Blessed Virgin Mary, blind Satan with your Flame of Love because he wants to lead me into a sin which cries to Heaven."

Satan had waged an insolent and foolish attack. I felt he had lost his head and did not know what to do while I was praying. The heavenly Father, in his merciful goodness, annihilated these demented and daring temptations of the Evil One.

– Note that I always write 'Satan' because he repeatedly says that he does not send anyone else. He himself wants to make me totter, he does not give this task to another.

LIVE IN HIS WILL

January 18-19, 1963

Today, I went to confession to Father X. Since December 24, the last time I went to confession, I took strength from his one word, "Suffer gently." I begged him to free me from the evil spirits which continually surround me. He calmed me down, saying that in those moments, I should pray and ask the Blessed Virgin to place like a curtain around me. He also told me to maintain the quiet and peace of my soul because Satan is watching and he wants to strip me of the grace of abandonment to God. My confession to Father X always gains me wonderful graces. This happened again today. Beforehand, my soul was so much troubled by Satan's continued annoyances that he also admitted that he could neither see nor understand clearly the matters I had told him. I told him: "Father, I come here precisely because you help to orient me in my spiritual state." He told me to live a life pleasing to God and that His Will will become clear for me. With this advice, peace returned to my soul and I experienced a day of great joy.

NEVER LEAVE ME WITHOUT YOUR SUFFERING

Some months ago, the Lord Jesus said:

Jesus: "My little one, never leave Me without your sufferings."

For several days, He repeated this many times. His words gave birth to a very passionate desire in my soul. I longed so much to suffer. Right before Communion, He unexpectedly said:

Jesus: "Beginning today, I will allow continuous suffering in your soul, which will go beyond all that you have suffered until now."

Great happiness filled my soul. Finally, His desire will be fulfilled. He had already asked if He could place me in the furnace of sufferings. Now, by His grace, I will be able to do this. "Now that You have arranged for continual sufferings in my soul, after many obstacles and in spite of them, I have finally come to You. Now, finally, I thirst being close to You..."

This is the spiritual torment that I am continually fighting. A part of me wants to spread the messages of the Blessed Virgin, and the next moment, another part holds me back. "Do nothing without your spiritual director." I am going back and forth between two forces. One voice eggs me on: "Burn it. Throw it into the fire. If you do not, your soul will have no calm." Then I thought of the words of Father X: I must not allow these disturbing thoughts to come close to me.

BLINDNESS AND CLARITY

January 20, 1963

The Savior told me:

Jesus: "In your soul, blindness and light will alternate just as the night alternates with the day. I will not change this. Just abandon yourself to Me. In all things, My Will shall prevail. Be attentive and wait until I give you the signal to begin."

In recent days, the Lord Jesus and the Blessed Virgin intimated to me many times to no longer delay the decision to take the first step. The Lord Jesus added the following:

Jesus: "Amid these contradictions, I want to assure you that this Cause comes from us."

As a result of this, my sufferings went to a higher level. Just as the Lord Jesus said, once again, because of the struggles, I could hardly stand. At some moments, the Lord's wonderful brilliance lights up my soul and I see things clearly. When these short moments pass, I return to my painful state.

January 24, 1963

I received a new order from the Lord Jesus.

Jesus: "Act! Do not set aside My request."

These words were forceful. My heart shuddered. Then the Blessed Virgin said:

Mary: "The resistance against my words comes from your human doubts. By these doubts, you limit your soul's capacity to act. This causes you spiritual harm. If you do not put them away, they will destroy your abandonment to us."

January 26, 1963

In these sufferings which flavor and give a rich taste to my life, a change that wants to demolish everything in me has come about. From now on, there is no more in me the good part which undertook an ongoing struggle in my soul against my evil 'self'. At present, there is only the evil that overwhelms me completely. The good has almost entirely disappeared in me... Oh, if the Lord called me to Him right now... Oh, how I feel such a terrible fear of death because I am hardened in sin! "O heavenly Mother, pray for me now and at the hour of my death."

A BURNING LOVE

February 1, 1963

I went to visit the Sister who was my companion to give her the messages of the Blessed Virgin, and concerning these, we spoke of a different subject. Then I went to the parish church to ring the bells. After the nighttime Hail Mary, I walked home so I could meditate about how to spread the Flame of Love of the Blessed Virgin. The Flame of Love of the Blessed Virgin fills my whole being and all my thoughts. I caused Sister to doubt if she is truly the one whom God has put with me. Now, my soul is penetrated by a marvelous perception. We have no reason for worry. We must just do God's Holy Will. We are small instruments. God's grace feeds and strengthens us. And I felt immediately that we have no reason to worry. When I arrived home, – It happened on the threshold, even before having entered – the Lord Jesus was at my side suddenly and unexpectedly. I did not see Him. He put His hand on my shoulder, touched my right shoulder twice and said:

Jesus: "My little one, persevere by My side and suffer with Me."

While saying these words, He allowed me to feel His Divine Presence in me. He usually does this to prove it to me, but only for brief moments.

Upon arriving in the room, my feelings vanished. But the amazing spiritual force that had revived in me during these moments filled my heart with an ardent love and the desire that the Flame of Love of the Blessed Virgin be enkindled.

In the following moment, a thought arose: "What would I be if the Flame of Love of the Blessed Virgin ceased to flood me with its effect of grace?" I realized how deprived are the people who do not receive that outpouring. These torturing pains increased in my heart this wish with an inconceivable power.

THE POWERS OF HELL WILL BE SHAKEN

In the evening, I went to bed, but I could not find rest and sleep did not close my eyes. A tremendous buzzing arose in my head, and after a few moments, I heard a noise like a siren bringing a bad omen. A terrifying smoke started to spiral up in which unrecognizable figures were moaning, jostling and staggering, terrorizing each other. Amid the smoke rising up in spiral appeared an enormous figure that I could not see because of the grayish smoke, but I could feel it was Satan.

With a frightful howl, he shouted for help. He did not know what to do. His resistance was weakening, all his tricks failed and all his attempts proved to be vain. This lasted only a few minutes.

Then the grace of God strengthened in me the conscience that the Flame of Love of the Blessed Virgin must ignite, for it will shake the powers of hell. This vision so exhausted me that I could hardly free myself from its effects.

The next morning, crossing the threshold, I came to where the Lord's presence overwhelmed me the night before. I knelt down in the new-fallen snow and thought: "How holy is this street He honors by His presence."

How many times, while kneeling at the Lord's Sacred Feet, He freed me from terrible worries. When I am not thinking about it, He suddenly appears. His Person remains invisible, but He makes His presence felt. In spite of all this, my sufferings remain.

I am now in an anguished state because I think that my sufferings have no merit and are of no value. In this frightful darkness, I asked: "My adorable Jesus, I ask that in this great dryness, my soul does not lose confidence in God."

ACCEPT HUMILIATIONS

February 4, 1963

The Lord Jesus would not allow me to suffer without consolation. In His infinite goodness, He spoke extensively to me, instructing me and exhorting me to continue suffering with perseverance.

Jesus: "Do not be surprised if certain people I love and who also love Me will receive you with distrust. They will treat you with suspicion and set you aside. Simply abandon yourself to Me. The way to the Golgotha was covered with obstacles. I had to cut a way for myself with great difficulty. You are now accompanying Me to the Calvary on the road of humiliations. Our dear Mother comes with us and has you share in her sorrows. Accept this great distinction, those she shares with are very few. You are her little Carmelite, her chosen one. I am obliged towards her and I can refuse her nothing because she invokes her Flame of Love. I am always close to you, even if you do not feel it."

I meditated on all that He suffered at Gethsemane. He interrupted me and said:

Jesus: "Permeate yourself with My terrible suffering. You see, this is the reason I asked My disciples to pray and to keep watch. Their vigil would have relieved My sufferings. The heavenly Father sent Me an angel. In your sufferings, I, Myself, bring you relief."

And once more, He referred to the Flame of Love of the Blessed Virgin, who obliges Him.

Jesus: "Be grateful to our dear Mother. I beg you again: Do not withdraw from anything that I ask you. Simply abandon yourself to Me. Even if the torments caused by Satan increase, I am the One allowing it. Do not fear. His power extends only as far as I determine."

He then spoke of Saint John the Baptist, who prepared His way. He mentioned his sufferings and his constant perseverance.

Jesus: "Whoever serves Me, My little one, cannot be a reed bending in the wind. She must persevere firmly at My side with an unshakeable determination. Your soul cannot bow to anything that does not serve Me. Again, My little one, I ask that you persevere with Me. You know how much I love you."

During this discourse, he placed a power in my soul. Before Holy Communion, at the moment of consecration, Satan began to torture me so much that he almost bound up my words and thoughts. His commotion, his taunting laugh, his insolent words caused a great upset so I would know that he has power over me. He said that he could do a miracle for me, but not even Heaven considers me worthy of it. Also, that he could take possession of me because he has all the power to do so. However, if they expelled him from me, it would be an embarrassment. And since he does not take possession of me, he prefers to continuously torture me. He kept torturing me this way for the whole day. Only by total abandonment to God, can I bear these torments that exhaust my whole being.

LOOK ONLY AT ME

February 7, 1963

During the afternoon, the Blessed Virgin again urged me to spread her Flame of Love. She asked me not to fear any difficulty. She is with me. Every disgrace and humiliation that comes will help the Holy Cause.

This same day, the Lord said:

Jesus: "You are too immersed in earthly things, My little one."

(The Lord Jesus told me this because after Satan's trials, my soul experienced a certain kind of abatement.)

The Lord's words shook my heart and I grew sad. But He, in a loving tone, consoled me with words filled with love.

Jesus: "I did not say that to discourage you. I want to encourage you so that you do not seek relief by looking to the earth in your battles. Look only at Me. I want that, while snuggling yourself right against Me and surrendering to Me in your arduous struggles, you never stop looking only upwards."

He showed me what my life would be if I followed only the desires of the flesh without any eternal purpose. He also described how my life will be after an existence saturated with suffering.

Jesus: "I and My Mother await you. This is the reward of your merits."

I cannot express the Lord's words any more. I have written these words to record how the Lord's goodness comforts me in my difficult hours.

INCREASE YOUR SUFFERING UNTIL MARTYRDOM

February 9, 1963

After ringing the bell for the evening Angelus, I prostrated at the Lord's feet to say my prayers. I had just begun my prayer of thanksgiving, when the Lord said three times.

Jesus: "I will increase your sufferings until martyrdom."

A great silence followed. Immersed in His infinite goodness, I asked pardon for my offenses and for those of my family and my parish. I offered reparation for all who had offended Him in any way, and I always referred to the Flame of Love so that the Virgin would pour out its effects of grace on all. In silent recollection, I thought about His words. Again, He repeated those words three times.

"O my Mother, Most Holy Sorrowful and Immaculate Virgin, I give you thanks. By the effect of grace of your Flame of Love, you gave me the great opportunity to merit." The joy of that moment lives continually in my soul. O come, blessed suffering, by which I can give my life for the Holy Cause.

DO NOT LEAVE ME ALONE

February 10, 1963

I hurried to come into His presence and began to pray the Little Office of the Virgin. I wanted to finish before it got dark. Besides, I started to feel cold. I did not spend much time in prayer because our church is very cold and made out of cement. However, the Lord Jesus, almost begging me, insisted that I stay.

Jesus: "Do not leave Me now. I am alone and without consolation. Oh, how often I am alone!"

He asked:

Jesus: "Tell Me, since I have been sharing My house with you and I have granted you entry at any time, when you came to Me, have you ever encountered anybody in My house?"

With my head down, I tried to remember. "No one, Lord! During this time, I saw no one." This sadness broke my heart. He continued to ask.

Jesus: "You see why I say, 'Do not leave Me alone!' Let Me give you abundant graces which are stored up in the immeasurable love of My Heart. May our souls be in harmony. May our hearts beat to the same rhythm. Draw many souls to Me. May our hands gather in unity. When you also are abandoned, I will never abandon you, I will be with you in every difficult situation. Besides, today I will accompany you with the penetrating glance of My eyes."

"My adorable Jesus... give me Your grace so I can withstand Your penetrating glance." His love so fascinated me that the cold and the tiredness ceased. Only His sad request filled my soul.

THE SOULS OF MY FAMILY MEMBERS

February 12, 21 and 28, 1963

The Blessed Virgin revealed that the light of her Flame of Love filled not only me, but all my family members, and the Evil One could not lead them into sin. That is why their souls are strengthened and prepared to receive even more graces.

February 21, 1963

The Lord spoke in the morning.

Jesus: "I was here during the night and I blessed every member of your family because of the prayer of our dear Mother. She is the one who fills your whole family with the effect of grace of her Flame of Love. How much we love you, My little one!"

February 28, 1963

My little daughter is sick. I thought of going to the doctor to know what to do. The Lord calmed me down.

Jesus: "Do not go anywhere. It will be for the good of your daughter if she is not cured."

These words depressed my heart because she has a husband and a child. The Lord Jesus also told me why He would not cure her.

Jesus: "Your daughter always has temptations. By a long sickness, I will fill her with abundant graces. Her soul will be purified of the great temptations, and from now on, she will undergo sufferings with patience."

CAPTIVATED BY GOD'S CLOSENESS

February 13, 1963

When I woke up in the morning, the Lord filled me with His wonderful peace. My prayer was to listen profoundly in silence. Even after Holy Communion, I did not speak. I know no name for this marvelous grace.

This wonderful grace increased every minute. I must write that it pulled me up from the earth. When I finally was able to open my lips to speak, I asked: "My adorable Jesus, what are You doing with such an unworthy person?" With an inspiration as soft as a sigh, He poured out in my heart the feeling that, at that moment, in a direct soaring, He was drawing my soul to the infinite love of His Divine Being.

Jesus: "I do this because I love you very much."

My soul was so united to Him, it was as if I had left earthly existence. My body did its daily tasks (that day, I was particularly busy because I had to take care of my daughter's house as she was seriously ill). However, these many occupations did not disturb the union of my soul with God. It was as if my soul had been floating in some high place from which it was looking down on the demanding activity of my body. This extraordinary state kept increasing like waves upon my soul.

Because I had promised to make daily reparation in the Sanctuary of the Blessed Virgin from noon to 1:00 p.m., I interrupted my household chores. Later, my son asked me to put some official business in order. All these pursuits were the labor of a single day. I had to do all these necessities with great attentiveness. Yet, during this time, my soul was flying high in its nearness to God.

LIVE A MORE HOLY LIFE

The graces of these days totally saturate my soul and I am nourished with wonderful strength. When I arrived home after Holy Mass today, I did my household chores while being immersed into an adoration of thanksgiving.

Gently and silently, He somehow made me sense that He was smiling, and that filled me with joy.

Jesus: "Yesterday, you were surprised that you were allowed to come into the nearness of God, as if you had taken flight from the earth. This was a reward for your persevering effort. You can see that we appreciate your efforts and the difficult combat which you accept for Heaven's Cause. By your perseverance, you will always arrive at a higher level of grace."

March 5, 1963

The Lord Jesus said:

Jesus: "Live a very holy life because so many graces that you receive from Me give you greater strength each time. Strive to live a holier life with all your strength and see how I intensify My graces in you."

NO TIME TO LOSE

March 11, 1963

Mary: "Because you give yourself to the effect of grace of my Flame of Love, my motherly heart rejoices. How long since we spoke! Is it true that you suffer much from those who misunderstand you? Is it truly burdensome to put up with so many trials? Do not spare yourself any hardship. Go and tell those concerned that the impetuosity does not come from you. I am the one who continually pushes you. Remember what I said: In spite of your littleness, your ignorance and your humility, my Flame of Love will be enkindled."

Once more, she related with what crazed rage Satan torments even those whom he suspects that her Flame of Love enlightens.

Mary: "We permit him to use all kinds of temptations against those who want to put into practice the Flame of Love, my Holy Cause."

Later, during the conversation, she repeated that we cannot delay for decades this time of grace that she wants to put into effect.

Mary: "We have no time to lose. A definite time is determined before my Flame of Love will ignite, exactly the time Satan needs to test the excellent twelve chosen priestly souls. Let them hear my voice. They should not fear, I will be with them. I will help them to gain victory over Satan's temptations, just as I did for you."

My heart burns with the desire that the Blessed Virgin's longing be fulfilled as soon as possible. Now, I am living very difficult days. Many times, the Blessed Virgin told me to go to Father X and tell him that she is the one asking him to consider it his obligation to direct my soul. On one occasion, when I heard these words, doubts assaulted me. I confided in the Sister who accompanies me. She told me to go. Now, she does not hold me back from going.

DOUBTS OF THE PRIEST

March 23, 1963

I went to confession to Father X. After confessing my sins, I gave him the message of the Lord Jesus and the Blessed Virgin. He still maintains his former position and does not accept being the director of my soul. He feels that he does not have enough strength to accept this. He appealed to his recent illness, to his growing difficulty in hearing, and above all, to his doubts...

He told me that I am very stubborn, have no flexibility, and am attached only to my own will. I told him that by my own will, I do not have the strength to take one step. I come to him only by Heaven's invitation. I told him that, even today, before leaving home, I sought advice from the Sister assigned to accompany me. After that, I thought about his statement about how he found me to be impatient. I am fully convinced that this impatience is not from my own willpower because I have no personal interest whatsoever in all of this. He answered with just one word, "Fine."

If he did not want to be my spiritual director, he should send me to another. Although convinced that I needed constant spiritual direction, he would not help me. He said, "Somehow, it will happen."

He told me to read the life of Saint Thérèse of the Child Jesus and the Imitation of Christ by Thomas à Kempis. I answered: "I accept your advice, but I have difficulty reading because I studied very little. Also, if I read a phrase which touches me, I meditate on it. The material for my meditation these past months has been one phrase: "And the Word became Flesh." This is an inexhaustible theme and I always meditate on it. At the end, he said: "Now, my daughter, I bless you with all my heart." I left with peace in my soul.

Afterwards, doubts assailed me again. The priest does not at all believe me; moreover, what I said raised doubts in his soul. I thought that he will also have to undergo the suffering of doubt just as I have. How humiliating was this rejection! This is just as well. Let God's Holy Will be done. If the Lord Jesus wanted me to suffer this humiliation, I receive it with joy from His holy hand.

Today, I went to Him. After I remained silent for a long time, the Lord Jesus said:

Jesus: "My little one, I ask everyone to be careful not to lose the state of sanctifying grace. It is the beauty of your soul by which you charm Me. Should you lose this sanctifying grace, do not delay in recovering it. Oh, with what love I suffered for all to obtain forgiveness for your sins from the heavenly Father. I beg you to help Me, so that many souls may recover this beautiful garment of grace which they received at Baptism." (His voice was imploring.)

THE SPIRIT OF POWER

March 24, 1963

I was still quite perturbed by the great humiliation and the flat rejection I suffered the previous day when I went to confession.

Jesus: "Elizabeth."

That gripped my heart and it seemed strange He would speak to me that way.

Jesus: "Do you believe in Me, in us? Do you believe that I and our beloved Mother have accredited you before her beloved son? Tell Me, do you believe this?"

I immediately answered in my heart: "My adorable Jesus, You know about my faith better than anyone else."

Jesus: "Are you confident you can fulfill the destiny for which we have chosen you? I am asking you again: Do you accept the many humiliations and sufferings that accompany the task of asserting our Holy Cause? Do you know that the sufferings you have received so far only served to prepare you to achieve the goal that we set for you? You are an instrument in our hands. Do you want to continue being an instrument? Do you want to climb with Me the Mount of Calvary, the Golgotha? If so, your place is beside the Mother of Sorrows. The Flame of Love of her heart that she wishes to enkindle on earth through you demands a total commitment on your part. Do not answer right now, meditate and prepare yourself to the answer concerning the great Cause."

At home, during the morning, He went on saying:

Jesus: "I can see to what extent you were shaken by the fact that they did not believe your sincere words which, in truth, come from Me. I have noticed with what level of fortitude you received this first great suffering that was a kind of general rehearsal for the beginning of suffering. This time of grace is destined for the whole world, however, it is through you that we want to initiate this Holy Cause, but it cannot start on feet of clay. It is only with a soul as hard as steel that it can be ignited."

As He was saying those words, a powerful stream of His graces entered my soul. The Lord Jesus asked if I understood. With His enlightened words, He poured out the wonderful grace of the Holy Spirit, the Spirit of Power, and the wonderful light of the Holy Spirit enlightened my soul.

The Lord Jesus told me that He had just given me, with wonderful strength, the grace of faith and confidence, because without these two virtues, no other virtues can take root in either me, or in any other soul. That is the fundamental pillar of this great and Holy Cause, the only way it can be ignited.

Jesus: "Meditate deeply on the importance of My words. What just happened was the first movement of faith in your soul because you could not overcome this complete rejection by a person living a holy life. You must not worry about that. I am guiding you, and if you worry, I might get the idea you are not happy with Me."

Listening to these words gripped my heart. "My adored Jesus, what are You doing with me? How humble can I possibly be before You? How painful it is for me to have offended You."

THE EARTH WILL KNOW GREAT TRIBULATION DUE TO LACK OF FAITH

The Lord Jesus had a really deep conversation with me. He asked me to urgently take the messages to the bishop. (It was March 27, 1963, and I did that.)

He spoke to me at length about the time of grace and the Spirit of Love quite comparable to the first Pentecost, flooding the earth with its power. That will be the great miracle drawing the attention of all humanity. All that is the effusion of the effect of grace of the Blessed Virgin's Flame of Love.

The earth has been covered in darkness because of the lack of faith in the soul of humanity and therefore will experience a great jolt. Following that, people will believe. This jolt, by the power of faith, will create a new world. Through the Flame of Love of the Blessed Virgin, faith will take root in souls, and the face of the earth will be renewed, because "nothing like it has happened ever since the Word became Flesh." The renewal of the earth, although flooded with sufferings, will come about by the power of intercession of the Blessed Virgin.

WITH THE BISHOP

At this time, the bishop was confirming in a nearby town. I went there and asked his secretary to give me the opportunity to have a conversation with him. While awaiting the reply, I grew anxious and asked the Blessed Virgin to touch the bishop's will in this urgent matter so he would listen to me. Receiving me, he told me to come to Fehérvar, to the episcopal palace, on Wednesday, at 10:00 a.m. On Wednesday morning, we spoke for one hour and I gave him the written document, saying that it was a message from the Lord Jesus and the Blessed Virgin.

GREAT SUFFERING

April 15, 1963

I remained thoughtful, my soul in pain.

"My adored Jesus, the Blessed Virgin planted her Flame of Love in a sinful family, where You receive so many offenses." The Lord Jesus answered with sweet consoling words.

Jesus: "I have not come to save the just, but sinners. This is why I suffered a cruel death. This is why I chose you to be My collaborator in the work of Salvation. Suffer with Me, as I told you before, even to martyrdom."

April 21, 1963

The Lord Jesus said:

Jesus: "Do you know the greatest suffering? To be misunderstood. This is the greatest torment. This will also be the sorrow of your soul, even until death. I endured it also during My entire life. You should not be greater than I, My little one. May our souls be in harmony and our lips beg together our heavenly Father."

Suffering keeps my soul in great dryness. During these moments, suffering seems senseless and even slightly dull.

Jesus: "I must give you a gentle reproach. How hard it is for you to comprehend the value and the meaning of your sufferings! Suffering is truly meritorious only if the soul accepts it with a full self-giving."

"You know, my Jesus, what You are asking is beyond me. My soul seeks continuously to serve You, but my body is in continual battle. In spiritual dryness, I can never see God's Holy Will clearly."

SALVATION OF SOULS

May 16, 1963

While I was cooking, the Lord Jesus said:

Jesus: "I beg you, in the future, do not think about yourself. May your thinking be only: us! If you come to Me and if you think of Me, think that the two of us are one. Let there be no gap between us. I will fill with grace the empty parts of your soul, and you, deny yourself so that, although you keep living, it will be I who live within you and you live only through Me."

Then, He said again:

Jesus: "How we love you, My little one!"

A few days later:

Jesus: "And I tell you: From now on, no longer speak of yourself. The 'I' in you must cease completely. Let there be only Me for you. That is your real life."

May 17, 1963

In the morning, I knelt at the Communion rail, but when the priest saw that I was the only one to receive, he did not give me Holy Communion. I said, "Oh, how painful this was for us!"

Jesus: "That is true. Let our joys and our pains be as one. Now, we both feel that we have been set aside and we are in pain. Let us endure this grief together."

Now, this is easier to accept. A deep feeling for Him overwhelmed my soul.

Jesus: "You are My little drop of water. Immerse yourself in the intoxicating wine of My infinite Divinity, both in its life-giving power and in its sweet aroma that you pour out for Me. May My good aroma pour out around you. When others perceive it, they will be led to Me. You see, we must be one. Do not be bound by the clay of the earth filled with worms. Let the earth be only that for you. Look at it as such and let us save souls from the worms that threaten and swarm them. Do penance and pray for them. Your acceptance of the sacrifice is the salt that, once poured over the swarming worms, they will fall like dead leeches. Let them be shriveled and annihilated. Let us have just one thought: the salvation of souls."

THE FEELING OF THE PRESENCE OF GOD

May 18, 1963

Jesus: "Always give Me new and abundant sacrifices. I am sowing in your soul the seed of My graces, My holy doctrine. Cultivate it in your soul by your prayers, mortifications, and a continual acceptance of sacrifices. Do not forget how painful for Me is the fate of the seeds that fall by the roadside. Pull up the flowers growing in your soul and bring them to Me while they are fresh. Here, in My presence, they will give off their sweet aroma. I only want flowers that are cut, not those which are still in a pot. A flower in a pot cannot please Me because it represents a victim which draws strength and wisdom from the earth."

What I will write now did not come from an intervention of words. I write it because the Lord Jesus asked me to. On one occasion, as I was taken up in prayer before the altar, the fire of God's love burned in my soul. While I was adoring Him, someone came near to me (a religious Sister). She became wrapped in that same love that was burning in my soul and maintained me in the presence of the Holy Majesty of God. The Lord allowed me to feel in what great measure the Sister also experimented this effusion.

At that time, the feeling of the presence of God so filled her, that the Sister whom I mentioned above lived almost for weeks sharing with me this effusion of grace.

On another occasion, I met a priest in the street. Suddenly, he greeted me. When I came closer to him, the Divine Presence poured forth from my soul and filled his soul. This happened to another priest on numerous occasions. However, when compared with the other priest, his outpouring was much weaker. When these outpourings happen, I am overwhelmed.

Jesus: "I am the One who radiates these graces upon you, and through you, on the souls that come to you. The Flame of Love of Our Mother obliges Me."

REPENTANCE

May 19, 1963

The Lord Jesus:

Jesus: "All of you must discard your false humility that keeps you away from Me. I say this because you stay far from Me by claiming that you are not worthy. Really, your sins cause you to starve for My love. So, make yourselves worthy by repentance. To you, I say: Suffer for them, especially when the suffering seems so dark. Let all come to Me with confidence. Suffering is dark only when you are close to earth. My little one, are you beginning to understand?

At your birth, I wrote about suffering in the story of your life and I will continue to write it until your final day. But I give the light of My grace so you can see its value. The closer you come to Me, the more I will enlighten you with My brightness. When you arrive in Heaven before the Most Blessed Trinity, you will see the value of your sufferings that will last forever and never become obscure. There, I will reveal them to you like a movie, filled with merits and wonders. This transformation united with My merits and the Spirit's illumination will plunge your soul into the most beautiful ecstasy.

Remember the decals you used to play with when you were a child. You had to wet them and rub them a little. After a few moments, a magnificent picture of living colors, a prince, a dragon, or whatever, appeared. You look at Me with amazement because I am relating such childish details to you.

My teaching, My little one, is simple and unaffected. I do not speak a scientific language that saves no one. My teaching is for those whose soul is childlike, simple, innocent, and does not give weight to anything, those who listen to Me with admiration and believe in Me. I tell you, My Kingdom belongs to those who are such, the multitude of those who welcome faith. Offer the sufferings I propose you for those without faith... Don't be lazy, keep writing! When your written words and your sufferings for My work of Salvation have risen to Me, My living rays of the sun will shine upon you. With the dawn, the sun rises, but the valley is still in the shadow. The early risers are filled with ecstasy as they contemplate the magnificent beauty. That is enough for now. In conclusion: live by My new teaching and return it to Me as a prayer."

This happened early in the morning, before the altar.

I, THE BEAUTIFUL RAY OF DAWN, I WILL BLIND SATAN

After the long conversation, a brief pause and silence... The Blessed Virgin made her voice heard in my heart, and somehow her words were intertwined with those of the Lord Jesus.

Mary: "You also, my little one, were among the early risers. When your soul was still in the darkness of night, I made my Flame of Love shine on you, and by its smooth, caressing warmth, I gave you a new strength. Many souls are asleep out there like yours was, and I also want to project on them the life-giving rays of my maternal heart, the effect of grace of my Flame of Love. Listen, currently, earth is like nature before a storm. It can also be compared to an erupting volcano which smothers, kills and blinds with the infernal smoke and its falling ashes. Its tremors disturb everything around it. Such is the terrible situation of the earth at this moment. The crater of hatred is boiling. Its deadly sulfur ashes change souls created in the image and likeness of God into gloomy and colorless creatures.

And I, the beautiful ray of dawn, I will blind Satan. I will free this world darkened by hatred and contaminated by the sulfurous and steaming lava of Satan. The air which gave life to souls has become suffocating and deadly. No dying soul should be damned. My Flame of Love is already lighting up. You know, my little one, the elect will have to fight against the Prince of Darkness. It will be a terrible storm. Rather, it will be a hurricane which will want to destroy the faith and confidence of even the elect. In this terrible turmoil currently brewing up, you will see the brightness of my Flame of Love illuminating Heaven and earth by the effusion of its effect of grace I am passing on to souls in this dark night."

SEEKING LODGING

Mary: "You remember, do you not, what I already said? My Flame of Love is seeking a refuge because of the hatred of Herod. Do you know who the persecutors are? The cowards, those who want their own comfort, the cautious and the lazy. Those who, under the guise of prudence, interfere and extinguish my Flame of Love, just as Herod acted against the little body of the innocent Jesus. But just as the heavenly Father took the Child Jesus under His protection, so does He now protect my Flame of Love."

The Blessed Virgin's words moved my soul and made me feel that she is the most powerful Sovereign in the world. She is the Queen before whom all must fall on their knees in repentance. After a brief pause, I again heard her voice in my soul.

Mary: "Do you understand this, my little one? I lift you up and lead you into the eternal homeland that my Divine Son acquired for you at the cost of immeasurable sufferings."

I never heard the Blessed Virgin speak in this tone of voice which was filled with the majesty of someone who is totally determined. I listened to her words with unspeakable admiration and trembling. A few minutes later, the Blessed Virgin spoke in a totally different tone, with her sweet motherly voice.

Mary: "You must put this into practice, my little one. Do not fear, my little instrument, trust in my motherly power."

I CALL ALL

May 24, 1963

I was praying for a soul who had not gone to confession for decades. I learned that this person was seriously ill. One day, we got the news she had already received the anointing of the sick. "My adored Jesus, thank You for Your infinite mercy." He replied:

Jesus: "Trust. I have always told you that whatever you ask for in confidence, consider you have already received it. Do you think that if you asked Me for souls, I would not grant them to you? May our hands gather in unity. Ask! Never grow tired of asking and desiring for Me. If large numbers were asking, how many would be converted. All of you have been called to My work of Salvation, fathers and mothers, learned and ignorant, the well and the sick. All can work for Me, the free man and the one suffering in prison. What is important is the availability of the soul and the spiritual freedom which constitutes the culture of the soul. Especially the sick, yes, in truth, these can fly on the wings of absolute trust in Me. With a single request, they can obtain a massive conversion of souls."

(When the sick offer their sufferings, Satan is blinded and souls are set on their way to salvation.)

THE SOUL'S BREATHING

June 2, 1963

After Holy Communion, Jesus said:

Jesus: "Your soul needs to breathe as much as your body. The soul's breathing comes from external and internal humiliations. In this month dedicated to My Sacred Heart, I will shower you with many graces and increase in you the virtues of humility and meekness. These two you need the most."

WITH THE DOCTOR

June 24, 1963

I had a difficult day. I went to Doctor H, a neurologist, to get his advice. Both my spiritual director and the religious Sister advised me to go. The Sister asked the doctor if she could be present. The consultation was very surprising. The doctor did no physical examination, but asked questions. I was surprised because I could tell that he was a very spiritual man. His questions covered everything and showed his good will. He was very moved when I revealed my spiritual life. During my conversation, I mentioned a doctor who for many years had lived without the Sacrament of Matrimony. I told him the grave circumstances of his death and that the Lord Jesus promised me that his soul would not be damned. The Lord had promised:

Jesus: "If you ask for souls, can I refuse your petitions? No. Otherwise, I would be acting against My work of Salvation. I always hear your persevering prayer."

The doctor heard my words with joy. After our two hour conversation, we left. He said that he would send his report to my confessor.

LIGHT OF MY EYES

July 9, 1963

During my nighttime adoration, I made reparation and asked Him to cover us with His Precious Blood. Before I left, I asked for His blessing. In an emotional strain, the Lord Jesus said:

Jesus: "May our feet journey together."

On the road, I said, "You are the apple of my eyes." (In Hungarian: "You are the light of my eyes.") He allowed me to feel the exultant joy of His Heart. He said:

Jesus: "You have not said this to Me for a long time. I never tire of hearing it. One cannot grow tired of love. Do you find yourself bored if I say the same thing often?"

His last words were:

Jesus: "My little one, I love you very much. Many are without light. I want to enlighten them with My Flame of Love, so that they understand the importance of the work of Salvation."

In the Sanctuary of Máriaremete, the Blessed Virgin said:

Mary: "You must go to the bishop."

Then she warned me to be cautious.

July 22-23, 1963

Jesus: "Do you realize how many times I take you by the hand? I lead you so that you are not timid. The abundant grace that gives you strength and courage is Myself. My clarity lights the rocky roads that you must walk.

This light, which keeps you from walking blindly, reminds you that I walked a similar road.

All do not walk this road in the same spirit as you do. Many are without light."

Then, the Blessed Virgin said:

Mary: "I want to enlighten them with my Flame of Love. The abundant love of my motherly heart went out to you who have an immortal soul and are the sweet fruits of my Son's redeeming work. You pray: 'The fruit of your womb, Jesus.' He is my fruit and you are His fruits. You, the elect, my little Carmelite, are special delightful fruits. There are other fruits produced by a wild tree. Graft yourselves onto every trunk on which you are able, through means of the fruits produced by the sacrifices of your hidden life, by which the wild fruit also becomes more noble.

Sacrifice and prayer! These are your instruments. The goal is to bring about the powerful work of Salvation. Oh, if your desires reach the throne of the heavenly Father, the results will be abundant."

SUFFER WITH LOVE

July 24, 1963

I was resting in the garden, thinking about the many sufferings that fill my body and soul. The Lord Jesus surprised me with His enlivening words.

Jesus: "Suffer with courage, perseverance and a sincere abandonment. Don't ponder if the suffering is large or small. All that you can still do for Me on earth is meritorious. Time is short, little sister, and never returns. What you do not accept at a given moment will never again become available to you, because I think that you would not receive it willingly. On everything you do, place the mark of your love and the seal of your decision. Do everything with a selfless love. In this way, you will joyfully share in My work of Salvation.

Every small drop of suffering accepted from sacrifice and love delights the Most Holy Trinity. In the company of the Trinity, you will enjoy it. This will be your reward which is not from this world."

CALMS THE SORROW OF MY HEART

July 26, 1963

Jesus: "Again, I must complain. Listen to Me. My Heart is in great sorrow. Hell is swallowing those souls created in the image and likeness of My heavenly Father. They fall into the clutches of Satan. The Flame of Love of My Mother can soothe the sorrow of My Heart. My little one, you also contribute to soothe this terrible spiritual torment. Therefore, I ask you to accept all the suffering I offer you."

Immediately, the Blessed Virgin said:

Mary: "My little Carmelite, whatever the difficulty confronting you, do not give up the fight. By virtue of my Flame of Love, which now I send upon the earth, a new era of grace never known before begins on earth. Be my faithful collaborator."

July 28, 1963

Sometimes, I suffer overwhelming spiritual sorrows and can hardly stay on my feet. I suffer for the dying so they are not damned. Amid these fearful sufferings, the Lord Jesus spoke.

Jesus: "Are you truly suffering much? I am the One who wants it that way and I know that you always want what I want. You must be abandoned, misunderstood and despised to truly share in My work of Redemption which saves many, many souls. In My abundant grace, your sufferings become more and more meritorious."

THE BUSH THAT IS NOT CONSUMED

August 1, 1963 - First Friday

I was tormented by both bodily and spiritual sufferings. While I was kneading the dough, the Lord said:

Jesus: "No matter how painful, accept this suffering. You are receiving graces that other souls would only receive over a period of several decades. Be very grateful for that. My Mother's Flame of Love is always compelling. I told you many times, you have been chosen as one of her most favorite."

While doing my work, He told me various things. From time to time, family members came to me with their problems. When they came, the Lord was silent. He is infinite kindness.

At 2:40 p.m., I looked at my watch while thinking of His agony. Once, He complained that He endured the most atrocious pains twenty minutes before His death. That same day, at nightfall, He said:

Jesus: "You no longer doubt that I have chosen you to be a worker of Redemption. Many missionary priests cannot do more than you do. Your constantly renewed sacrifices and unceasing efforts are most pleasing to Me. Your living faith in Me keeps your soul in a continual freshness and makes you ready to receive abundant graces. Hence, My little one, do not serve anyone but Me."

According to the Lord, this also applies for all those making sacrifices for His work of Redemption. The first Thursdays and first Fridays of each month are special days of suffering. On those days, the Lord Jesus pours them out in a greater measure. Today, He said:

Jesus: "The harvest is bountiful but the workers are few, especially those who, with full heart and soul, enlist among My workers. You understand, do you not? Do not do unwillingly what you are doing. Burn like the bush that burned but was not consumed. I need a similar sacrifice which is never consumed, and of which the flame burning from love touches Me."

MARY WILL BE EVEN MORE VENERATED

August 4, 1963

Jesus: "I must tell you, My daughter, that My Mother will not have been as venerated ever since the Word became Flesh, as she will be once she spreads the effect of grace of her Flame of Love in hearts and souls. The day her Flame of Love prevails, all the prayers and supplications addressed to her anywhere in the world will be joined in one single supplication for help. In this way, humanity will prostrate at the feet of the Mother of God to give her thanks for her unlimited maternal love."

The same day, He also said:

Jesus: "Pass My words on to those concerned and plead with them not to impede this great river of grace which My Mother, through her Flame of Love, wants to run over the earth." (On March 13, 1976, He also asked me to pass them on.)

YOU CAN GET ANYTHING FROM ME

August 6, 1963

Jesus: "Do you know what makes the soul to live in truth? The continuous exercise of prayer and sacrifice. Without these, your souls are sick and will die. Yes, it is necessary to give the body what it needs. The soul also has needs. But between the body and the soul is the Evil One, who stirs the soul on one side and the other. If the soul doesn't hang on firmly to the reins, it is unfortunate, but it will hurt itself."

Later, the same day:

Jesus: "Ask often and ask for much with respect to intentions and needs and you will receive accordingly. Even more, if I perceive your trust, I will fulfill your requests and so repeatedly. I cannot be outdone in generosity. Don't you also have that feeling, My little one? This provides you with great strength. Even though you stumble, your reprimand would be brief. Do you know why? Because at your own request, I chained you to My feet. I would not have done this without your asking, the free will is yours. If I see your confidence, I am obliged to you, and you can have anything from Me. I do not restrain Myself, and I stay right before you with the love of My Heart to make you happy."

REPENTANCE AND THANKSGIVING

August 7, 1963.

Jesus: "My love is almighty. Be permeated by this great miracle: I am continually at your disposal. With Me, you do not have to wait for your turn nor ask for a time and place to meet. I am present everywhere and at every moment. If you call on Me, My ear is already against your heart and attending for you, I cherish you and I heal you. I do not ask for the patient's file, I hunger only for the voice of repentance. Repentance is the only step that brings you closer to Me.

I know that many will fall again, but if I see you are not going astray as you distance yourselves from Me, I can quickly raise you from your prostration since My Divine Hand is close to you. Then, as I raise you, the sin falls away instantly and you become lighter again. Gratitude is all I want in return. Tell Me just one word: 'Thanks.'

You ask, 'How often?' Every time I raise you! Surely, this is the least you can do. However, if you thank Me for others, then you are well engaged on the road of progress. Also, My Elizabeth, I want you to pray so the number of repentant and grateful souls may grow from day to day."

CLEANSE YOUR SOUL

August 10, 1963

When I went to Holy Mass on Sunday, I noticed a dress with an interesting design and wanted to examine it more closely. The Lord Jesus admonished me.

Jesus: "Hold back your gaze. Am I not enough to look at? May our glances melt in one another."

August 13, 1963

While helping to clean the chapel, I said with joy, "I am here, sweet Jesus." He replied:

Jesus: "What a good time we are going to have!"

The next day, with a dust cloth in my hand, I knelt before Him and asked: "As I am now preparing for confession, please cleanse my soul of dust so that I see Your Holy Will more clearly and be more worthy to serve You." Later, on the trolley, I also spoke with Him, thinking how clean His house was now. He surprised me in my thoughts.

Jesus: "I also would be happy if the soul of those who belong to My house would have so little dust and be as clean as My holy house is now."

I asked Him, "Is it not that way?"

By a painful sentence, He let me know about it.

Jesus: "Unfortunately, no."

I was very emotional and thought about the sorrow in His words. Instead of speaking, the Lord Jesus breathed on my soul.

Jesus: "May our souls be in harmony."

August 17, 1963

During lunch, it was very difficult to make my meal tasteless. So, I decided to eat one half and to make tasteless the other half. Our Lord sadly observed.

Jesus: "I accepted sufferings without a thought and I saved you from all your sins, not just from some. Do not be stingy. May our hands gather in unity. Give Me your oily seeds and they will become more fruitful and more filled. Only your full commitment will squeeze the drops of oil from them."

THROUGH SUFFERINGS AND HUMILIATIONS

August 22, 1963

On the feast of the Immaculate Heart of the Blessed Virgin Mary, I was in bed with a high fever until noon. While praying the Rosary in honor of the Blessed Virgin Mary, the Lord Jesus honored me with His words. He surprised me by speaking about the great humiliation and suffering that I had suffered a while ago. As a result, my peace of soul and my confidence in the Lord were shaken.

During those days, I asked the Lord many times if I had only imagined that He and the Blessed Virgin had sent me to Father X to be my director. Since Father X had often rejected this role, I asked the Lord if I had fallen victim to my false imagination. Since I never received an answer from the Lord, I suffered much. But afterwards, it disappeared from my daily preoccupations, and I did not think of it anymore.

Jesus: "My little one, I appreciate and look very respectfully and with understanding love at your sufferings and humiliations that until now you had to sustain with patience. The priest I sent you to has his free will. He told you that he has doubts. I tell you that even now, he does not see the matter clearly. However, he has not removed the question from his mind nor has he forgotten it. In his heart, the fixed decision by which we decided to send you to him continues to be obscure. But he will understand that it is quite authentic. Nevertheless, he, also, will have to suffer. I told you that whoever knows something about the Flame of Love of Our Mother can only deserve being worthy of serving our Cause through sufferings and humiliations."

August 26, 1963

Mary: "In September, you must begin to spread the Flame of Love even more. Do not speak on your own, only give my words to the bishop. I am asking him to assume my Holy Cause. You should answer only if you are asked. Be very humble." (My confessor did not let me go to the bishop.)

REMAIN LITTLE

August 30, 1963

Jesus: "Do not seek to be more greatly noticed. Why do I say this? See clearly My rules of correctness. Record My words the best you can, without any need to correct them. I rejoice that you venerate My words but there is no need to honor them with rules of neatness and spelling. Remain small and ignorant! I already told you that you are dear to Me as you are. Do not look for anything that would make you look intelligent. Had you been pleasing to Me as such, I would have provided the means and possibility for that. Through your smallness and ignorance, and above all through your humility, we want to put our Holy Cause into action through you. Be careful, do not let vainglory come near. That is why I am bringing it to your attention: be very humble, work hard at it, as through this, your efforts will consolidate."

COMPASSION FOR HOLY SOULS

August 31, 1963

I assisted at the evening Holy Mass and stayed a long time with Him. I asked Him many things. The Sister sacristan did not realize I was in the church and she locked the door. God and I were together with my prayer of supplication. I interceded for the souls in Purgatory because my heart burned with a great desire that many be freed from this place of suffering. The Blessed Virgin responded to my great longing.

Mary: "My little one, I reward the great desire and compassion you have for the souls in Purgatory. Up until now, you have recited three Hail Mary's in my honor thereby liberating one soul. Now, to fulfill your burning desire, ten souls will from now on be liberated from this place of suffering."

I could hardly imagine such kindness. Instead of pouring myself out in thanksgiving, only a sigh came from my lips: "Holy Mother of Mercy, thank you for so many graces."

I AM GOING TO LOOK FOR HEARTS

September 1, 1963 - Monday

Today is my fast day for the priestly souls. The Savior has asked me to fast each Monday on bread and water to free a priest soul from Purgatory. Although the fast weakens me, I can do my housework and help with the children. After dark, when I finished my work, I went to the Lord Jesus. My union with Him was unexpectedly disturbed by a problem I was feeling. I had to leave the Lord Jesus. On the way home, He said:

Jesus: "I'll wait for you at home. When you arrive, I will be in our little dwelling."

I was very emotional and I ate my little dinner of bread in His presence. The Lord Jesus was there with me. Although I did not see Him, the feeling of His presence assured me. My great tiredness did not allow me to kneel up straight for a long time. With infinite goodness, Jesus said:

Jesus: "Rest now. I will stay with you a few more minutes. Feel My blessed presence and the pain of My Heart that I share with you. May our hearts beat to the same rhythm."

I broke forth in tears. This increased my sorrow for sins. Who would not cry in the presence of such goodness and kindness? In the silence, He remained next to me and then left.

Jesus: "Rest in peace. I am going to look for hearts."

As I felt His presence leaving me, I called to Him, "Where are You going, my adored Jesus?" He answered me with a troubled voice.

Jesus: "I am just going. First, I visit the souls consecrated to Me and offer them My graces again and again."

LIFE OF PRAYER AND SACRIFICE

September 2, 1963

At lunch, the magazine 'Vigilia' fell into my hands. I began to read an article. Then the Lord silently made His voice heard.

Jesus: "Put it away! Did you forget that I wanted you to renounce all distracting literature? Let your life be one of contemplation, prayer and sacrifice. It would hurt Me if you do not want to be a true Carmelite. Is renunciation difficult? Do not worry, I will repay you."

I repented of what I did and quickly began to work while adoring Him. When I left the garden to hang up the clothes, He said:

Jesus: "I will await you in our little dwelling. Come quickly and be with Me."

When I entered the small room, His presence filled me with holy devotion. After adoring Him briefly, I continued my work. The Lord Jesus asked me:

Jesus: "Do your task and then come back. I await your return."

I returned quickly and prostrated. He filled my soul with His Divine Presence and said:

Jesus: "Love only Me and serve Me even more. You already know these words, do you not? You know, I always ask you what My Heart desires the most."

EFFECT OF GRACE FOR THE DYING

September 12, 1963

After a holy confession, the Lord Jesus filled me with great alternating torments. I once had to suffer because doubts were overcoming me. Another time, at the request of the Blessed Virgin, I had to suffer the agony of the dying and their fight against Satan. The Blessed Virgin spoke again.

Mary: "You see, my little one, once the Flame of Love of my heart lights up on the earth, its effect of grace will also spread out to the dying. Satan will be blinded, and through your prayer at the nighttime vigil, the terrible struggle of the dying against Satan will end. Coming under the gentle light of my Flame of Love, even the most hardened sinner will convert."

While she was telling me this, my suffering increased so greatly that I felt I was on the verge of bursting to pieces.

DOUBTS AND INTERIOR HUMILIATIONS

September 14, 1963

While I was working, the Blessed Virgin asked me to plead her Holy Cause. I was so confused that a resistance which I had never felt began to torture me. I asked: "Is this truly the Blessed Virgin's voice? Have I fallen victim to my imagination?" This happened because after my confession two days ago, I gave the Blessed Virgin's urgent petition to my spiritual director. He told me not to go to the bishop and that he would take responsibility before the Blessed Virgin. He even added that, if it is urgent to the Blessed Virgin, that she herself would take the means. Besides that, I should wait until the bishop returns to the city and then speak with him. I told my spiritual director that I submit myself fully to what he said and I will do nothing without his permission. Meanwhile, the Blessed Virgin kept urging me.

Mary: "Go quickly!"

I asked: "O my Mother, where and in what direction must I go? To whom?"

She gave a clear response.

Mary: "Go to Father E and ask him if he knows when the bishop will come."

I was completely confused by these words. This was unexpected and I felt incapable of making a decision. I foresaw great difficulties because the bishop usually does not come at this time. What would Father E say if I came to him with my question? However, the urgency was much stronger than my power to resist the request.

I interrupted my housework and went quickly to speak with Father E. He was not surprised and answered: "We expect the bishop on Monday to bless a tombstone." Since the response was not precise, I asked him if he could tell me the exact time, because I wanted to speak to him if he comes. Then I knelt and asked for his blessing. When I ask Father E for his blessing, he is always surprised, but I consider it quite normal.

...Since the priest did not tell me the date and time, I had great inner humiliation. I did not understand the reason for this. Even though the inspiration I followed was true, the anguish of the doubts still continued. If this inspiration did not come from the Blessed Virgin, then what power made me do this?

OVER ALL PEOPLE AND NATIONS

September 16, 1963

The Blessed Virgin spoke again.

Mary: "My little one, I extend the effect of grace of the Flame of Love of my heart over all the peoples and nations, not only over those living in the Holy Mother Church, but over all the souls marked with the sign of the blessed Cross of my Divine Son."

Further annotation in the diary: "Also over those who are not baptized!"

(The Blessed Virgin repeated these things also on September 19 and 22.)

FAMILY HOLY HOUR

September 24, 1963

Afterwards, on September 24, 1963, she called me again.

Mary: "My Flame of Love which I desire to spread from my heart over all of you in a greater measure extends even to the souls in Purgatory. Listen closely to what I am saying. Write down my words and give them to those concerned: For those families observing a holy hour of reparation on Thursday or Friday, if someone happens to die in the family, the deceased is freed from Purgatory after a single day of strict fasting observed by anyone member of the family." (Let's understand: if he died in a state of grace.)

Note: Strict fasting does not mean suffering from hunger. It is permitted to eat bread and drink water.

The Lord Jesus:

Jesus: "You please Me a great deal at this moment. You ask why? Continue to do you your best. What did your guardian angel tell you? Increase the adoration and homage to the Holy Majesty of God. You see how by your resolve to examine your conscience every hour, your soul is refined to become more apt to immerse itself in God and worship Him. Your homage also is greatly gaining in standing with the Holy Majesty of God. This proposition on your part requires a very great peaceful contemplation. But to the one who loves, nothing is impossible. I have provided you with sufficient examples of that.

Your bad temper will go on, but out of this evil nature, I will accomplish a masterpiece if you agree to submit to My Divine Hand. Simply surrender to Me like the wine grapes that are pressed and transformed into wine, which will become My Precious Blood. You also will be intoxicated with My Precious Blood, but only if you are transformed and purified, just like the must, or like the wheat transformed in My Sacred Body, once it has been ground. You also will transform yourself only once you have been ground down and your miserable nature divinized. You understand that, do you not? We have already meditated at length on that together. Whoever eats My Body and drinks My Blood remains in Me and I in him. He in whom God dwells will be divinized. Permeate yourself with this grace so great, My daughter."

I AWAIT YOUR ARRIVAL

October 2, 1963

The Lord Jesus told me:

Jesus: "Do not let the earth attract you to itself. By the many graces which I give you, you are an arrow which flies straight to Me. By these graces, you can stay in flight. We do not allow any relapse because My graces keep you in a continuous flight. The moment is near, so be patient. I can hardly wait for your arrival. My Elizabeth, My little one! I draw you close to My Heart. You will receive a tremendous reward for all the sufferings that you have accepted for My work of Salvation."

October 9, 1963

The Most Holy Virgin also asked me kindly:

Mary: "Keep vigil over the silence of your soul, my little Carmelite. Give no entrance even to a whisper that might disturb the silence of your soul. Our words will continue to echo if you listen with humility and holy devotion."

These words of the Blessed Virgin resounded in my heart such as when we mothers admonish our children and watch over them with an anxious and apprehensive love.

ONLY A MOTHER CAN UNDERSTAND

October 18, 1963

During the nightly vigil, the Blessed Virgin began to speak. While she did, she spread the boundless pain of her maternal heart into my soul. While my heart was filling up with the sorrow of her maternal heart, she continued to speak.

Mary: "My little one, only a mother can understand the anguish and sorrow of my soul. That is why I am speaking to you. You know about anguish and you understand me. Oh, how many of my children are damned! I crumble under the weight of the pain and I want to share it with you just so you hasten to set into motion my Holy Cause. You are also a mother and the anguish of my heart is also yours."

While this motherly pain was growing within my heart, she asked me again not to refuse any fatigue and not to neglect her request that will go forth through me.

October 19, 1963 - Saturday

When I arose in the morning, the Blessed Virgin told me with her moving words:

Mary: "Go, my daughter, and hurry! Each minute means the loss of souls. Go, my child!"

She repeated it again. After Holy Communion, she asked the same thing.

Mary: "Do not be trapped by the heavy feelings of doubt. These are just obstacles to my plans. Now, before long, I will take my Holy Cause to those who will propel it widely."

In spite of these words, a heavier doubt came upon my soul. "O Mother, I have taken so many initiatives and have satisfied your requests with all my strength. Yet, everything has remained the same. Forgive me. I do not want to follow my own imagination. Completely strip from me all of my thoughts. I want to think and do only what you want. If I can ask even more, take from me everything that makes me a victim of my own imagination."

The Blessed Virgin was content to say:

Mary: "Believe in my maternal power."

I then felt that I must begin. I must do what the Blessed Virgin asks. Her request resounds continually in my heart as a dark omen.

DURING THE WORSHIP OF THE MOST HOLY TRINITY

October 22, 1963

After returning from Holy Mass, I began to do my housework. My holy guardian angel asked me to go and adore the Most Holy Trinity. At his request, I went into my little house at the foot of the garden. I cannot speak of or describe the wonderful graces that I received from adoring the Most Holy Trinity. They must be experienced because all human words fail completely. It happened on previous occasions that I could have described in some way, by its splendor and illumination, the transfusion of graces sent out in the form of rays by the Most Holy Trinity, but those experiences are pale and dark compared to what they now allow me to feel and live.

October 23-24, 1963

I spent two days immersed in adoration of the Most Holy Trinity. Meanwhile, doubts greatly disturbed my soul and I could not free myself of my depressing spiritual torments. I am the foolish victim of my own imagination. Who can set me free from that? This is not a temptation of the Evil One because a long time ago the Blessed Virgin blinded Satan in my soul. Am I the source of these battles? Right now, I do not have the possibility to consult my spiritual director. He could give me some explanation of these disorders and doubts that dominate my soul.

I felt as if my soul was climbing a mast so high that I was getting dizzy, and I only had to climb to the top or to throw myself into the abyss. But I could no longer fight this long battle... In the midst of my sufferings, I felt that immersing myself in the Most Holy Trinity was the only way to avoid giving up forever the exhausting struggle, which despite everything I did, refused to leave my soul.

As the night was falling, I went to the Lord Jesus to receive some rest for my soul. Suddenly, the Spirit of Love overwhelmed me with a feeling that caused me to tremble.

I must write that all feeling of space and time ceased in me, and in this spiritual ecstasy, the Lord began to speak. His voice spread an extraordinary strength over me. His words reached my conscience through a very humanlike locution.

Jesus: "My little one, as a reward for these great struggles, the Most Holy Trinity took possession of your soul to a greater and greater level. It brought all your human strength to the highest level of tension. Do not be surprised by what I am going to say or the way I will express it. Just so you understand the meaning of My words, I must use expressions that are familiar to you: Both in quantity and in quality, you have responded to the Divine Demands."

Coming from Him, these words made my soul experience unimaginable joy.

Jesus: "Because your soul has been purified of the anguish of doubts, you now have been given the power to rise to the heavenly Father and be immersed in the delightful and joyful contemplation of the Holy Trinity. I will speak to you less frequently. Your frequent immersion in the Most Holy Trinity will raise your soul towards God and it will remain in the company of the heavenly Father. This is the reward for your suffering representing indestructible value.

Instead of your doubts, I will now grant you the gift of another category of sufferings. From this point forward, you will fight an uninterrupted struggle against the demands of the body pulling strongly towards the earth the inner desires of your soul which long for Heaven. It is by resisting them constantly and by confronting them that you will remain in possession of the Spirit of Love. I will improve the sacrifices of your struggles and your fatigues in support of the twelve priests called upon to promote and set into motion the Flame of Love of My Mother."

At this moment, the Blessed Virgin intervened with immense love and said:

Mary: "My little instrument, I will make prevail in your soul the certainty that my words are authentic. Humility and sacrifice! These two virtues jointly predominate in your soul. Trust, at last, in my maternal power by which I will blind Satan and free the world from damnation."

A FIRM HELP

October 28, 1963

At night, I went to the Lord Jesus... On the way, I was immersed in Him and I wanted to take advantage of the silence that surrounded me… I asked the Lord: "My adored Jesus, are there any words that I have written that come from my imagination? If so, please show me because this causes me unrest."

At this moment, He came to my side and placed His blessed hand on my shoulder – I did not see Him but I felt His presence. Smiling, He said:

Jesus: "There is no reason to think that."

After saying this, He intensified the experience of His presence.

November 1, 1963

During my work, the Lord Jesus spoke and increased the intimate devotion that dominates my soul. I must write about this. I live, but only the Lord's Will makes me live. What I am writing now was very surprising to me.

Jesus: "My dear little beloved one! Does He who is calling you so tenderly really surprise you? You please Me when you surrender totally to Me. Always do this because it keeps you continually close to Me. In your uselessness, I will be your strong support. That great experience of God with which I gifted you recently compensates for Satan's great temptation that was unleashed against you. Do you know what I am talking about?"

And He reminded me of the struggle which lasted several days.

Jesus: "I, the Master, saw and was satisfied. Now, I place your soul in a special state of My graces because of that great battle. You know, My little one, even here on earth you receive a foretaste of Heaven's delights. As I already said, this is your reward for the sufferings which have eternal value."

ITS EFFECT WILL ENLIGHTEN ALL THE SOULS

November 7, 1963

During these days, the Blessed Virgin continually urged and asked.

Mary: "I can no longer hold back my Flame of Love in my heart. Let it leap out into all of you. Make all the preparations to set out. Only the first step is difficult. Once it will have been accomplished, my Flame of Love will sweep away with uproar the distrust of souls. Encountering no resistance, the Flame will illumine souls with a gentle light. Those accepting the Flame of Love will be intoxicated by the abundance of graces and they will proclaim everywhere, as I said before, that such a torrent of grace has never been granted since the Word became Flesh."

November 19, 1963

The Blessed Virgin said:

Mary: "Once the doubts that torment you will have ceased, you must take up my Cause. You cannot rest. Be neither weary nor uncommunicative. You have to make the most of your mission through that person who has also been assigned to accompany you.

Come together, all those who already know it! How clumsy you are! Have no fear, trust in my power!"

November 21, 1963

The Blessed Virgin insisted again.

Mary: "...Now that my Flame of Love has conquered your soul, you must seek with all your might everything I have entrusted you. I give to everyone the power to act. By the effect of grace of my Flame of Love, I will enkindle a light in your soul so that your initial thrust remain courageous."

Here, she reminded me of those to whom I must speak.

Mary: "Do this! I am the one who urges you."

UNITING FORCES TO BLIND SATAN

November 27, 1963

The Blessed Virgin spoke again in a very human voice.

Mary: "Tell me, my little one, how long will you remain here without moving forward?"

Instantly, her words conveyed a feeling of helplessness and misery in my heart. Then, I once again heard her words which sounded so wonderful, in a way I had only once heard before. They resounded majestically, stern and urgent.

Mary: "To whom, do you think, will I ask to render an account for having set up obstacles? If someone among you was to set up obstacles, defend my Flame of Love with all your might.

You must dedicate yourselves to blind Satan. The coordinated forces of the entire world are necessary to accomplish this. Do not delay because someday you will be called to account for the work entrusted to you, for the fate of a multitude of souls. I do not want even one soul damned. Satan will be blinded inasmuch as you work against him."

Here the Blessed Virgin added that the responsibility will fall not only on the priests, but on all those who, seeking their comfort, did not enroll in the fight to blind Satan.

Mary: "Put immediately into action the outpouring of graces of my Flame of Love. To your group, I give a wonderful strength to all and to each one in particular. Your responsibility is great but your work will not be in vain. There must not be a single soul missing in this common effort. The soft light of my Flame of Love will light up, spreading fire over the entire surface of the earth. Satan, humiliated and reduced to powerlessness, will not be able to exercise his power. However, do not seek to prolong these birth pangs."

Later on, she asked me again to make sure to bring her message to the bishop. (I sent him a letter on November 28, 1963.)

THE BLESSED VIRGIN'S INSISTENCE

November 28, 1963

I took this letter to Father X a few days earlier. The Blessed Virgin insisted so much that I almost did not know how to fulfill the task.

Reverend Father,

Please do not take offense at this letter. I am a nothing and a nobody, just a small instrument in the hands of the Blessed Virgin. I do only what she tells me. She has great power and she is the one who urges me. I am just her humble daughter. I also obey you with all my will, and I do all that you tell me. I am exhausted from the Blessed Virgin's urging that never ceases in my heart. She is the one who asks that we send her petition to the bishop. She speaks of how he welcomed her Flame of Love. What more can I do than to write and to take, or send through the religious Sister, the words the Blessed Virgin told me to send.

When I was with the bishop for the second time, he gave me this advice. I am transcribing it word for word: "Try to get a regular spiritual director. After he gets to know you, – your extraordinary spiritual state will draw his attention anyway – he will know what to do. If he comes to me, I will talk with him."

You, Father, must seek an opportunity to meet with the bishop. The Blessed Virgin asks that you meet as soon as possible. I write this because of the continued urgent pleas of the Blessed Virgin. I greet you with humble respect.

DO NOT BE PASSIVE

December 2, 1963

After Holy Mass, the Blessed Virgin spoke.

Mary: "Do not be passive about my Sacred Cause. It will be through the few, the little ones, and the humble that must begin this great outpouring of graces that will shake the world. None of those called must excuse themselves or refuse my invitation. All of you are my little instruments."

(This message was received in the hands of Father, and it is always sent by personal courier in the form of a letter, as the Lord Jesus or the Blessed Virgin request in each case.)

MY SOUL WAS ENRAPTURED

December 10, 1963

The Blessed Virgin sent me to Father E to ask him to go to my spiritual director. She said nothing more about this. Her words on this matter were short and firm. Thereafter, her voice changed and she began to speak with such tenderness that I can do nothing but rewrite that my soul was enraptured. I cannot describe but with few words what happened within me. On previous days, I struggled with vehement spiritual torments… The Blessed Virgin shared her maternal sorrow with me. So greatly did these sufferings come upon me, that I had almost no strength for other tasks… The conversation with the Blessed Virgin was almost uninterrupted.

I cannot write what the Blessed Virgin said during the ecstasy… The Lord Jesus now speaks rarely, but He had already warned me about that. Now, the Blessed Virgin fills my soul with her special love and brings about the ecstasy…

DO PENANCE

December 15, 1963

The Lord Jesus was grieving while instructing me.

Jesus: "With what great faith, hope and love, I made the greatest sacrifice for all of you. I believed and hoped that I would have disciples who would correspond to My sacrifices made with boundless love. In My agony, when I was sweating blood, the heavenly Father's consolation gave Me renewed strength to drink the cup of suffering to the bottom. It is as a Man that I suffered, refusing any help from My Divinity, so My Heart would feel as yours do. As a Man, I experienced every type of suffering, and I walked the road of sorrow motivated by the hope I had in all of you. I saw many infidelities as well as your loving commitment. It was your commitment which motivated Me, and even today it still moves Me to mercy and forgiveness. Whenever I encounter one righteous soul, I forgive many. Therefore, do penance so that My hope placed in you may produce for you the fruit of salvation."

December 1963

One Friday afternoon, while I was already lacking strength due to the difficult mortification, the Lord Jesus suddenly surprised me. He poured out graces that made me tremble. With great kindness, He said:

Jesus: "To you! What will I not grant to you! As you have asked, I will increase My graces. Through your sufferings, you have widened your soul. Now, everything I want to give you fits in your soul. Each sacrifice is a new bank deposit in Heaven that you will bring with you. Through Me, the multitude of souls will receive its interest after your death."

THE DUSTY ALTAR

December 22, 1963

While immersed in His infinite goodness, I was cleaning the chapel. In my joy, I thanked Him for being in His presence today for so long a time. He told me that He also felt the same joy. Meanwhile, He began to complain. When I started to clean behind and at the foot of the high altar, – which for so many years had not been cleaned, and where the layer of dust was as thick as a finger and my white work blouse became grey – the Lord Jesus made this bitter complaint:

Jesus: "You see, such is the soul that recollects before My altar but which, for years, has not kept itself clean. It does not look within, it comes into My presence out of habit. It also comes before Me with a layer of dust as thick as a finger on its soul."

He then allowed me to see a priest that He had pointed out to me once before, and He asked me to suffer for him because He strongly desired this priest to come in His presence. He constantly avoids the reason why he was chosen by God. At that time, I was overwhelmed, and to this day I am still quite moved. Now I continue where I left off.

Jesus: "Indeed, you would not have suspected the existence of a thick layer of grey dust behind My altar. You also only clean the surface. Now you can see why I complain so much of souls consecrated to Me. They come before My altar, but their souls are grey and dusty. Not looking within themselves, they see only the outside beauty. Just as your white gown became grey, so by their bad example they soil many, many souls. And they do not even realize it! They should not admire themselves as they do not look at the splendid altar in their soul. They look beyond and over it. They avoid what is difficult, and as the years go on, their soul becomes grey and covered with dust. Woe to them, because through example they influence others. From the one who knows little, little will be asked; they know a lot, however they consider themselves satisfied with the knowledge, they do not feel with Me. They do not care – as I already told you – to leave Me only a few crumbs. Of course, for each crumb received, I only give one crumb back. They are only giving Me what they no longer need in their life. Yet, they think that for the crumb that they threw to Me, they are entitled to something in return. I very much love small sacrifices, the tiny crumbs, provided that the one who gives them is not proud. I am pleased with the humble soul, and even if the sacrifice offered is very insignificant, they will receive a great reward. But I demand the effort.

My little one, I return to the subject of dust where My reflection started. The world is an altar covered with a layer of dust like this one. I am the victim. Moreover, you raise your eyes up to Me, you see My splendor and rejoice over its beauty, you take advantage of My kindness, but you do not even think that behind all that, there is an ocean of suffering. You simply savor only the good that is offered to you, but it does not even come to your mind that you should respond in turn.

You see, this is the pain of My Heart. May our thoughts be in unison. Oh, I have complained much, but do not be depressed about that. A shared grief is half a grief. However, I also share joy with you. Even sharing in My sorrow becomes a joy for you because in doing so, I grant you My Divine Confidence. Tell Me, little sister, can you understand this? Perhaps not? This is of little importance. I just desire that our hearts beat to the same rhythm. The mind cannot comprehend as readily as a compassionate heart does, being constantly enlightened by the splendor of sacrifice.

The light dims down for whoever remains in the dust, as he cannot see the grief in My Heart. Let both of us implore the heavenly Father on behalf of those dusty souls."

I GUIDE YOU

1963

I do not remember when the Lord told me the following. I only found one fragment.

Jesus: "...I guide you. Naturally, this does not mean that the words of your spiritual guide do not come from Me. On the contrary, I emphasize that they do come from Me. Accept his directions with the greatest humility and do what he says. His words flow from My Heart. Hopefully every soul would understand and follow this advice."

THE GIFT OF GRACE OF THE BLESSED VIRGIN MARY

"I want to place a new instrument in your hands. It is the Flame of Love of my heart. With this Flame full of graces that I give you from my heart, ignite all the hearts, going from one to the other. Its brightness will blind Satan.

My Flame of Love is so great that I can no longer keep it within me; it leaps out at you with explosive force.

Sublime mission: to propagate the Flame of Love.

To propagate it should be the principal purpose of your life, my little one. Help me to propagate this devotion!"

My Most Holy Mother, by the love which the Holy Spirit granted you, save me from falling into sin. Make me live and die in your blessed company. Gloria...

Pray constantly to the Blessed Virgin with this prayer:

Our Mother, spread the effect of grace of your Flame of Love over all of humanity. Amen

Each time you pray invoking the Flame of Love for all humanity, Satan is blinded and loses his dominion over souls: "Help me to save souls."

"My Flame of Love will blind Satan to the same extent that all of you spread it around the world."

* * *

Chapter four

1964

A TORRENT OF GRACES

First Sunday of January 1964

I went to the hospital to visit one of my children. It was very cold, and as I returned home, I could hardly walk. I then realized that the adoration of the Blessed Sacrament will begin at 5:00 p.m. and I wanted to be present for this community adoration.

Overcoming the coldness that made my feet feel almost numb, I rushed to go near the Lord Jesus. As I walked, with His silent and thankful words, He began to speak.

Jesus: "I am very glad that you came to keep Me company. You try so hard to please Me. This will gain for you a new and abundant torrent of graces."

During the adoration of the Blessed Sacrament, He asked me to offer Him reparation for the offenses committed by so many people paying very little attention to His inspirations. Oh, immediately, my sins came back to mind. I was one of them having offended Him very much. Can anyone think of this and not shed tears?

"Lord, forgive my sins." Many, many times, I experienced the repentance that the Lord's mercy brought forth in my soul. "I want to repent for my sins like no one ever has repented until now. I want to love You like no converted sinner has ever loved You until now."

While I was repenting of my sins, He continued:

Jesus: "You know, the great sin of the world is to ignore My inspirations. It is because of that and lukewarm consecrated souls that the world is walking in darkness. They could help Me, but they are not even aware how dangerous their tepidity is. I beg you, communicate the desire of My Heart to your spiritual father. Hopefully, he and those who guide souls will follow My inspirations with greater fidelity, and bring souls to understand the importance of this, because otherwise it is impossible to lead a spiritual life. Regardless of how great their perseverance may be, if they set aside My holy inspirations, their souls will become corrupted just like the ones entrusted to them."

THE GREATEST RICHNESS - HUMILITY

January 13, 1964

During my meditation, the Lord Jesus said again:

Jesus: "Be careful, My Elizabeth, your soul will be the battleground of a great and prolonged combat. The Evil One wants to uproot the greatest riches in your soul. He wants to destroy your humility. He knows and he sees that this is the unique value he has to attain. This is the only way that he can destroy the constancy of your soul. He will attack you with a terrible power and he will use all the resources of his hatred against you. The Evil One will disturb your thoughts, he will make you unsure of your actions. By his words, he will suggest every kind of foul deeds and he will flood you with terrible torments. He wants to deceive you so you abandon your humble devotion."

A few hours later, the troubles of the Evil One began. If the Lord Jesus had not told me ahead of time, I do not know how I would have remained stable in confronting these revolting thoughts. I could not expel him from my thoughts. He rushed on me with all the force of his hatred. My heart languished and was incapable of acting. It is only the Lord's warning that prevented me from doing something wrong.

NOT ONE SOUL DAMNED

January 15, 1964

The Lord Jesus told me:

Jesus: "Do you know, my little one, that the number of readers is very great? Frequently, many are those who read about My holy doctrine, but without getting anywhere. The electrical light, the sunlight, light up only the letters. Only the souls that come to Me understand truly the meaning of My doctrine. By My Divine Brightness, I give to the soul that prostrates before Me the intelligence of My Divinity, and through it, their mind can understand my eternal desire, which is the salvation of souls.

Desire to share in My work of Redemption! Let this be the supreme goal of your lives, the most valuable gift that you can bring to Me. Take advantage of every opportunity and every means to save souls. Work at it! Remember what you once read: 'If each Christian would save just one soul, no one would be lost.'"

When the Lord Jesus concluded, the Blessed Virgin spoke these sorrowful words:

Mary: "My little one, I want that not one soul be damned. You should want this together with me. For this purpose, I place in your hands a beam of light that is the Flame of Love of my heart."

When she said these words, I experienced more deeply the sorrow of her heart.

I AM THE GREAT DONOR OF BLOOD

January 16, 1964

During Holy Mass and after Holy Communion, the Lord Jesus spoke of the power of His Precious Blood.

Jesus: "I am the great Donor of blood. By virtue of My Divine Blood, you can be divinized. Can you understand that? Truly, it is difficult. I am the sole Donor of blood in the whole world. Permeate yourself with My love, My almighty love. Meditate on that now in the light of My holy brightness. Can't you feel this Precious

Blood? My Precious Blood warms up and sets into motion the frozen, paralyzed energy of your souls. I am pouring it out and will continue to pour it in all the men in the entire world inasmuch as they submit to the holy treatment of My Divine Hand. Allow Me to act within your soul. Why should you desire to remain men with coarse souls? If only you accepted to become divine, I would find My joy in you, and live with you.

My table is always set. I, the Amphitryon, have sacrificed everything. I give Myself. After receiving My Precious Blood, examine your souls and become aware of the exhilaration that the power of My Precious Blood brings about in you. Do not be so insensitive. Let not routine lead you to my holy table, but rather the fervor of sacrificial charity, which ignites through contact with My love. Through Me – inasmuch as you remain united to Me – it will burn sin out of your souls. Oh, how I have longed for your decision and your voluntary love. When will you finally come to Me?"

These Divine Experiences maintain my heart in such a state that, on these occasions when the disturbing power of the Evil One cannot make any gain, they become completely annihilated in my heart.

EACH HOME SHOULD BE A SANCTUARY

January 17, 1964

Today, the Lord Jesus spoke about His home in Nazareth, which was the warm and cherished living place for the Holy Family.

Jesus: "You know, this is where I prepared My Soul for the great Sacrifice, for the sufferings I endured for you. You also had to mature in the holy enclosure of the family. As you were an orphan, it is in your home as a married couple that your soul was prepared for your great vocation, which could only mature in a family setting. I know your qualities and that's why My Divine Providence ordered everything to make you ready to communicate My message to the world. It is from the family sanctuary that all of you set out for the difficult struggles of life.

It is to the warm solidarity of the family sanctuary that souls come back to, after having strayed far. It is there that they come to find themselves and they once more return to God. It is necessary for you, mothers, to extend the warm understanding of your hearts to your children even once they have established their own homes. Great is the responsibility befalling on you. Do not think that once a child has become an adult, he no longer needs his parents. My Mother accompanied Me everywhere with her love, her sacrifices and her prayers. You must do the same, and I will bless your efforts. My beloved Mother obliges Me to that. By her powerful intercession, she obtained from Me for families this great effusion of grace, which she also wants to extend to the whole world. As she said: 'Nothing comparable to this has happened ever since the Word became Flesh.'

She places the healing power of her maternal goodness at the root of evil. She did not want to perform a spectacular miracle as does occur in the large famous sanctuaries of the world, giving rise to great admiration. She wants every family to be a sanctuary, a wonderful place where, in union with you, she works miracles in the depth of hearts. Going from heart to heart, she places in your hands the Flame of Love of her heart. Through your prayers and sacrifices, it will blind Satan who wants to rule over families."

The Blessed Virgin added the following:

Mary: "Through you, my little Carmelite, I want all to know the anguish that springs up from the boundless love of my maternal heart because of the danger threatening the entire world by the disintegration of the family sanctuaries. I direct my maternal cry to all of you, and in union with you, I want to save the world. I allow you, my little one, to be the first to feel this immense effort I am beginning to deploy in order to blind Satan.

Until the day of your death, I will share with you the anguish of my heart. Your compassionate heart makes you worthy to spread my Flame of Love. And all those who will share in my sorrow will also have the right to receive this great grace by which we will save souls from eternal damnation."

RENOUNCE YOUR ENTERTAINMENT

January 18, 1964

I was with the Sister that had been assigned to me. She was listening to one of her favorite concerts on the radio. When she had a task to do, she gave me the hearing device saying that I should listen. Immediately, I became absorbed in the beauty of the music. After a few minutes, the Lord spoke some soft words.

Jesus: "Do you not think that during these occasions I am jealous of you? What did I tell you? That there will not be one hair between us!"

His words dominated my soul and drowned out the beauty of the music. He continued imploring me.

Jesus: "Listen to My heavenly words through art and musical beauty of the world also. Renounce yourself and your own entertainment. Think about how I work within you, My little sister, and do not allow any passing diversion into your soul. Take good care to not dispel the recollection of your soul by the makings of petty worldly artists. For you, only one thing is necessary, your uninterrupted sharing in My work of Redemption. Let this be your diversion! Do not say that I am very strict. Have I not asked you many times to renounce yourself? You must do this moment by moment. You cannot stop doing this even for a short time. I am your way and your life. Everything passes away, only your work for souls remains."

SOME LIGHT FOOTSTEPS

January 19, 1964 - Sunday

Today, I attended only one Holy Mass. My old chilblains on my feet began to bother me again, keeping me away from the evening Holy Mass and I couldn't do the evening adoration either. I thought that I should rest today. So, I spent the afternoon and evening in my little warm house, doing minor tasks. At some point, I went out into the garden, and immediately, I heard some light footsteps on top of the icy snow. I looked around thinking it must be a small hungry animal looking for food, and I went on walking a few more steps. Then suddenly the presence of the Lord filled my soul. I was startled because He allowed me to feel that He was present next to me. My whole body was shaking under the effect of the graces emanating from Him. My physical strength abandoned me so much that I almost collapsed. It is only hesitantly that I was able to take a few steps. Many times now, the Lord has surprised me with His presence, but this time went beyond all the previous ones. My body shook as never before until now. I did not see and I do not know how, nevertheless I perceived the touch of His garment. It was like an extraordinary breath of graces filling my heart with the feeling of God's presence. All this happened in the garden covered with snow. When I returned to my tiny dwelling, I realized how long I had been gone. Afterward, the Lord Jesus began to speak kindly to me.

Jesus: "You know, I was alone, and since you were not coming, I came to you. I rejoice to be with you. I am grateful for the number of times you think about Me. Oh, how it pleases Me when you meditate on My Precious Blood with such devotion and when you make reparation and adore Me. I gather that it is only fair on My part to honor you in this particular fashion.

Oh, the loneliness! The loneliness and coldness are surrounding me constantly. That is why I stay close to you now. I do not disturb your rest, I am here with you in silence. May our hearts beat to the same rhythm. Keep on doing what you are doing. I will stay with you for quite some time because… what would I do all by Myself. No one comes to worship Me, or to make reparation, or to ask, or to give thanks. I know that you never miss without a valid reason. You never have any unjustified absence. My Elizabeth, I am giving you the gift of My Divinity. Hold Me close to your heart because I also have human feelings. I wanted to give you as a reward the sacred surge that you felt just now, as a sign of My gratitude towards you."

WHOEVER READS THIS

January 20, 1964

Jesus: "Write what I say: Any person, in any place, who will read this Divine Emanation with which I honored you yesterday, will also – nobody excluded – share in the outpouring of My graces that I will pour out over the souls by virtue of your merits united to mine, as a payment in advance for the drops of oil flowing from your sufferings."

I TOOK YOUR SOUL

January 28, 1964

What I write now happened some days ago. It pained me so much to write it down because I hardly succeed in understanding what He said.

Jesus: "Do not try to understand. What good does it do? You cannot understand the long road that you had to travel for your soul to be lifted to these heights. All the astronomers in the world cannot describe the road that you have traveled in such a short time. Even the saints and the angels of Heaven are in admiration.

Can you understand how easy it is for Me to bring this about? I snatched you with My love so that you fly straight like an arrow to Me. I repeat, straight like an arrow. This is the road of love which has no detour and does not calculate. Because you accepted this love I offered you and held on to it with all your strength, you are now here with Me. Do not wonder for one moment about how I respond to your love. Because you understood the sacrifice offered by My love, My graces act in your soul with no obstacle. If I lift you to Myself, do not even reflect on it. Take it as My gift, do not try to understand. At any rate, it pleases Me greatly that you be immersed in your misery. Even this you cannot attribute to yourself because it is a fruit of the extraordinary graces that I offered you. And as you cannot understand with your intelligence what happens during this separation with earth that occurs during the ecstasy, in such way you will neither be able to account for nor provide an explanation concerning the abundance of graces received, that will leave a great many dumbfounded. Because I took your soul in hand, you are the exclusive work of My hands. I prepared your soul and all praise belongs to Me. Furthermore, I did not give you a spiritual director because I wanted to personally train you for your great destiny. As for allowing you to fall many times, that was required of you by Myself in order to thus temper your soul for this great humility without which I would not have succeeded with you.

Even today, I guide you. This naturally does not mean that the words of your spiritual director do not come from Me. On the contrary, and I say this strongly, accept all his directions and do only what he says. His word is My word. He receives all that he says from My inspiration. Oh, if only each soul understood that and conformed itself to it humbly and obediently!"

GOD'S UNFATHOMABLE PROVIDENCE

January 29, 1964

A few days ago, the Sister assigned to me wanted me to ask the Blessed Virgin if some Sister who was very ill was going to die. Her eventual death would prevent the progress of various difficult matters. I told the Sister that I was not accustomed to ask the Blessed Virgin in matters of that nature. The Blessed Virgin did not answer my question that I asked only at Sister's request and against my will.

Some days later, when I was not even thinking about this, the Lord Jesus surprised me and said:

Jesus: "Why does your Sister companion want to know matters that do not concern you?

Who I call and when I call him, that is My business. In any case, I arrange everything for your good. My Divine Providence works hard, with diligence, and without any interruption for the good of all humanity. As to those who are Mine, it is even more pronounced, and I frequently show it by very delicate manifestations of My love, but not to satisfy your curiosity or to calm your immediate concerns. In any case, My Providence remains unfathomable to you. Trust! Bring Me all that is difficult and obscure, and I will ease your burden and enlighten it every day."

THE FEW WORKERS

February 8, 1964 - First Saturday

Jesus: "Look around and check. Who is gathering with Me?"

What He taught me during my work is interesting. He showed me a very strange surface which was rotating, and irrespective of where I looked, I could only see this surface. I saw countless souls in expanses impossible to take in at a single glance. Those souls were suffering in body and soul. The Lord Jesus pointed out:

Jesus: "I am showing you this so you see how abundant the harvest is. You, My beloved; you, My great collaborator, may our hands gather in unity. Continue working for the salvation of souls. This vision that I laid before your eyes shows you who is gathering with Me. Do you see how great is the harvest and how scarce are the workers? This shows you why you must dedicate all your strength to your mission. Isn't it that you now feel an acute pain in your soul? Accept it wholeheartedly! For a time, this pain will remove the exhausting afflictions from the devil, which I could see were wearing you down.

Gather with Me, Elizabeth. I have few laborers despite the great rewards I keep offering. Those volunteering their services are few. Be My good worker, go beyond what is asked."

A TRANSPARENT SOUL

February 12, 1964

The day before, I went to the Sanctuary of pilgrimage Máriaremete. I was very moved by the splendor of the newly painted church. The following day, He said:

Jesus: "Did you delight in seeing My house? You have seen how it can be covered with one glance. May your soul also be simple and may it contain nothing but Myself."

WE GAINED NEW STRENGTH

February 13, 1964

The following happened last week, but it is difficult for me to write it down. I resolved that I would apply myself this year and not allow the Lord's words to be unwritten. But there are times when I think that the Lord Jesus said that just for me, and He would say something else for others. Yet, He insisted that I write down His words because, through me, He distributes His graces to others, but also for me to be His collaborator in that too.

I acknowledge that because of lack of schooling, I lack both an ease in writing and an ability to spell. Therefore, it is difficult to put everything into writing. I keep many things in my memory for myself. However, since the beginning of this year, I try hard to write down everything.

The following short conversation took place last Thursday. The days before, I had pain in my ear and throat, accompanied by a fever. I could take no solid food. And precisely on Thursday, I observed a day of strict fast (only bread and water). When the Lord Jesus saw my painful efforts, He said:

Jesus: "Since the two of us have been so exhausted, let us eat something hot."

I prepared some hot soup and felt much better. While I was eating, He praised me using few words but much feeling.

Jesus: "Is it not true that we now have both gained new strength? I also suffer with you. Could you imagine that I would leave you alone? No! I would never do that. Our souls are always in harmony."

I EXPAND YOUR HEART

February 14, 1964

Jesus: "I expand your heart by the fire of My Divine Love, so I can place in it an even greater abundance of graces. Heat expands iron, and the more it becomes incandescent, the more easily it can be shaped and expanded. Since you also worked in this field, you understand that, do you not? That is why I say: The more you are close to the ardent love of My Divinity, the more easily I shape and expand your heart according to My Divine Pleasure."

TO SUFFER MARTYRDOM

February 15, 1964

As I returned home after Holy Mass, He said some unexpected words.

Jesus: "My little sister, I pour over you the burning fire of My love that makes you worthy of even greater graces. These are not new to you, but as your remember My words, you will again surrender to Me and accept My petition. You must suffer all the way to martyrdom. Accept My words as a definitive and irrevocable proof of the Divine Love."

These serious words led me into deep thoughts. On the same day, the Evil One, with irritating boldness, interrupted the silence of my soul. With his infernal violence, he attacked me and shook my soul: "I am obliged to admit and even to recognize that the Cause entrusted to you is true. Nevertheless, I can assure you that you will never be able to suffer enough to bring about its progress. First, because you are buried in false humility, you do not take a single step. And even if you did, you would just repeat your failures. Also, your confessor does not like you, so do not hope to gain anything through him. You must advance without him. Do you think you will make progress by your austere life? You are mistaken. If extraordinary, external signs accompanied your human effort, it would be different. However, as you are now, no one will believe you. I cannot understand why you are sacrificing your life. Nothing of value will come about."

This grueling attack of soul and body lasted for hours and kept my mind in a dark torment. Although this happens often, I rarely write about it.

On that same day, I spoke with someone about a person whom we both knew. My companion said, "She is no leading light." Although she did not say this to hurt, it did hurt me because I have thought highly of the person she was referring to for many years. To avoid sinning against our neighbor, I immediately turned my thoughts to my beloved Jesus. I wanted to say to my companion that the person was a guiding light for me. However, there was no time. On the way home, I was consumed in adoration when the Lord Jesus answered my thoughts.

Jesus: "How it pleases Me when your heart suffers with Me and is thrilled at the slightest trifle. Your continual docility to My inspirations floods your soul so quickly with light. 'I am the light of Christ.' All can lift their gaze to Me. I am the majestic greatness of sacrifice, the inexhaustible depth of mercy, the abundance of example, the God of invincible patience, the inexhaustible goodness that flows from Me to all with overwhelming abundance. Who else could say this of himself? Only I, the 'Light of Christ.' I am one nature with the Father. I, who did everything for you in order to be 'the Light of the World' that you must follow; I, the Dispenser of strength to human weakness, I have convinced the world by showing, through My human nature also, the road that you must follow."

TEMPTATION OF THE EVIL ONE

February 17, 1964

During the day, the Lord Jesus said:

Jesus: "May our thoughts be in unison! Love this prayer I taught you, so that having recourse to its words, which your soul needs at this precise moment, you can find the necessary strength in all circumstances. Believe, My daughter! Let nothing lead you to abandon your goal! Your faith and confidence in Me will save you. Without faith and confidence, you are really very weak. This is why I chose you to be the instrument of our heavenly messages, so that the world will see how prevailing is the Divine Will that wants to be manifested only through the weak.

I do not change the order of nature nor do I suspend it in your circumstances. I act according to My Divine Wisdom and the necessity of the Cause. The temptations of the Evil One, by which he disturbs your soul and mind, must not deviate you from the road of faith and confidence in Me. Although you feel so weak, that is not an impediment, because neither the manifestation of your weakness nor your constant effort will bring our Cause to a successful conclusion. Your humility is the only instrument in your hands that helps the Cause to succeed."

IN PLACE OF OTHERS

February 20, 1964

A bad flu still tortures me. It has now attacked the cavities of my eyes and my face. During the night, I found myself in such a state that I could only spend a half hour with the Lord Jesus. I was struck by fever again. In the morning, I felt better. My heart was beating strongly when I prostrated myself before Him. I wanted to tell Him so many things, but He preceded me.

Jesus: "Welcome, My little one. I greet you!"

He allowed me to feel the beating of His Heart, which is well known to me. The silence that filled my soul was interrupted by the Lord Jesus.

Jesus: "Be indulgent! Once again, I will bring you My complaints. In this moment, may our hearts beat to the same rhythm and our thoughts be in unison. Today and tomorrow (it was the day preceding the first Friday) will be good days for Me. I look forward to these special days when people offer Me reparation. In these days, graces pour out like a refreshing dew descending upon dry and dark souls. Yourself, you must only want to; as for the rest leave it to Me. Results do not matter. What makes someone a saint, what saves, and what keeps the person close to Me is the continual desire of the will. That also makes your soul beautiful. Again, I say that I will have a good day because I see your good will. I am without pretense and easy to please. If you do not succeed, it matters little, providing you are willing to try again unceasingly. This effort dispels My pain.

I know that you are not bothered by My complaints because our souls are in harmony. You also, do as I do, assure Me of your constant love that the blazing fire of your continual acceptance of sacrifices keeps burning. It is of little importance to Me what you can do on a certain day or how much you can accomplish, only do not take a break, because that would cause Me great sorrow. So often I am sad because souls make Me feel that the burden I place upon them is heavy. You, the joy of My Heart, never tire of hearing My complaints. Even this gives Me rest. Console Me in place of the others."

MY DROPS OF BLOOD

February 22, 1964

The Lord Jesus said:

Jesus: "I wanted to speak to you last night, but I saw that you went to bed early because you were tired. This moment is more favorable. You know what I did for you because you immerse yourself often in the contemplation of My Sacred Passion. Oh, how happy I am to realize that I did not suffer for you in vain. I truly rejoice. Your souls, you who live in the mud of the earth, cannot free themselves. I take you from the mud of sin and wash you with My Precious Blood.

Prostrate yourselves at the feet of My Holy Cross and let My Precious Blood fall upon you. The drops of My Blood are a blank check in your hands; you need only to collect it. This check is valid until the end of the world. The soul that lives in God's grace can cash it anywhere, at any time until death, even if she ignores the day. As frequently as possible, each soul must make use of this check, which is the ransom paid by My Precious Blood. If you put this off until the evening of life, there will be just a short time to gain its full value. Take advantage of it while you still have your full vigor. For Me also, it was in the fullness of age that I gave My life for you. This is what I want and what I accept with the greatest thanks. How many times I hear this sigh rising up from your souls: 'O my Savior.' Unfortunately, it is only pure habit. Oh, how it wounds My Heart; this insensitive sigh is but indifference and indolence! Do not love Me in this way!"

BLIND SATAN

February 23, 1964

What I am writing now is something special. One time at the Sanctuary of Máriaremete, the Blessed Virgin led me to give the Flame of Love to a priest whom I did not know. Then the Blessed Virgin asked me to write down the names of all who have some knowledge of her Flame of Love. In the sacristy, I learned the name and address of this unknown priest. As I left the sacristy, I sensed that the address was not correct, but I paid no attention to this inner inspiration. I kept the address and, as the Blessed Virgin asked, I put it on my list. However, I experienced a restlessness that would not go away.

When I was again in the sanctuary, the Blessed Virgin gave me a decisive command.

Mary: "Go and learn immediately the correct name and address."

I could no longer resist, so I went to the line of confessionals. Someone I know said that the priest was no longer hearing confessions. This happened at a time when it is not customary to go to confession. To my surprise, the priest returned and I grew peaceful. Clearly, the request did come from the Blessed Virgin. Entering his confessional, I told the priest that I had not come to go to confession. Instead, I told him of these extraordinary happenings and that more than a year ago, I had written them for him to read. The priest remembered immediately and answered: "Yes, I know. It treats about blinding Satan." And he added that he recited the prayer with fervor. This surprised me because this priest understood the essential message, which is 'to blind Satan.' This is the principal and only purpose of the Flame of Love of the Blessed Virgin. She, herself, promised an outpouring of graces so great as have not happened on earth since the Word became Flesh.

I asked the priest for his name and address (hospital X...), as the address I was given in the sacristy was that of a church. Then I understood the reason for the firm command of the Blessed Virgin. At the end, I asked the priest to bless me and the feeling of unrest left me.

ENTER WHERE I AM

February 24, 1964

At 7:30 p.m., I passed by the church in the district of Christina. It was already late and I did not intend to enter. The Lord Jesus said:

Jesus: "Come near Me and greet Me."

I went in. To my surprise, the priest was simply standing before the opened tabernacle. He had his hand raised to close the tabernacle. When I fell prostrated, He said:

Jesus: "How much I waited for you! How kind that you have come."

The priest closed the tabernacle and bowed three times. From this, I realized that he was a Catholic priest of the Greek rite. He said a prayer in Hungarian. He turned twice to the people and blessed them twice with the chalice. Before the last gospel, he gave the final blessing. While I was adoring the Lord Jesus, He lovingly said:

Jesus: "You see that I called you here to receive My repeated blessings. Are you happy with Me?"

So great a condescension! "O my Lord Jesus, I can even no more annihilate myself before You."

Jesus: "How good this is, My little one! Often, I call the souls. How I yearn for them! How I hope that they accept My Divine Inspirations! Continue to be My atoning soul."

UNDERSTAND THE ARDENT DESIRE OF MY DIVINITY

February 25, 1964

The next day, when I returned home after Holy Mass, I was doing my household chores. He continued the previous night's conversation.

Jesus: "If you had not followed My call yesterday, you would have missed multiple blessings. I am happy telling you that these actions are further evidence of your attentive love. Oh, how many reject Me in one minute. If I find no rejection, My Heart rests there. Your most reverent effusive thanksgiving which you continue even at night obliges Me also.

While you were there with Me, I delighted in your devout thanksgiving. Now that you have returned from My place, I have come to show you My gratitude in the middle of your work. Understand the ardent longing of My Divinity that I want to calm down here with you. I delight to be with you because I feel that every beating of your heart is Mine. I am with you all day. Do not tremble from My presence. The experience lasts just an instant. You need your bodily strength to fulfill the obligations that you have undertaken."

WHAT WOULD I NOT GIVE TO A SOUL THAT RESPONDS TO MY LOVE

February 28, 1964

During the nighttime adoration, I renewed my self-offering: "Sweet Jesus, I live and I die for You."

Jesus: "I also! I also! For you I was born, for you I died."

Every word I said to Him returned like an echo. I continued: "I adore You, I bless You, I exalt You, I glorify You on behalf of others who do not." During this prayer, He responded with a great love.

Jesus: "My little sister, for this great praise, I bless you wholeheartedly, your family, and all those in whose place you offered it. I pour out upon them My abundant graces."

I wondered if I had misunderstood His words. If so, I would retract them.

Jesus: "No, do not do that. Understand Me, who am Love so often unreckoned, even if your mind could not succeed in penetrating this! What would I not give to a soul that responds to My love! I allow My loving Heart to be driven by 'madness'. I use those words so you can understand Me as Man. I know that you do not love Me only with your understanding, that would not be as pleasant to Me. This love differs from an intellectual love that measures, considers and ponders. Now, do you understand Me? I am accessible to you in a way that is quite human. If only this gave rise in you to a trust similar to Mine."

SUBLIME VOCATION OF MOTHERS

February 29, 1964

"My adored Jesus, accept me the way I am."

Jesus: "You also accept Me with My disheveled and sticky hair, My beaten body, stripped of its clothing, My hands and feet pierced by the nails, My opened wound on My side."

Somehow, He made me meditate with Him on His sad words and then said:

Jesus: "Wrap Me with your love that gathers My Precious Blood flowing from the wound on My side. Contemplate Me! Contemplate Me! During your lifetime, have you ever seen such a pitiable creature? Do you see how I became a wreck? You can never do too much for Me. Just as our hearts beat to the same rhythm, so may our thoughts be in unison.

Write down again My teaching which corroborates the teaching of the Holy Father. We have not yet meditated on that, but it is very important. Should you have forgotten about this, then I want to remind you."

The Lord was speaking about what I first wrote on May 24, 1963. After writing it, I never thought of it. Since the doubts in my heart were very great at the time, I never dared to read it again. Now, the Lord Jesus made me record it.

Jesus: "For My work of Redemption, I have great need of all of you."

I was hanging on His words. It is as if I were barely able to put them in any order in my thoughts. When He mentioned my person and spoke of my work as something important destined to complement the work of the Holy Father, doubts emerged in my soul. The Lord, with gentle words, continued speaking.

Jesus: "What I am saying now is for you and all mothers who work according to My Heart. Your work is not of less value than that of persons raised to the highest priestly dignity. Mothers of families, you must understand your sublime vocation to populate My Kingdom and to fill the places left vacant by the fallen angels. Each step of My Holy Mother the Church starts from your heart and your lap. My Kingdom grows inasmuch as you, mothers, nurture the created souls. You have the greatest work requiring a heightened sense of responsibility. Be fully aware that I have placed in your hands the task of leading a multitude of souls to eternal salvation."

GREAT GRACES TO FATHERS

March 1, 1964 - Sunday

During Holy Mass, He meditated with me on the words He had pronounced the previous year. And in the profound silence which filled my soul, with moving and kinds words, thus spoke the Lord Jesus:

Jesus: "I give you My special blessing for this work that carries such great responsibility. Through your spiritual director, send My petition to the Holy Father."

While I was writing, the Lord Jesus asked me to write these messages in red and to join them to the other ones.

Jesus: "Send My petition to the Holy Father because it is through him that I want to grant My blessing which carries great graces. At each opportunity, let them give a special blessing to those fathers who, in this great work of creation, collaborate with Me and accept My Holy Will. This unique blessing is reserved only for fathers. At the birth of each child, I pour out extraordinary graces on these families."

After those words, I no longer felt the anguish of doubt, but my heart was moved by a flow of extraordinary graces. "O my Jesus, how unspeakable is Your goodness and mercy."

He flooded my soul with the graces which mothers who bring children into the world and educate them according to His Holy Will do receive.

HIS PEACE

March 3, 1964

At the morning Holy Mass:

Jesus: "My peace I give you. Do you know what My peace is? The peace which the world cannot give. Only those who subordinate the body to the sublimely beautiful needs of the soul can enjoy it. These, indeed, enjoy My sublime and life-giving peace. Live this spiritual tranquility that lifts you up and calms you down."

TRUE GOD AND TRUE MAN

March 6, 1964 - Friday

Prostrating myself before Him, my soul breathed words of profound humility that He aroused in me. "Blessed be God! Blessed be His Holy Name! Blessed be Jesus Christ, true God and true Man." He did not let me continue.

Jesus: "Your homage pleases Me, My little one, but I will explain the words, 'True God and true Man.' If this were not true, how could you come closer to Me? I let Myself be known to you as true God and true Man. Not only you, but all those who eat My Body and drink My Blood. As true God, I penetrate your heart and as true Man, I speak to you because My human Heart beats at the same rhythm as My Divinity. Your heart beats to the same rhythm as My Heart. Do you know what this means? It means that you participate in My Divinity.

All who feel with Me and whose thoughts are My thoughts will receive this participation. Whoever lives this way can only bless. This blessing increases the effect of My work of Redemption. This effect makes you saints. You see, this blessing is an eternal circular movement between Heaven and earth. Your sacrifices unceasingly rise up to Me and I shower My abundant graces upon you and upon all who dedicate themselves for the glory of My Holy Name. Patient, persevering love never blunders."

The following happened a few days ago, but I am just now writing it. The Lord Jesus called my attention.

Jesus: "Yes, My daughter, what you need most is the Spirit of Fortitude. Be careful! Be careful not to lose your strength of soul. The Evil One continually watches, not taking his eyes off of you for one moment. Frequently, and seemingly for no reason, he creates confusion in your soul because he has not yet lost hope. Let your hope be nourished by the Spirit of Love whose power frightens Satan. This is My petition and My inspiration that, if you accept it as your own, will silence Satan's disturbing uproar that cries out so loudly in the silence of your heart."

MAKE SACRIFICES

March 11, 1964

While meditating on the infinite mercy of His Sacred Heart and desiring souls for Him, I recommended my family in a special way to His mercy. The Lord Jesus spoke with a gentle and lively voice.

Jesus: "Heightened trust represents a significant guarantee. Tell Me, Elizabeth, can you imagine that I would not grant you what you are asking on behalf of souls? If it were so, would I not be the One hindering My work of Redemption? I see that you are dwelling on these thoughts, so I will answer your inner questions. Obviously, I do not call everyone in the same manner. I expect more from the one who has received more. But this is not the most important thing for you. The essential is to make sacrifices on behalf of those you want to lead along My road."

MAKE SACRIFICES FOR PRIESTS

March 12, 1964

Jesus: "Pay particular attention to the extraordinary importance of priestly vocations. Coming from Me, this is not new for you. And now, with special devotion, make sacrifices for this purpose.

Because not only do I commend to your special attention the vocations that are yet to come, but furthermore the present priestly vocations. Make many sacrifices for these."

The same day, during the nighttime adoration:

Jesus: "Tell that to your spiritual director."

My heart began to tremble. Then the Lord Jesus spoke in a thundering voice.

Jesus: "Before the difficult times are upon you, prepare yourselves for the vocation I have called you to by renewed tenacity and a firm decision. You must not be lazy, uninterested and indifferent because the great storm is brewing just ahead. Its gusts will carry away indifferent souls consumed by laziness. Only those souls with a genuine vocation will survive. The great danger that will soon erupt will begin when I will raise My hand. Give My words of warning to all the priestly souls. Let My words that warn you in advance shake them up, and My severe request..."

DESIRE IS A MARVELOUS INSTRUMENT

March 14, 1964

Jesus: "Do you wonder how the eternal thought of My Divinity is so clear for you? Every soul which, having committed to a life of sacrifice to fully share in My work of Redemption, will receive it from Me. Sacrifice gives glitter to your works and you can recognize My desire at their light. I have already given you various instructions on that subject. Desire is a wonderful instrument that already contains the concept of sacrifice. For instance, a child wanting to be an excellent student will accomplish this if he studies tenaciously. A mother desiring a new child is also accepting the related sacrifice. A scientist conducting research also implies sacrifice. An athlete wanting to be the best will undergo endless sacrifices. A father building a house for the family expects to make great sacrifices. That is why I continually urge you to fill your heart with desire, because that carries within it sacrifice. They are inseparable."

THE PRESENCE OF THE EVIL ONE

March 17, 1964

Due to the cold weather, I spent a few days with my daughter. I had just returned to my little house two days ago and I was enjoying the happiness of my quiet solitude. Abruptly, the door opened. I looked outside and sensed the presence of the Evil One. With a mocking smile, he said: "I have come to visit you and to see how you are doing." That is all he said. His paucity of words surprised me. At other times, he would torture me for hours. Now he could not do this because his power was stripped away and he was blind. He was close to me but deprived of his diabolical power. In fact, he was forced to remain close. "Is it true that you have no power to harm me?" (I said this because on one occasion after he hit me, the Blessed Virgin said: "He will not be able to do this anymore.")

Then I answered his question concerning what I will do here in my quiet solitude: "I will have more opportunity to adore God. I want to serve Him for all those whom you have turned aside from this road. Even if it pains you to have to hear this, I will make reparation to the Lord Jesus for the many times that I offended the God of infinite majesty and mercy when I was influenced by you. He is so merciful that He forgives every repentant sinner. If you would get rid of your stubborn pride, recognize God's majesty and power, and repent of your perversity, He would pardon you, also. But because you hold onto your stupid pride, you must suffer. But the time will soon come when you will be blind and stripped of your power. As much as it pains you to hear this, it is true."

The Evil One had to hear my answer. He suffered from his lack of power. The Lord Jesus allowed me to experience that the powers of the humiliated Evil One were gone. Then he disappeared without a trace. Neither his presence nor his departure awakened any fear in me. The Lord was present, and the Evil One must have felt it. Then, Jesus said:

Jesus: "And now, let us be immersed in sweet solitude. May our thoughts be in unison, our hands gather in unity, and our hearts beat to the same rhythm. In this way, we will rest."

YOUR HEAD ON MY HEART

March 18, 1964

Jesus: "For now, I will not say much, just this: Those who truly love each other need only a few words to show their love, and their hearts already beat to the same rhythm. Place your head on My Heart and let this nearness fill you with strength for your future battles. I do not want to console you because you suffer from joy, and whoever suffers from joy does not want to be consoled. I give you My Divine Strength, you certainly need it. The sacrifice that I await from many is made only by a few. This translates into a setback for My work of Redemption."

March 21, 1964

After some difficult days of fasting, the Lord Jesus gave fresh life to my soul. I began to eat but I took no pleasure. A long time ago, the Lord had asked me to abstain from food for the pleasure it provides, but to take it only for my body's nourishment. My children provide me with an abundance of food. I always take what they previously gave me and do not eat what they recently cooked. At lunch, the Lord Jesus assured me of His presence and said:

Jesus: "Think of Me, My little sister. How rare it is that a fresh soul has come to Me which, rather than having had a taste of sin, had a taste of Me. May our souls be in harmony. Offer this to Me. Taking your food without any taste is a sacrifice from your heart which is tasty for Me. In this way, our hands gather in unity. Is it not true that you also find this wonderful?"

OUR EYES AND OUR GAZES

March 22, 1964 - Sunday

I was kneeling before the tabernacle in the chapel dedicated to the Holy Spirit. The Lord Jesus said:

Jesus: "Look into My eyes! I allow our eyes to look at one another and our gazes to be as one. Do not see anything else. Read in My tearful eyes that I rest on you the anxious desire of My love.

Make reparation! This is the only consolation you can give Me. I, the Man-God eager for your hearts, I need your consolation."

THE URGENT IMPORTANCE OF THE CAUSE

March 23, 1964

I asked the Lord Jesus if I could publish His messages and those of the Blessed Virgin during my lifetime. He answered with brief and gentle words.

Jesus: "Why do you ask such a thing? This strikes Me as if you asked if you could share in My work of Redemption during your lifetime. Must I tell you again what I am constantly urging you to do? I lifted you up like an arrow in flight coming to Me, so you would be ready as soon as possible to spread our messages. Did I not already put pressure on you in the past three times? In My imploring words, I put My Divine Stress on the urgent importance of the Cause."

It is true that in the past, the Lord Jesus asked me three times to give His messages as soon as possible to my spiritual director.

SUFFER WITH ME TODAY

Holy Thursday and Good Friday

I wanted to spend the whole night in prayer in the chapel, but I had no way to do this. The Lord Jesus saw my disappointment and said:

Jesus: "Come! When you arrive home, I will be waiting for you in our small room."

His kind, unexpected and thoughtful goodness surprised me. I did not dare to think about it. On the way home, I was absorbed in constant adoration. When I entered my small room, I greeted Him, "Praise be Jesus Christ." With the lightest of sensations, He made His presence known. This lasted just a few minutes. Then He filled me with a heavy anguish and a sorrow filled with worry. He did this so much that I had to hold onto something not to collapse. The Lord spoke with sorrow.

Jesus: "I have you partake in My suffering of Soul and Body just as I had to as a Man. I did not use the power of My Divinity, it was only as a Man that I lived the horrors of the night of Gethsemane. I honor you with the extraordinary pains in My Body and Soul. In truth, this suffering means that you participate more deeply in My work of Redemption."

While He said that, He was next to me. He complained for a long time and, because of His words, sorrow increased in my heart. Meanwhile, it was midnight, but I cannot do a vigil at this hour unless I have taken some time to rest beforehand. At midnight, I had to recover my strength to share, while kneeling, in the sufferings of the Lord. I hardly persevered for fifteen minutes in this position because a great spiritual sorrow came upon me and dried up my strength. After a short time, I was curled up on my little kneeler and I was able to meditate on the sufferings of the Lord. The suffering that He gave me totally weakened me. Before 2:00 a.m., I went to bed but could not sleep. I thought only of the Lord's sufferings. In the morning, the Lord Jesus said:

Jesus: "Do not withdraw. Today, all day, suffer with Me."

THE BEST SERMON

Easter Monday

Today's sermon was the best I had heard in my whole life. And while I was thinking about these simple and spontaneous words, the Lord Jesus said:

Jesus: "Do you know why this sermon was so beautiful? Because I flooded the priest with abundant graces. This grace went from him to the faithful in the church. Every eye was filled with tears. The tears flowed and the hearts were moved by the effect of these extraordinary graces. Now, you see the fruits of your sharing in My work of Redemption. For a long time, I have asked you to be the representative of your parish community. And as such, I want to show you the result of My graces which flow from your works united with My merits."

All day, I recalled the words of the Lord Jesus and gave Him thanks. I will describe the sermon of Father E in a few words.

"The two disciples walked the road to Emmaus with heavy hearts. They were discouraged and did not know what to do." Here, the priest quoted from the meditations of Prohászka: "The soul of the disciples was like the burned grass left behind a shepherd's bonfire in a green pasture."

He compared these disciples to souls who live without God and without hope. Then he recalled war time when a young soldier was taken to the hospital with serious wounds. He knew that he had no hope to live. After he went to confession, the soldier asked the priest to sing with him. The priest asked him: "Maybe a beautiful hymn of Our Lady?" With eyes bathed in tears, he said with difficulty: "Let us sing to the Blessed Sacrament." And he added: "How happy I am to have come to know the Lord." While preaching, Father E had a lump in his throat and his voice became softer. In those moments, God's grace poured out upon everyone.

The final words of Father E touched everyone. "How unhappy is that man who in the final moments of his life does not know the Lord, the infinitely good and merciful God!"

During the day, I anxiously awaited the night so I could go to the church and thank Him again in the name of our parish community for the grace that He poured out upon us through the love of His merciful Heart. While I was immersed in the profound silence of adoration, the Lord Jesus said:

Jesus: "I am grateful that at least you came to give thanks for the numerous graces. Reflect deeply upon this terrible tragedy. Our Mother wants no soul to be damned. Therefore, all must share in this great saving work whose purpose is to save souls."

PATIENCE, PERSEVERANCE AND FIDELITY

April 6, 1964

He spoke about His teaching, about persevering patience and fidelity.

Jesus: "Patience, perseverance and fidelity, Elizabeth. That's what keeps you close to Me. And by these means, you can also bring others to Me. The reward of your tireless fidelity for you and for all who share in My work will be what eye has never seen, ear has never heard, and the human mind cannot comprehend. Then our glances will melt in one another and our hearts will beat to the same rhythm."

A BROOM IN MY HANDS

April 9, 1964

Jesus: "You, Elizabeth, are a broom in My hands. The Divine Hands use your sacrifice to sweep clean. All who surrender themselves with loving renunciation and entirely forget themselves are a broom in the Divine Hand. Only by accepting unceasing sacrifices they become worthy of being taken up in My hand so they can clean effectively. Through all of you, I sweep the streets, the flower-filled meadows, the leaf-filled forests, and any place where there is sin. Do not be surprised that My words sound so human. As the proverb says, 'Let everyone sweep in front of his own house.' Keep this before your eyes.

He who feels that his soul aspires to something greater, let him serve Me with utmost faithfulness. When it pertains to working for Me, no one can exaggerate too much. Even if it seems that I always repeat the same things, just simply write them! I beg you, carve this in your mind: the Word of God is always the same… Through it, I seek the salvation of souls."

YOUR MASTER CARES FOR YOU

April 14, 1964

When I arrived home and went into my small room, the Lord Jesus was waiting for me.

Jesus: "I wait for you here, and at each genuflection that you make with adoration and thanksgiving, My Heart beats with joy. By continual repentance, your soul always remains alive. I implore you, Elizabeth, do this in place of the others also. As you see, I am honoring you again. At your request, I come to bless your family and the whole neighborhood. I have brought My peace. Trust! Do not give way to discouragement! I unite your sufferings to My merits. Your children's salvation is assured. I will stay here because I enjoy the silence of your small room. Our hearts beat to the same rhythm. Without you, it is difficult to suffer, and I know that you feel the same. Oh, happy moment! I know that you also hope for the moment when nothing will separate us anymore. I wait for you with all My riches. We will be totally one, indivisibly. I know your heart is beating with joy and I rejoice with you. Your Master takes care of you. If you stumble, My hand will raise you immediately. Your constant repentance obliges Me to pour out upon you My constant pardon."

MUSIC OF MY HEART

April 15, 1964

After midnight, the Most Holy Virgin awakened me, but in a way that never happened before. The ease with which I arose surprised me since I had only gone to bed at 11:00 p.m.

After this short sleep, I felt no tiredness and I could prolong my prayer. I was unable to completely grasp the Lord's visit of yesterday afternoon. I was touched deeply because the Lord Jesus promised that, from now on, He would wait for me in my small room.

All morning, I meditated on the infinite goodness of the Lord. "Adorable Jesus, my Divine Master, You know what I want to say but words do not come to my lips. Only my tears fall silently. Tears of repentance! I would like to write beautiful verses to describe Your infinite goodness, but I did not receive this gift. Conscious of my misery and my nothingness, I always think of what I can give You. Lord, my Jesus, I once more give You my sins again and again, and the monotonous flow of tears from my heart imbued with graces. Please listen to me. This is the music of my heart and the only gift I can offer. I know that this is also a gift from You and I thank You a million times. In every beat of my heart there is repentance. My Lord, my Jesus, it is very little because my heart sometimes misses a beat. Therefore, I ask You that in each grain of dust that You have created, I can place sorrow for my sins. In this way, the wind can take them to You and You can see how much I love You. This is my hymn, my poem and my music. This is all that I can give. Accept me as I am."

Jesus: "My little one, your profound sorrow for sins will move many to repentance, and sinners will return to Me."

DO NOT SET ASIDE OUR URGENT PETITIONS

April 18, 1964

Jesus: "My little one, ask your confessor to see to it that the Cause is presented to the Holy Father by Pentecost of 1965. Do not neglect the messages of My beloved Mother and Mine, they are urgent!"

The Lord's petition was very powerful in my soul. Conscious of my misery and nothingness, I was trembling and thought that I must deliver God's words and make them known. I am a little grain of dust! Can anyone accept this task without trembling? Now, I have no doubts in my soul. The Lord Jesus removed them, but I am always conscious of the misery of my soul.

I AM YOUR ALL

April 20, 1964

While doing my housework, I was consumed in adoring Him and giving Him thanks. He began to speak.

Jesus: "My little sister, by calling you this way, I invite you to trust Me and to believe in the One who calls you 'little one'. When I speak this way, I guarantee you My loving care. I will give you all that you need and I will defend you at every moment. Are you not touched that I care for your needs in such a simple way?

I do not want to become your debtor. Above all, I want to make your thoughts and your work pure and unselfish. I, your Master, will care for you. I will free you from every worry. I only want to be everything to you so that nothing ties you to the earth. You can see by My solving your problem, your heavenly Father knows what you need."

STIR UP THE FLAME

May 16, 1964

The Blessed Virgin said:

Mary: "I speak with you, my little Carmelite, with all the love of my motherly heart. Fan the Flame of Love of my heart with your sacrifices! Do not allow the Flame of Love which I poured out on you in such a privileged manner to flicker weakly in you."

Because I did not know why the Blessed Virgin said this, I asked her. She gently answered.

Mary: "So that you use well the time that has been given to you, with a growing desire to lead a life of sacrifice here on earth."

THE REWARD FOR THE MONDAY FAST

May 18, 1964 - Monday of Pentecost

I attended Holy Mass, and right before Communion the Lord Jesus said:

Jesus: "Since I see your firm determination to which you are faithful even on feast days, I have prepared a happy event for you. Today, from midnight on, at every hour the soul of a priest suffering in Purgatory will be released."

The Lord Jesus said this because, at His request, I fast on bread and water on Monday. I do not skip the fast even when it is a feast day. I am happy to keep the strict fast on Mondays because He promised that, by fasting on Monday, one priestly soul would come into the Divine Presence. When I heard that one soul each hour would be freed, my soul was overwhelmed with the suffering that these souls still endure before coming into the Divine Presence. This suffering only lasted one or two minutes, but I almost collapsed from these sorrows.

After Communion, the Lord permitted me to experience the freeing of one soul. My feelings went from one extreme to another. After experiencing the depths of suffering, I was overwhelmed with the sublime joy of that soul who arrived in the Divine Presence. The state of my soul, trembling from this rapture of graces, made me feel freed for hours from the force of the earth's gravitational pull.

May 22, 1964

The Lord said only this:

Jesus: "Only through sorrows and sufferings does My Holy Cause make progress."

THE POSSESSION OF THE MOST HOLY TRINITY

May 28, 1964

While getting ready to go to bed for the night, I prostrated myself one last time before the image of His Holy Face. In this moment, I felt an extraordinary transfusion of His Divine Majesty. That lasted just an instant but I was shaking intensely. I could not understand what this intense transfusion was all about. At that moment, earth ceased to exist for me and I was entirely in the presence of God. I repeat, this only lasted just an instant.

The following day, the Lord spoke for a long time but I could only record a few words. During the conversation, He explained that this moment was to be in the possession of the Holy Trinity and that would be my situation once my eternal salvation has been achieved.

Jesus: "I only permitted this for an instant because you could not stand this experience while you are still on earth. In this case, you could withstand this only through a special power of My Divine Grace."

June 2, 1964

Jesus: "For My Cause, you must undergo great sufferings and you must continually battle for souls. Outside of this, My little one, do not waste your strength on anything else."

THE MAIN PURPOSE

June 15, 1964

The Lord Jesus said:

Jesus: "My little one, spreading the Flame of Love should be the main focus of your life. It must flow smoothly like a stream of water that nothing and no one can stop. This stream of water is My grace which purifies, which destroys when need be, or saves and gives life. But it must run because God wills it. Pass this on to your spiritual director as My request for him and all those called upon to set this Cause into motion."

NEW SUFFERINGS

June 17, 1964

Finally, after a great interior battle, my soul saw clearly because the Lord's words strengthened me. I went to my spiritual father and told him of the Lord's request. He told me what he had said many times. As long as he does not feel something in his heart that confirms the authenticity of this matter, he will take no steps. His words caused new sufferings that tortured and overwhelmed my heart.

THE EFFECT OF HUMILIATION

June 28, 1964

At night:

Jesus: "Now, I will intensify your sufferings even more."

When I was adoring Him before the tabernacle, He said:

Jesus: "It is urgent for you to go to your spiritual director. Tell him that I am the One who is prompting him to get in contact with Father E."

The Blessed Virgin also spoke of this urgency.

Mary: "...My little one, even though it is very difficult, you must go. The humiliation that overwhelms you actually moves our Cause along."

LOOK INTO MY EYES

June 29, 1964

In the morning, when I knelt before the tabernacle, I could only say an ejaculatory prayer to the Lord Jesus, because He interrupted my words.

Jesus: "My Elizabeth! Oh, how much I waited for you! This loneliness is so long. I knew that our 'goodbye' last night would lead you to be the first to greet Me today. You fill My Soul with happiness. You and I, we two! I delight to be with the children of men. Unfortunately, I am welcomed only by few.

My little sunflower! Do you know what you are receiving from Me now? I give you an increased measure of My love, which until now has been unknown. I promised you this. Accepting it demands a very great sacrifice. Because I am pleased with you, I put this before you. By this extraordinary sacrifice, you can also prove your great love. You and I! Because of our union, joy fills your heart. I know that you give Me thanks untiringly. I see also the thoughts that distract you. Do not be concerned about that. Look at the plants in your garden, they always climb and try to reach higher. Their flowers wither quickly, but soon new ones open up. The withering of the flower does not show its uselessness because the chalice of withered flowers contains the fertile seed which reproduces the plant.

You understand, do you not? If there were no battle, what would then give value to things? Always try to go higher. Do not feel sorry for the withered chalices in your flowers.

Unite your thoughts with Me so our hearts can beat to the same rhythm. Do not look to the right or the left. Look only into My eyes. That will invite you to be recollected and help you to obtain the victory for the success of My work of Redemption. Thank you, Elizabeth! Your understanding love touches the deepest part of My Heart because My Divine Heart also feels with human affection."

"My Lord Jesus! Now that You have placed Your Divine Words in my heart, allow me to thank You especially for the extraordinary sufferings, and for the kindness and love with which You want to honor me, and that You did not make me feel until now. Your words, my adored Jesus, have stunned me, especially when You said, 'You and I.' You have reversed the order. Your unlimited condescension has confused me and my face has turned red. How can You do this to me who am small and nothing?" When He saw that I was getting carried away with thanksgiving, instead of speaking, He flooded my heart with the love of His understanding Heart.

THIS USEFUL LITTLE TIME

July 17, 1964

My daughter-in-law asked me to get her some medications for her sick son. I had to wait more than an hour for the medicine... While waiting, a newspaper article caught my eye... I started to read a few lines when the Lord Jesus made a gentle request.

Jesus: "My little sunflower, help even more to free the suffering souls. I always share with you My eternal thoughts. Realize that even this short time is useful. If you put aside the newspaper article, you can help suffering souls come into My presence. This sharing in My work of Redemption is filled with merits. You see how I simplify what I ask of all of you. Everyone can fulfill My eternal thoughts. Write them down! As you communicate My words to others, many souls will benefit."

FILL EACH DAY WITH MY DIVINE LOVE

July 21, 1964

While I was watering the flowers on the altar:

Jesus: "You see, as you water the flowers daily, in a similar way, hearts should daily be filled with My Divine Love that will keep their soul fresh and would make it capable of making sacrifices."

YOU ATTRACT ME BY YOUR REPENTANCE

July 26, 1964

On coming home from Holy Mass, the Lord Jesus said:

Jesus: "My little one, accept the extraordinary manifestation of My love that you deserve by your continual repentance. This is the shortest road to come to Me, making you fly like an arrow. This humble, uninterrupted repentance keeps you in flight… I overlook everything. By your repentance, you attract Me to you like a magnet, and any soul doing that will attract Me. Oh, I beg you, draw Me to yourselves. Repentance is the most perfect instrument in your hands by which you totally oblige Me, and I grant you virtually anything. During those moments, I pour out boundless graces on you."

REPENTANCE INEBRIATES ME

July 27, 1964

I was polishing the marble floor of the presbytery. The Lord Jesus encouraged me with these words:

Jesus: "Very well! With your sacrifices, My little sunflower, polish the souls in whom the brightness of My grace is obscure."

When I left for home, He said:

Jesus: "Now we are home by ourselves. Do you know that your small room is My sanctuary? I enjoy being here with you because just as I gave you shelter in My house, you provide Me with a home. What unites Me with you? Your inexhaustible repentance!

Yes, this is what inebriates Me. Poor little soul, listen to My words giving recognition to what you are capable of. You inebriate the most high and all powerful God. Understand this great marvel: you can make Me happy by your repentance for your sins."

I NEVER LET GO OF YOU

August 3, 1964

Jesus: "My little one, whenever a magnet attracts something to itself, it does not let go because that would be against the laws of nature. So, I never let go of you or of anyone else because that would be against the law of My Divine Tenderness.

I accepted you and sheltered you in My Heart. By the abundant nourishment of My graces, I offer you the continual love of My Heart. Let us pray together the eternal Father so that He may grant His mercy to those who pull themselves violently away from the field of attraction of My Divinity."

SORROW MAKES YOUR SOUL PLEASING

August 11, 1964

The confession desired for such a long time, I made it today. I revealed to my spiritual father the torments of my soul and asked him to treat me severely because I know that I am presumptuous, proud, untruthful and misleading, and that I want to deceive him. For weeks, I have no peace day or night because of this.

He calmed me down, saying that this was not true. The devil does this because he finds no other way to harm me. If these accusations were true, he would have rebuked me severely. As long as I am sincere and obedient, I do not have to worry because this is good and pleasing to God. In the future, I should continue to reveal with sincerity the difficulties of my soul. In this way, the devil will accomplish nothing by his temptations.

Later that night, I was kneeling before the tabernacle and adoring the Lord Jesus. He spoke silently.

Jesus: "I knew that you would overcome your tiredness and come. If only you knew with what happiness I await you! A soul, among the many, who loves Me… How pleased I am with you! I want you to feel this joy in your soul. You, beloved! You! Your sorrow for sins makes your soul – and that of all who come close to Me with true sorrow for sins – beautiful and pleasing."

I WILL INCREASE YOUR SUFFERINGS

August 13, 1964

The Lord Jesus came to me in the morning.

Jesus: "By the merits of your sufferings, I gave great light to your confessor. From now on, he will see clearly that My Holy Cause is authentic. However, your sufferings will still be necessary. After a short rest, I will again intensify your sufferings. Do you accept this? Answer Me with your words and by your committed surrender. I want to be the one and only ruler of your soul…"

"I understand You, my adorable Jesus. You seek my total surrender. How can I prostrate at Your Divine Feet? All my members are so united with You that I live only for You. My adorable Jesus, accept me as I am, with my nothingness and my constant sorrow for my sins. I find no other words than these ones: I love You very, very much. I want to love You as no other repentant sinner has ever loved You." He interrupted me.

Jesus: "Repeat them! Repeat them, My Elizabeth! They delight Me. For these words I suffered and accepted a painful death. I would like to hear them from everyone's lips. You understand well. Teach this to others also…"

PRAY FOR SINNERS

August 15, 1964

The Lord Jesus said with a lamenting voice:

Jesus: "My dear child, wish Me many, many souls. This is My only request. Souls! Oh, how I long for sinners! Oh, how I suffer from the indifference and the contempt of souls. Tell Me, Elizabeth, is it difficult to love Me?"

When He asked, I could only answer by my own sorrow for sin. The Lord Jesus continued:

Jesus: "The great repentance of your soul, Elizabeth, renders the souls fruitful. Do you know what your repentance is like? It is like the bee that gathers the pollen, flying from flower to flower. This is your repentance! And the more you pray for souls, the more I pour My abundant graces, and they will repent for their sins. You see, if the bee does not cooperate, the bee and the flower are useless. Nothing results.

Look! The sinner is passive doing nothing just like the flower, which is hoping to be pollinated. You understand, do you not? Your repentance for sins allows My graces to be active in souls. Just as the collected pollen transforms into honey, so the tears of your repentance, through My grace, transforms into sweet honey in the souls of sinners. Give Me great joy!"

Then He stayed silent and I heard His sigh of longing in the depth of my soul. He made me experience His great desire for souls.

August 18, 1964

While doing work in the house, we pulled down the Lourdes grotto. I thought that I would reconstruct it with the old rocks. During this work, I continually adored Jesus. At night, my heart beat with joy. In adoration, I was thinking that I would go near Him very soon and that I would continue my adoration prostrated at His Sacred Feet. Meanwhile, the Lord Jesus said:

Jesus: "You and all who constantly adore Me increase the joy of My Divine Heart. If there were only more of you! You, My little friend, with what joy I look at you. I thirst for every one of your words because these quench My yearning for souls. I have written My teaching and My thirst for souls deeply upon your soul. While I was hanging on the Cross, I cried out in a loud voice: 'I am thirsty.' I say these same words to all, especially to the souls consecrated to Me."

LIKE A SPRING

August 19, 1964

Jesus: "Your soul is like a spring from which the purest water gushes, a water that not only refreshes but also purifies. It refreshes Me, and through your desires, purifies the sinful souls. I am grateful to you, Elizabeth, because you quench My thirst for souls."

LOVE ME ABOVE ALL THINGS

August 22, 1964

For several days, because of many family duties, I could not go near Him for the evening hour of adoration and reparation. Sighing, the Lord Jesus said:

Jesus: "May our feet journey together. I follow you, and you follow My footsteps. I love you much, My Elizabeth. I want this love to penetrate your soul deeply. I, the Lord, make this confession and I anxiously desire your reciprocal love."

Later, He almost shouted in my soul.

Jesus: "Love Me above everything! Your love filled with repentance intoxicates Me, little sister. Desire with ardor that the repentant love of other souls also intoxicate Me. Your desire is not without fruit."

THE DIGNITY OF A MOTHER

August 27, 1964

The Blessed Virgin said:

Mary: "My little daughter, this maternal suffering and the injury that you must endure from others are another opportunity for you to see why I chose a mother to transmit my messages. Only a mother is able to sympathize with me. These multiple sufferings have matured you, and through your experience, you understand better the supreme importance of your participation in the work of my Divine Son.

Without it, you could not make great sacrifices since the true preparation for sacrifices can only mature in sufferings. Ponder deeply this vocation to which you were raised due to the only dignity of being a mother. Maternal dignity is at the same time a vocation saturated with sufferings, and that is what I share with you. I thank you, my little one, for your participation that is continual and filled with sacrifices. I, as a loving Mother, can assure you of your heavenly reward."

WHAT DO YOU PREFER?

August 30, 1964

During my little chores on Sunday afternoon, a newspaper fell into my hands. I began to read an article on Spanish customs. After I read a few words, the Lord Jesus said:

Jesus: "I have reserved you totally for Me and you have accepted this by repeating on many occasions your surrender to Me. Now, despite all this, you prefer this reading that distracts you. This is not good, My Elizabeth. May be you do not receive all what you need from Me? Why do you want to know more than you need for your eternal salvation? I do not demand this from others with such strictness, but you are My preferred one. You did not make yourself worthy. I, God, thought you worthy of your call. Even one instant is too much for you to be occupied with something else. My love does not rest. May our thoughts be in unison!"

JESUS COMES TO ME

September 1, 1964

The Lord Jesus told me many things, but I was so immersed in this love with which He overwhelmed me that I could only remember His beginning words. The rest of His messages melted together in my mind and I cannot put them into words. Meanwhile, a great depression came over me and I said: "My adorable Jesus, I will not have the strength to go near You tonight." With His calming and kind words, He said:

Jesus: "Well, I will come to where you are."

This produced in my heart a greater dejection. I stayed up late into the night; and my adoration time that I concluded in His presence was prolonged past midnight.

The next day, I spoke with the Sister assigned to me and I told her what happened the previous night. She listened with distrust and said that anyway, it would be better if I went to the Lord Jesus, as it is possible that it is not authentic, that it could be pure autosuggestion. This confused me greatly. Sadness and insecurity covered my soul and anguish filled my heart and my soul.

At night, I went to the Lord Jesus and asked: "My adorable Jesus, was it my imagination that You were with me and that You filled me with the joy of Your presence? I do not know how to bring about autosuggestion. If this was true, I could never prevent such suggestions from arising in my heart." Kneeling in the silence of the night, His words were tied to mine.

Jesus: "Calm down, My little one. There is no reason to lose the peace of your soul over such a question. I am lovingly increasing your sufferings while you nourish My love, which I pour over you for your continual sacrifices. Tell Me, what comes from your imagination? This is a supernatural process. Understand this simplicity by which I come close to you. I do this to give you the strength to offer, in your human misery, continual sacrifices. It is not doing great things that maintain the outpouring of My graces, but this continuity that you do not interrupt. Is this clear to you?"

MY LIVING PYX

September 3, 1964

From the small chapel, I brought the pyx (empty!) to the parish church of the Holy Spirit. While I carried it on my way, I was also adoring and making reparation to the Lord. He was moved and said:

Jesus: "You are My living pyx. The Father sent His only begotten Son to redeem everyone. But you must also do your part in My work of Redemption. Take it out with love from the depth of your heart; there it is dormant. Do not be lazy. Go ahead, awaken it and be fed with My Precious Blood.

I ask you to forgive Me for having bothered you so often in your time of rest. However, no one else is around and I so much wanted to pour out My troubles to someone. My little sister, serve Me according to My pleasure."

I want to record what happened on June 13, the 51st anniversary of my Baptism. At night, when I entered my small room, the Lord Jesus flooded my soul with His presence. I was so moved because He was standing so close to me. He said:

Jesus: "You see, My little sister, this fine veil, like a breath, is all that separates us from one another. Do you know what this is? It is your life that still keeps you captive on earth."

I was thinking during my meditation: "My adorable Jesus, my sins! Oh, forgive me so that nothing separates me from You." He answered me.

Jesus: "Trust."

Then I spent a long time before Him. I cannot describe the joy that I felt through the words of the Lord. When I wrote that He was near, in front of me, I did not see Him. He just allowed me to feel His presence. I write this to avoid misunderstandings.

I CAN HARDLY WAIT

September 14, 1964

At nightfall, while I was preparing to go to the hour of adoration, the Lord Jesus began to speak.

Jesus: "Come, just come! I can hardly wait for your arrival. The greater and more numerous are the sacrifices that you make, the happier you make Me. Believe Me, everyone has the power to make God happy. I passionately await this happiness. I am in debt to you for this happiness and I continuously rain down My graces on you, like dew."

TORMENT OF DOUBTS

September 18, 1964

During the morning, at Holy Mass, the Lord Jesus spoke. However, because of my spiritual torments I was not able to write. Later, I only wrote what the Lord expressly commanded.

Jesus: "I am very, very grateful, Elizabeth, for you to have accepted much suffering."

My soul was relieved. Hearing the voice of the Lord Jesus, the power of the Evil One ceased in my heart, but one hour later, he overpowered me so much that were it worse, I would have gone crazy. At night, I could withstand no more. I went to the Sister assigned to me and I confessed to her that I was a liar and asked forgiveness for my continual lies. She tried everything to calm me down: "I cannot believe that you would want to deceive." But this brought no peace.

On the morning of September 19, I went to my spiritual father so I could confess my awful doubts that make me suffer so much. Surprised, he listened to my confession, and he almost did not recognize me. He did not grasp what was happening to me. I continued to confess that this torment is nothing new. I have come under these sufferings for long months and I cannot withstand any more. With this heavy weight continually on my soul, I do not dare to receive Holy Communion. Many times, I drown in my tears because I cannot free myself from my sins.

Father, with his kind words, did everything to calm me down. "Go to Communion in peace. I take the responsibility because I am convinced that you commit no sin." He said many things – that he is certain of his judgment and that I should be convinced that this is the Evil One who wants to keep me far from God and push me into despair.

While listening to his words, I calmed down. However, as soon as I left the confessional, new tormenting doubts came within me as never before. The evil spirits burst upon me a hundredfold. They screamed like a chorus at me, saying that yes, I am a liar, and with my whining I am misleading even my confessor. If this is true, my lies are even more serious. One can imagine the terrible spiritual torments that came from this. I recommended my soul totally to the infinite love and mercy of God. I drew near to the Blessed Virgin: "O my Mother, cover the multitude of my sins before the eyes of your Divine Son, so He is not saddened because of me..."

PUT YOUR EARTHLY THINGS IN ORDER

September 20-23, 1964

The Lord spoke at various times.

Jesus: "My daughter, put your earthly things in order. Time passes quickly and you are flying to Me without sensing your speed. There is an immeasurable distance between your soul and the earth. Beloved, I am waiting for you with a loving heart. God is calling you with His infinite love."

UNTIL YOUR DEATH

September 24, 1964

Jesus: "My daughter, after a period of relief, do not be surprised if sufferings again flood your soul. You are experiencing the temptations of the Evil One. Do not worry. I am with you and I act within you. All around you is dark and your inhibitions are appearing once more in your soul. I have already said that this is how it will be until your death. Just as night follows day, so light and darkness will alternate in your soul. I do not allow the night or the day to reign continuously in your soul. I do not want you to enjoy continual light. Believe Me, this is how it must be. I know what is suitable for the good of your soul. Just keep surrendering yourself to the demands of My Divine Pleasure."

PRAY THE ROSARY

October 5-7, 1964

At the Lord's request, for three years now, I have kept this strict fast on Mondays to free priestly souls.

Today, Monday, when I returned from Holy Mass, my body was so weak from pain that within a few hours a great hunger came over me. I did not resist it and I took some food. I experienced great pain that I could not help the priestly souls come into the presence of God. Because this compassion was increasing more and more in my soul, I asked the Lord Jesus what I had to do. There was great darkness and silence in my soul. The Lord Jesus did not reply.

Even on the third day, I woke up feeling compassion for the priestly souls in Purgatory. And while I was thinking about it, the Blessed Virgin made her words of kindness heard in my heart.

Mary: "My little Carmelite, pray a complete Rosary and attend a Holy Mass for the priest. In this way, you can regain what you owe because of your weakness. The soul of the priest will come into the presence of God."

With tearful eyes, I thanked our heavenly Mother that in my weakness I was helping to free these souls. Strength and peace returned to my heart.

That same morning, the following happened. On my way to Holy Mass, my thoughts were distracted a little, even though this only lasted a few minutes. Then the Lord Jesus spoke to me.

Jesus: "You are My beloved. Do not let your thoughts wander. Think only of Me, because it grieves Me if you don't. If I correct you, do not be upset. You know how it pleases Me that you are always attentive to My Divine Words. Even a minute is a long time for Me if you spend it on something else. I will help you so that I, and nothing else, fill your thoughts.

Do not let any creature come between us. My Elizabeth, My beloved, receive My Divine Words. Gather them in a bouquet. Write them down, so that others can realize that they can only possess God if they come far away from all earthly noise. Do not believe that this is impossible because you are a living proof. I placed you in a family setting, so others could see how they can and ought to live. You serve both the family and God at the same time. My little Elizabeth, your oily seeds are already ripening. I am ripening them with joy. Rejoice, because the more abundant and ripe they are, the more numerous will be the souls on whom the drops of the oil of grace will fall after your death. This is My gift. The value of your sufferings will never be lost. By My grace, they will never dry up. Meditate on this generosity which manifests the unlimited love of My Divinity. It will find its full value only in Heaven."

CONSECRATED SOULS

October 9, 1964

Jesus: "Allow Me to start over asking and complaining. Think highly of Me because the Divine Love thinks highly of you and honors you. I confide in you so you can tell My complaints to others. O souls, love Me and reflect on all that I have done for you. I, the Man-God, plead with you with such simple words. It hurts Me that you so often offend Me. I am so abandoned. What hurts most is that consecrated souls set Me aside. They have no time to spend with Me. They devote their time to everything but to Me. O, you foolish ones! Every minute passes. The time that you devote to Me is never lost. It is saved for an eternity of infinite value.

You will easily render an accounting for time dedicated to God. Why not do everything for Me? This is so easy. All you need is a pure soul. The purity of your soul makes you divine. He who eats My Body and drinks My Blood remains in Me, and I in him. Immerse yourselves in My words. If God is in you, My little Elizabeth, how can you not also become divine?

I outpour upon you the clarity of the Divine Mysteries so you can meditate on the mysteries of My Divinity. I take you step by step. Even while you are still on earth, I make you begin the road to this wonderful world. That is why, I pray you, esteem Me still now more than anyone or anything here on earth. Do this always!"

THE CLARITY OF DIVINE MYSTERIES

October 10, 1964

Due to my extreme tiredness, I could not reflect on the conversation of last night. In the morning, I meditated on it. I wanted to express this in words but I am completely incapable. These things cannot be expressed in words. While I was trying to do so, the Lord Jesus began to speak.

Jesus: "Do not try anymore, My little sister. All would be in vain. On one occasion, I told you: 'Immerse yourself in Me like a drop of water in wine.' I am the wine, you are the water. Now, I have placed some drops of the mysteries of My Divinity in your soul. Just as you cannot separate the drop of water from the wine, so you cannot explain the Divine Mysteries.

And now, I ask you to come to Me today as soon as possible. Do not wait until the evening! Let nothing be more important for you than I."

BLINDED SATAN

October 25, 1964

The Lord Jesus spoke at great length, but because of circumstances in my family, I could not take notes. Now, a few days later, I only record what I remember exactly. These are words from the Lord Jesus:

Jesus: "Once Satan is blinded, the decrees of the Council will be fulfilled in an extraordinary way."

October 30, 1964

At Holy Mass on Friday morning, the Lord Jesus surprised me with words of thanks.

Jesus: "Oh, how happy I am because you assist at various Holy Masses. This is a great honor for Me. I pray you, tell everybody, because it is the expression of My opinion. Through it, I pour out My graces on you."

WORDS TO PIOUS PERSONS

November 8, 1964

For many days, the Lord Jesus instructed me on piety and He asked, or rather, lamented.

Jesus: "Listen to Me, and do not be surprised that I have complained for some days even about pious souls. Unfortunately, I have a serious reason for that. I want you to atone for them also, because pious souls who make no sacrifices hurt My Heart even more. Oh, how sad I am to see the multitude of devout souls living a pious life without earning much merit on behalf of their eternal salvation. So many of them do not attempt to come close to Me in any way as though they are afraid. The sorrow for their sins does not stem from love.

Write down My words, or better, My request to those who are indifferent: there is no progress without sacrifice. I am not happy with a sterile piety. It is like a tree that produces no fruit. I will add this, My Elizabeth: the pious people who are like this do not even think at what point their soul is gray and dark. The light of grace only penetrates and illumines the soul burning with love to the degree that they expose their soul to the transforming effect of My grace.

Do not be surprised that I speak in a severe tone of voice. This severity springs also from My love. I would like them to take at heart My words and that they prostrate themselves before Me in an atoning adoration and a repentant heart. For it is also a habit of pious souls to think that after having spent a good time at their devotions, they have already given to God what is God's.

Oh, you fools! If you could only feel the immense pain your pious indifference causes to My Divine Heart. I am the Victim and it was not by pious attitudes but only by a continual acceptance of sacrifices that I brought about My redemptive work. Repent! Repent! Repent! This is what I am asking you. The voice of repentance reaches up to the throne of My heavenly Father. It is the voice holding back the arm of justice of My Father."

PIOUS SOULS - REPENT

November 10, 1964

The Lord continued His complaints against the pious souls.

Jesus: "It seems to Me that you have forgotten that I already pronounced these words when I was carrying My Cross, and the holy women were weeping for Me more than for their own sins. Again, I ask pious souls to repent. Repent on behalf of others as well."

THE CONFESSOR

November 13-14, 1964

Jesus: "...Be at peace, My little one. I have irradiated such a great light in the soul of your confessor, that by its brightness he sees clearly the road he must follow to put into action our Holy Cause... We have gained one of the twelve..."

When I heard these words that evening, a great joy like I had never felt before filled my soul. I could see in my heart how Satan will be blinded and the good effects that mankind will receive. Because of this joy, I could hardly close my eyes the whole night. When a light sleep came over me, my guardian angel awakened me saying: "How can you sleep given this great joy that will shake the world?"

The Lord Jesus said:

Jesus: "Satan blindness means the universal triumph of My Divine Heart, the liberation of souls, and the opening of the way to salvation to its fullest extent."

TOTAL SURRENDER

November 16, 1964

In the morning, the Lord Jesus said:

Jesus: "By your total surrender, My Elizabeth, you have become My harp. The sacrifices which you continually accept are the chords of the harp. Now, I play the most beautiful melodies. Your soul, taken up in God, easily receives My wonderful melody. I have never played this before for anyone. Your sorrow for your sins inspired Me to compose such a wonderful melody. Listen to it attentively because I will repeat it often in response to your sorrow for your sins."

AFTER YOUR DEATH

November 17-18, 1964

While it was almost dawn, but still night, the Blessed Virgin said:

Mary: "My little one, I see that because of your great pains, you cannot rise for the nighttime adoration. In spite of that, you must regain all your strength. When you wake up, you will offer your sorrowful vigil for the dying."

And she again reminded me gently that I forgot to kiss my scapular before going to bed.

The morning of November 18, when I received Communion, the Lord Jesus said:

Jesus: "I waited with great yearning to enter within you. Do not be surprised that I fly into your heart without touching your lips."

Because I was not able to receive Him the day before, my own yearning had been great. On November 19, the same experience happened. He flew into my soul without touching my lips.

Jesus: "My little one, write down what I now dictate: ...You are mine and this is your guarantee. After your death, will abound in the treasures of your heart those who will know, bless and glorify God. God helped you with His boundless grace to have a life filled with treasures. Those who will live after you on earth can draw abundantly from these treasures. They will be able to follow the simple road of your life. By this path, they also can reach Me."

And returning His own words as a prayer, the Lord Jesus began to speak.

Jesus: "The water of My graces, like a stream, flows continually into your soul. Now is the moment to tell you why these abundant graces remain in your soul. By your sacrifices, you have dug a deep channel and the water of My Divine Graces, with its purifying power, has found a place in your soul. If you had not prepared this deep channel by your sacrifices, the purifying water of My graces would have drained off.

Do not grow angry, My Elizabeth, if I want to console you but that My words end up as complaints. This does not come from Me, your understanding heart leads Me to complain. Oh, how many, many souls receive My abundant graces, but they are not prepared, and the purifying water of My love drains out. Their souls lose this grace. How this hurts Me! But I will stop complaining because I must strengthen and prepare you for the battles that await you. The water of My graces have found rest in the channel of your soul. So now, the drops of oil squeezed from your sufferings float on top of the fountain of My graces. See how your drops of oil are shining upon the mirror of silvery water! They shine like pure gold. This vision flows from My Divinity. You also find it beautiful, do you not? Immerse yourself in this beauty."

For hours after this, I do not know what happened to me. When the bell sounded at noon, I recited the Angelus. Then the noisy announcements on the radio disturbed me. But more than this, I cannot write, because what happened in my soul might be what Saint Paul wrote: "Eye has not seen, ear has not heard and it has never entered the human heart..." Maybe I cannot write more because I do not have the intellectual capacity. That is to say, it cost me much to come back to the real life...

ACCEPT EVERYTHING FOR MY GLORY

December 2, 1964

The great spiritual trials returned. With a little sigh, the Lord Jesus spoke in my soul.

Jesus: "My daughter, accept everything for My glory. The suffering, the peace in your soul, its anguish and doubts, because all of that will appear in My glory. When your body leaves the earth, you will enjoy this glory with Me, impacting favorably on the souls living on earth. Repeat frequently with the angels, 'Glory to God.'"

This happened during the vigil, before dawn.

SUFFER WITH HEROISM

December 5, 1964

The anguish of my heart was increasing, accompanied by doubts of faith. Meanwhile, my soul struggled in darkness.

For a few minutes, the Lord Jesus calmed down the anguish prevailing in my heart and said:

Jesus: "Are you suffering much? Let your sacrificial suffering not stop! Do you know why? The same way I let the darkness of doubts and the spiritual anguish come over you, to the same extent I will put light and relief in the souls who are going to set into motion what I am communicating through you.

My Elizabeth, suffer with heroism, with perseverance and constancy. From time to time, I will lift the veil that hides My Divine Will. I will show you My satisfaction, so you can receive strength from time to time for your soul to be filled with the abundance of My Divine Grace that you must pass on to others, so that they praise and glorify God for His infinite goodness."

PUT OUT FIRE WITH FIRE

December 6, 1964

When Holy Mass began, the Blessed Virgin began to speak with maternal kindness.

Mary: "We will put out fire with fire."

I was very surprised by her words. A pause followed, and she continued.

Mary: "United with you, I will perform a miracle that the scientists of the world will try to imitate to no avail, being completely beyond their power. Only the wisdom of pure and God-loving souls will be able to understand that, as they possess God and His infinite secrets.

Yes, my little one, we will put out fire with fire: the fire of hatred with the fire of love. The fire of Satan's hatred hurls its flames so high that he believes his victory is at hand. But my Flame of Love will blind Satan. I have placed this Flame of Love in your hands, and soon it will reach its destination, and the flames which spring from my love will quench the fire of hell. My Flame of Love, with its unimaginable light and beneficent warmth, will wrap the earth. To accomplish this, my little one, I need sacrifice, your sacrifice and the sacrifice of many such that the minds and hearts where the infernal hatred is burning may receive the soft light of my Flame of Love."

Then she explained:

Mary: "Do you know what you represent? You are a sparkle of light enkindled in my Flame of Love. The light you receive from me enlightens souls. The greater the number of souls who sacrifice and watch in prayer, the greater the power of my Flame of Love on earth will be. Hence, line-up in close ranks because it is with the power of sacrifice and prayer that the flash of hellish hatred will be overcome. Evil will diminish gradually, the burning flame of hatred will be put out, and the splendor of my Flame of Love will fill all regions of the earth."

THE MERITS OF SOULS

December 10, 1964

So intensely did I experience the graces which the Lord poured into my soul, that I could hardly walk. Let no one who reads these words be surprised. When this experience happens, many times the Lord's grace burns softly my heart. At times, even others experience what is happening within me. However, not everyone experiences equally the graces that flow from my soul. I asked the Lord Jesus why this was. He told me that He grants the experience according to each one's merits. By these words, He makes it possible to deduce what would be the grade of merit of souls. This causes me pain and great suffering. But the Lord Jesus asked me with kindness:

Jesus: "Suffer with Me."

YOUR EAGERNESS FOR THE WORK OF SALVATION

December 12, 1964

On my way to Holy Mass early in the morning, the Lord Jesus, with extraordinary kindness, said these words in my soul:

Jesus: "I have many, many things to tell you, little sister. Do not be surprised that I, the Man-God, speak so much with you. Because your soul is like the pure water of a lake, My Divine Eyes can always see what is within you. The pebbles at the bottom of the lake shine with light and cause delight. They are your hidden sins and defects which your repentance has made bright and shining. I tell you, there is no longer any mud, any dirt in them, but only beauty for Me. My Divine Eyes look upon them with pleasure. That is what you felt, taking away your strength to walk. God's gaze rested on your soul.

And now I continue on an entirely new subject. Oh, My Elizabeth, allow Me to honor you as a preamble. How much I long for you to come to Me so that nothing disturbs our union. But now, I pass on to what I want to tell you. Our union here on earth reached such a level that the desire for martyrdom fills your soul; the martyrdom of suffering has reached its full development in your soul. My Divine Blood waters all the particles of your body, making it strong and able to withstand this great martyrdom that you suffer continually without a word of complaint. Now, I will reveal many things so that you draw strength from the tasty fruits of your sufferings.

When I offered you My graces, My Soul already rejoiced then for the high degree of availability to make sacrifices with which you embraced them. Your constant willingness to suffer with Me increased this transfusion of My graces. What does this mean? It means that according to the promptness and the degree that you share in My work of Redemption, to that same degree and promptness the Holy Cause we entrusted you will progress. In other words, the martyrdom that you are living in your soul prepares for the greater progress of our communications. My little Elizabeth, should you approach Me with only cautious and slow steps, that would do very grave harm to the Holy Cause... Now, beloved, you understand fully the value of your sufferings. Your promptitude will lead others to act rapidly, and My graces will soon triumph in those souls for whom you accepted martyrdom, with all its consequences."

When the words of the Lord Jesus died down in my heart, the love of the Blessed Virgin attracted me to herself. This was very pleasant. All morning, even as I completed my household tasks, it was as if I was not living on earth. The tasks did not occupy my mind. I was entirely possessed by the presence of the Lord Jesus and the Blessed Virgin. I could only write a few of the words of the Blessed Virgin. After the long conversation with the Lord Jesus, the Blessed Virgin spoke with maternal love.

Mary: "My little one, this is the reward of your faithful attachment. I await anxiously the moment when I will hold you on my heart."

And then, by God's favor and under the effect of graces, I was fully immersed in the knowledge of my nothingness and my lowliness. For me, this grace is the greatest by which the Lord Jesus honors me and inundates me. And as this is happening more and more deeply in my heart, the Blessed Virgin spoke to me again.

Mary: "My little one, I am so happy that you keep before your eyes my virtues of humility and simplicity."

At this moment, the bells began to ring for the Angelus. I wanted to begin this prayer that honors the Blessed Virgin, but she intervened.

Mary: "Now, your prayer must be to pay attention to my words. Meditate on them with your mind as a sign of your veneration."

THREE PARTS

December 21, 1964

The Lord Jesus said:

Jesus: "From now on, I will divide your life into three parts. The first part will be made up of pains and torments. Then I will fill you more and more with my strengthening graces, and this will be your reward in form of ecstasies. Then there will be spiritual dryness, that is, you return to your natural life. So far, your life has been quite similar to this. In the future, you will know ahead of time what will happen to you."

Chapter five

1965

DOUBTS

January 1, 1965

On New Year's Day, the Blessed Virgin said:

Mary: "By the outpouring of my Flame of Love, I will place the crown of success on the holy Council."

Since mid-January, I began to live in the middle of great dryness and spiritual darkness. In my abandonment, the idea more and more dominated me that everything up to now has been pure imagination and a lie. I have tried to get rid of this idea with all my strength. But the more I tried, the more I fell under its power.

In the midst of a great loneliness, this spiritual anguish was made worse by the disturbing thoughts of constant doubts against faith. With all my strength, I tried to safeguard the spiritual balance, which was already greatly reduced. In my weakness, my confused thoughts convinced me that everything was evil. This insecurity kept growing and causing waves in my soul. Then a violent hopelessness made me decide to radically end my continual lies, because if I do not do that, I will be damned. This thought caused me to shake. I do not want to sin. Once and for all, I uproot from my heart my deceitful imaginings, I leave behind all that deals with my lies. I will not speak with anyone who knows me. I will not speak any more with the Sister who has been assigned to me. I will never go to my confessor. I have the feeling that he is too easy on me and allows me to go on with my imaginary lies.

I did not dare to continue writing the words of the Lord Jesus, because I constantly thought that they were totally my own invention, and that I was writing under the impulse of self-sufficiency and pride. I was entrapped in extraordinarily great torments. When I stopped writing them, a new fear overpowered me. I was not fulfilling the request of the Lord Jesus. Struggling in the midst of these torments, I could hardly pray. In my spiritual darkness, I abandoned the fight for a short time. Then I heard the voice of the Lord Jesus.

Jesus: "Today, you have not yet said a single word to Me."

I jumped at these words. However, I could not tell if they were the Lord's words or the last vibrations of my lies. The next moment, I heard the Blessed Virgin sobbing in my soul. I took this as my imagination tempting me with past memories. I kept trying to free myself from these deceiving illusions which had reached their highest point.

I live now in a terrible spiritual world, but I will make a final effort to free myself definitively from these confusing lies. I tried to do this many times, but my will was too weak. Therefore, everything began again, or rather, I continued to make the situation worse. In vain, I asked the bishop, Father X and Father D to free me from evil spirits. None of them did. They calmed me down with the hope that the Will of God would become clear to me. For me, their words lacked strength and I continued with my lies. In vain, I asked my confessor to be severe with me. I felt that he was too kind and would not uncover my serious failings. I had some tremendous struggles. My confessions brought me no relief because I thought that he did not notice my lies. Sometimes, the unrest so tortured my soul that I did not dare go to Communion.

Crying, I pleaded with my confessor: "Father, do not trust me because I am a liar and a deceiver. My many sins keep me from receiving Holy Communion. Do you remember, Father, what you told me? That I should not hesitate to receive it because you took upon yourself the responsibility for my fault. And I, faithfully obedient to your command, dared to do it."

Afterwards, for a short time, I was able to be calm, but the feelings in my heart constantly changed. This struggle was unbearable. When I confessed the last time, you encouraged me to speak and to relieve my soul. But I could not tell you what was happening in my heart. Frequently and without warning, I felt some obstacle within and that you are a person of good faith... The best thing is not to continue to deceive you with my endless lying because both of us will be damned. This is a terrible torment! I can no longer withstand it. Until now, you guided me in all my thoughts and actions, encouraging me to accept every sacrifice for the Holy Cause. But no one can say whether this Cause really exists and does not come from me. I, myself, am not sure. The bishop already told me that it does not come from the devil. Father X and Father D said the same thing. My father also calmed me down. One time, Satan said to me: "This does not come from me, nor from God, but from yourself."

"My Lord, forgive my sins!" I do not want to be deceived any longer. I want to have peace. I see that all I have done lacks common sense and I cannot explain why I have been suffering only since that time. Since this comes from sin, it cannot be meritorious. "Free me! Free me from this terrible torment!" This is the only prayer I raise up to Heaven. Only death! Oh, happy death! This will be my salvation that will free me from the infernal torments that I suffer here on earth.

For years, I have been enduring this. Oh, happy death! I abandon myself to God's mercy. If He deprives me of my life, and if God forgets about me amid the souls in Purgatory until the Day of Judgment, I would gladly accept it because as long as I am there, I would not be able to sin. With death, my confused thoughts and my lies will cease, and I would not offend God any more.

When I heard in my heart the date when I would die and be among the blessed, I felt deep gratitude. To be freed from earth will be an unimaginable pleasure. Until this happens, I will go to a new confessor and will not mention to him the sinful imaginations that take place in my heart. I will leave these aside and be freed from my sins because my previous confessions – I feel it so – were filled with pretense. This thought caused a painful unrest in my soul. I do not want to return to my former confessor because the wounds caused by my past lies will be opened again. This would weaken my firm determination and would disturb the peace of my soul. I am living with terrible torments...

TRUST IN ME

January 7, 1965

The Lord Jesus said:

Jesus: "Don't think about who will be this strong soul who will put our messages into action. Myself, I have no need of strength. I choose humble and sacrificial souls. The important thing is that they draw close and have confidence in Me. Trust Me! I repeat, this is how you can enter fully My close circle."

CONFESSION

January 11, 1965

I went to confession. For two or three days, I was so relieved – no, I should not write it this way – because this lightness snatched me from earth, and during these days I felt an enthralling bliss.

My bliss was so great that I had the feeling of not being able to contain it within myself. During this period, I went to the Carmel and I stayed there for a few hours. I so wanted all to feel this ecstasy with me. I could hardly contain it. Stopping my work, I kissed the forehead of the Sister assigned to accompany me. The Lord Jesus permitted this Sister to feel the wonderful effect of the grace that lived within my soul. The Lord Jesus said:

Jesus: "The eye of God rests upon you."

HAPPINESS IN CONFESSION

January 15, 1965

Jesus: "Your soul, My little one, is the receptacle of My Divine Words. Do not tremble! It is thus, even though you feel unworthy. You know well that I make use or your littleness, your ignorance and your humility to gain My purpose. Above all, I stress your humility."

SATAN COULD NOT INCITE TO SIN

February 4, 1965

This morning, I woke up very relieved. The Lord Jesus said:

Jesus: "Peace be with you."

I couldn't not accept this word in my heart. At the words of the Lord Jesus, the desired peace entered my heart. This peace gave me an unmistakable strength. The Lord Jesus said:

Jesus: "My little one, have you suffered much? Satan, deprived of the light of his eyes, could not incite you to sin. A fierce anger overwhelmed him when he learned that it is you who were to transmit My Holy Will, and this is why he wanted to blot it out of your mind. It is through a merit of your sufferings that My Divine Splendor enlightens the Divine Origin of the 'demonstrated facts' in the souls of those called to transmit the Cause.

The opposing camp will be large and you will still have to suffer much so the Cause can triumph. Give an account of the state of your soul to your confessor."

BREAD FOR THE FAMILY

February 14, 1965

During adoration, the Lord Jesus reminded me:

Jesus: "Leave now. You must get bread for your family."

I had forgotten this completely. With deep gratitude, I thanked Him that His attention extended also to our earthly needs.

On the way, I kept adoring Him. When I entered the bakery, I remembered that it was Saturday and I asked, "Do you still have bread?" They said, "No." I was scared. What will happen now? When I was about to leave, I heard them call me. They had reserved a bread, but the one for whom they had set it aside did not come to get it. At once, I said, "My adorable Jesus." He said:

Jesus: "I am that one. Do you see? The time you spend with Me should not harm your family."

We walked home together in silence. I speak thus because He filled me with His presence. Immersed in Him, I kept adoring Him.

March 25, 1965

The Lord Jesus said:

Jesus: "Act with all your strength. This is what pleases Me the most about you. The more a bow is bent, the more accurately it can hit the mark. You also must extend your strength of will, and thanks to it, the arrow will not deviate from its goal which is nothing else than Heaven."

BEING WITH YOU

April 7, 1965

I spoke with the Sister who accompanies me and told her that the Lord Jesus is acting as if He had forgotten me. In those moments, I feel so far from Him. On that same day, while I was busy with my grandchildren at home, I adored the Lord Jesus in the depth of my soul and I made reparation. I felt that the words I spoke to Him had flown to infinite heights. Then He surprised me.

Jesus: "Why do you think that I am far away, in the heights above you? Really, I am standing right now next to you."

While the Lord Jesus was talking, through these waves of special feelings, my soul experienced the Blessed Virgin with her captivating love, saying to the Lord Jesus:

Mary: "She is my special one, also."

And they allowed me to understand that they were talking about me. The Blessed virgin was so merged in the love of the Most Holy Trinity that I could hardly distinguish her in my heart. I was surprised by that, and in my admiration, the Lord Jesus allowed me to be immersed in extraordinarily wonderful things. He said:

Jesus: "This is not ecstasy, just a form of it. Therefore, your bodily powers can endure it."

Meanwhile, He initiated me into heavenly things which I was unaware of until now. I cannot put these realities into words… On the following day, the Lord Jesus also spoke about this during Holy Mass, but I am unable to write about these things.

YOU WILL NEVER BE REFUSED

April 12, 1965

On Holy Monday, the Lord Jesus overwhelmed me with His complaints. His sorrow also increases because of my family...

Jesus: "Do you see My hand begging for help, My little sister? Many turn their eyes away so they do not have to bear the sad look in My eyes. I am the One who draws close to them. But they just keep walking stubbornly the path of darkness. This is why My Mother asked that her Flame of Love light up on the earth in order to enlighten souls. To accomplish this, she asks for the drops of oil of your sacrifices. I tell you and I promise with My Divine Word that whenever you pray for someone, you will never be refused, because the drops of oil of your sacrifices not only fall on the lamps of souls, but also upon My wounds which burn with fever. These drops are like refreshing balm. My Elizabeth, the Man-God thanks you for this.

Do not excuse yourself. I must act this way because I am also a Man and I share your feelings. When you make sacrifices for My work of Redemption, I am in debt to you. I can say this in another way: You buy Me with your favors and an overflowing happiness fills Me."

When He finished speaking, He allowed me to experience in my heart what He feels when He sees our compassionate love.

SUFFER FOR OTHERS

May 1965

I went to the doctor. After his first examination, he said he could find no illness. He said that the sufferings about which I complain do not come from any illness, but that I carry the sufferings of others. I have no problem with my nerves, they are completely in order.

So that the examination would be complete, he sent me for laboratory tests. They were completed within a week and I returned for the results. After reading the results, he said that I had a little anemia that is totally insignificant. Again, no sickness was detected and he did not prescribe any medication. He recommended a thermal bath in lukewarm water, but only when the weather will be warmer. His only explanation was that I take the sufferings of others upon myself and that my nervous system is extraordinarily sensitive and reacts in an extraordinary way to everything. This brings about the many sufferings. On this subject, I could not express another opinion. This doctor did not know me and he was not aware of any of the circumstances of my life.

One can imagine that my children, who knew that I was talking incessantly about my ill health and my continual weakness, were awaiting with very great interest the results of the examination. They learned with much surprise that, according to the doctor's diagnosis, I did not suffer from any illness. They found this strange, and I continued to suffer as before.

SPIRIT OF POWER

May 15, 1965

The Lord Jesus allowed me to hear His soft sigh that seemed to come from far away. By His sigh, the Lord Jesus allowed a faint light to enter my heart and it revealed the worth of my suffering. And while the sigh that I felt coming from afar crossed my heart, I felt the Spirit of Power act intensely in my heart. While this was happening, the tormenting illusions of uncertainty that almost – almost drained me, ceased in my heart.

Then, the Lord Jesus said:

Jesus: "Do not waver, My beloved, in this exasperating state in which I have placed your soul earlier."

Upon hearing the voice of the Lord in my heart, I welcomed His words: "O Jesus, how happy I am because You spoke to me. Do not let me go! You are the One who knows best because You give the suffering." Silently, He said:

Jesus: "Now, you must endure the suffering and darkness which My disciples experienced after My death. But as I sent the Holy Spirit upon them, I will also send Him upon all those for whom you must suffer. Now, in the middle of the sufferings, you comprehend what you did not understand before. This miracle is the repeated coming of the Holy Spirit that many await, and the light of His grace will spread and penetrate the whole earth."

When the Lord Jesus finished, the illuminating power of His words instantly disappeared from my soul and the dark suffering again covered my soul.

I WILL NOT INCREASE YOUR SUFFERINGS

May 20, 1965

At morning Holy Mass, before Communion, the Lord Jesus said:

Jesus: "Be very strong. I will not increase your level of suffering."

I was astounded by these words. I will not receive more sufferings? "My adored Jesus, does this mean that You are withdrawing Your love from me? This saddens me even more." And I sorrowfully complained to the Lord Jesus. "Suffering for me is when I do not suffer. Now, how can I come before You? Your love, made as one with sufferings, dominates my soul, and now it will not dominate it anymore. What will happen to me?" My heart became heavy and I asked the Lord: "Adorable Jesus, why do You treat me this way? Do I not merit sufferings? Am I not strong enough to undergo them?" I complained to the Lord Jesus for a long time. Again, He spoke.

Jesus: "I see that you did not understand Me. Until now, I gave you as many sufferings as your human strength could undergo. From now on, I will not increase them because you have already reached your limit. There is no room left in your heart and soul. I repeat, persevere and be at peace, you are the vase full to overflowing with the sufferings you have received. Besides, I will not lessen My love, but I will not increase your suffering. I already told you that I will not spare you. You must suffer until your last breath. And because you have so enthusiastically taken part in My work of Redemption, I am keeping you in My love. Peace be with you, My Elizabeth. No one can give My peace, only Myself. It is I who called you to be among the workers of Redemption. Now, I call you to be among those who have received the reward."

AFTER YOUR DEATH

May 30, 1965

The Blessed Virgin said:

Mary: "After your death, my little one, your place will be next to me. Your drops of oil gathered on earth – which by your lifetime of sacrifices, my Divine Son united with His merits – will fall back upon the extinguished lamps of the souls and will ignite them by my Flame of Love. At its light, they will find the way that leads to salvation. These drops of oil will fall also on the souls that have no lamp, and they too will know the cause for this and they will come to my Divine Son. Then you will have work even in Heaven, and you will continue your participation in my work of Salvation even after your death."

SATAN'S IMPOTENCY

June 4, 1965

A very interesting thing happened. Last night, as I was going to my little house, I had to listen on the road to the bitter groans and reproaches of Satan. He was lamenting that, for a long time, he suspected that I was going to cause him serious difficulties. Therefore, he always managed to keep his eyes upon me. And he went on lamenting that in spite of his effort, I always managed to escape from his claws. Even when he used every means, he was nevertheless baffled.

Until I arrived at my little home that is at the end of the garden, he came with me, or rather, he came furtively, because being blind, he is powerless. But there was a moment when I had to feel his eyes sparkling with hatred and vengeance which, at that moment, filled my entire being with fear.

NEW ATTACKS

June 5, 1965

There is always a great and continual longing for God in my heart. I accepted life, death and suffering according to His Holy Will. This filled me with such felicity words cannot express it. My heart throbbed with happiness. However, the following morning, none of this remained. Instead, an attack of the Evil One came upon me. I have never used this word until now, but I must write that the torture of these sufferings ripped open my heart. I will describe in a few words these attacks which the Evil One used to make me falter: "You believe that the foolishness you have invented is true. This great delusion has upset you and has made you forget that all is your pure invention. Recognize this and correct it. You are committing a sin by pursuing this type of life which is contrary to human dignity. Even your Beloved has abandoned you. Do not consider yourself as worthy of life or death. The only thing that is assured is your damnation and that of all those who agree with you. Yes, you are responsible for them because you led them into evil by your continual lies."

He attacked me with such great impetuosity that I immediately lost the security of my soul. That fight lasted several days. In this uncertainty, my only prayer was the Lord's Prayer. I asked the heavenly Father to accept my soul and my body. I want to serve Him with all my mind and fulfill completely His Holy Will. This is all I long for. I asked Him to forgive all my sins by the merits of Our Lord Jesus.

GOD'S DELIGHT

June 9, 1965

At night, I laid down to rest. Because of my weakness and tiredness, I could hardly think. Quite unexpectedly, the Lord Jesus surprised me with His words and started to converse. Never in my life had His words penetrated so deeply within me. I listened to them with a trembling heart and devout concentration.

The tiredness ended and the darkness of my soul also disappeared. Even so, I had difficulty in understanding His words. In the previous few days, a blinding darkness had come over me. Every moment was for me not only a corporal torment, but above all, a spiritual one. The Lord Jesus:

Jesus: "I take delight in the struggle of your soul. For you to fight a continual battle against the Prince of Darkness is My greatest joy. Whoever does this has assured his salvation. Beloved, I have dissolved the darkness of these past few days in your soul..."

BURNING VICTIM OF LOVE

June 10, 1965

When I woke up in the morning, the Lord Jesus spoke... and praised me. Before Holy Mass, every morning, I normally spend an hour in adoration. During this time, the Lord Jesus spoke again.

Jesus: "Feel the light of My penetrating gaze without which you cannot understand My Divine Word, and by which I am now giving you a particular strength. As I told you, I will not increase your sufferings any more, but I will not diminish them either. I will change the forms under which they will reach you. The fact that your death has not yet arrived is also a form of these sufferings. I gladly admit that I was very pleased when you renounced your life. This renunciation was fruitful both for you and for those for whom you offered it.

And now, I want something else from you. By your sufferings you have become a victim burning with love in whom the Most Holy Trinity takes delight. Do not fear that anything will separate you from us, even for an instant. Heaven is open for you. Of course, it does not mean that earthly torment will cease, and that explains why there was this darkness in your soul. I have placed your soul and your body under the full dominion of the Prince of Darkness, so that he could do as he pleases with you. Let him seize every opportunity to put you to the test. I have put at his disposal all the means to make you waver, for him to see with whom he is dealing: a soul that the Most Holy Trinity possesses. He had to admit that such a soul knows how to live, to die and to suffer in complete conformity with My Holy Divine Will. Is there any greater reward for you than to rest in the arms of the heavenly Father and be filled by the Most Holy Trinity? This is the reason why I say: You are a victim burning with love."

This morning, as the Lord Jesus was speaking, it was like a river overflowing with the feeling of God's presence. I saw nothing, I just felt it. This Divine Presence confirmed in my heart that I was not deceived by my own imagination.

Meanwhile, the Lord Jesus said:

Jesus: "Your burning sacrifice of love will lead souls to the knowledge and love of God. This is My delight. That is why I keep you on earth so you can be a burning victim of love. With My Divine Eyes, I look upon you with favor."

Following this, my soul enjoyed silence and peace, but only for a few days.

THE INFURIATING BATTLE

June 18, 1965

While attending morning Holy Mass, a great anxiety took possession of my soul. An infuriating battle arose within: these arguments are nothing but counter-arguments invented by my lies with which I blind myself. Not one word of all this is true, this is why my sins have so greatly increased that I cannot receive Holy Communion. In my anxieties, I come to the same conclusion. I must stop this and I must destroy all my lies. So, I resolved not to write a single word.

Ever since then, I heard that many times in my soul, but I did not write it down. But rather, I tried to remove from my mind the idea to leave all behind. This torment is such that I never experienced anything similar in all my life.

What a terrible life! I live always knowing that I am offending God and He has no desire to come to me. In this way, He helps me to understand how our unworthy union pains Him and how He experiences revulsion because of my sins. In this great spiritual torment, it is no surprise that I only want to die. Then I will be free of these continual lies which confuse even my confessors… Because I am living without God, my life has no purpose. For two weeks, I have not attended Holy Mass, except on Sunday, because of the obligation. I nourish my soul only with spiritual communion. All is dark and without any purpose. Life is strange for me. How can I live for God… without God? This does not work at all.

I beg you, Sister, go to Father G and speak with him for me. After that, what must I do? I am totally convinced that the Holy Father is the only person who, after he studies the Cause, can restore my peace. If he finds that it is not true, he can give me absolution for my imbroglio of lies. I want you to understand my very serious situation and to help me with your good will. With the little strength left in me, I will go to the Holy Father, even if you find this strange. I will overcome all difficulties because I cannot go on living and do nothing with this cruel and atrocious spiritual remorse.

It does not matter that you are not ready to give me a recommendation. Even so, I will do everything to regain the peace my soul has lost. I decided to do this because of my uncertainty and my feeling of abandonment. I will not continue to live this way. I am either a fool and a liar or what is happening in me is true. If it is true, then I cannot stand around with my arms folded while souls are perishing. I cannot be frightened by this question of blinding Satan. I must make whatever sacrifice is demanded.

OBEDIENCE TRIUMPHS OVER THE EVIL ONE

July 2-3, 1965

I was having lunch when the Lord's voice enlightened my heart like a ray.

Jesus: "Do you remember what your confessor told you at your last confession? If you find yourself in difficulty, go to him or call him."

At that moment, I gathered all my strength and called him on the phone. I received an encouraging and favorable response.

During the night of July 3rd, I could not sleep. As the saying goes, "I awaited the morning like a child at Christmas." And it has become a reality! Two weeks had already gone by without my daring to receive the Body of the Lord for the reasons described above. It was Sunday. Early in the morning, I set out with little bodily strength, but with great hope. After the favorable response the day before, the gentle peace of the Lord Jesus came immediately into my soul. This peace calmed the spiritual torments which I had experienced for a long time.

When I came to my confessor, the Evil One burst in again with his trials. By a cruel torment, he harassed my mind with great force and brought about chaos. With all my strength, I listened to my father confessor so I could understand what he was saying. Due to the Evil One's harassment, even during confession, the continual doubts I had in my soul weighed heavily upon me. During confession, I repeated several times: "I want to believe with all my strength in the validity of the absolution, but if in spite of this I'm not convinced, it no longer depends on me."

The priest was very understanding. When he heard that I had not received the Sacred Body of the Lord for two weeks because of these doubts, he ordered me sternly: "You must understand that this comes from the harassment of the Evil One and not from the contempt that the Lord Jesus might feel towards you." I must not let these doubts come upon me, and I must never stay away from Holy Communion because of that... When the priest gave me this order in Jesus' Name, I felt that he pronounced these words with all his strength. At the same time, the Evil One's attack was so great that I had to gather all my strength just to say, "Yes!" seven times to Father's repeated commands.

My mind was completely under the pressure of the Prince of Darkness. To accept Father's words, I received a power which is greater than anything on earth. By my affirmative answer, I wanted him to know that I would obey him with all my strength. Knowing that I would obey filled my soul with peace. Much later, the Lord Jesus entered my soul and flooded me with His presence.

OBEY YOUR CONFESSOR

July 7-8, 1965

The Lord Jesus spoke at length.

Jesus: "Do not set Me aside, My beloved soul. Concerning your confessor's advice, I only add what I already said on other occasions, 'His words are My words.' Always perceive his word as authentic because I have enlightened your confessor and he is the one who knows you, understands you, guides you, and will never abandon you. Therefore, do not be distressed and do not be afraid. Let My Will be clear to you. I will always tell you ahead of time what will happen. Did I not also say that I was going to release Satan upon you so he could try all his temptations on you? My Elizabeth, I rejoice that you promptly went to your confessor when I called you to order.

You see that you possess the Spirit of Love, something I have already discussed with you, and the devil cannot prevail against you. I allowed him to torment you, and what Satan wants to accomplish is that you pay no attention to My words of advice. He knows your weak points, however the instrument of obedience is in your power, and by it, you conquered him. The devil was powerless and blind at your side.

I'm so happy that you practice with great diligence this virtue, which is so contrary to your nature. My beloved Elizabeth, during those moments, you truly oblige Me. By My immeasurable grace, your soul becomes even brighter."

After that, I remained in deep thought concerning the words of the Lord Jesus. How holy and great is the virtue of obedience. Until today, I had not thought about it as I do now. Also, I pondered how my soul will become shining because of obedience. I made a firm resolve to accept with greater fidelity and surrender what I receive, whether directly from the Lord Jesus, or indirectly through my confessor.

THE NIGHTTIME PRAYER

July 9, 1965

The Blessed Virgin said:

Mary: "My little one, I ask you again to give immediately your confessor the instructions on how to make the night vigils united to the merits of my Divine Son. You have not yet given these to him. I want the holy night vigils – by which I want to save the souls of the dying – to be organized in every parish, so there is not even one moment without someone praying in a vigil. This is the instrument that I place in your hands. By this, you and your companions will save the souls of the dying from eternal damnation. By the light of my Flame of Love, Satan will remain blind."

YOUR HOUSE - A SANCTUARY

July 12, 1965

During Holy Mass, the Lord Jesus said:

Jesus: "You must live as someone who is divided in two. Are you surprised by this? Can the body's will and the soul's will be united? Never! I see that your soul is intensely fixed in Me to do My Holy Will. The body is a formidable opponent, and by its continual resistance, wants to impede the promptness of your soul to remain with Me and to collaborate with Me.

I accept and I give My unending blessing to your great will to love. Even more, I will take one more step. Beginning today, your little dwelling will be My continual sanctuary. I will honor with My continual presence this little dwelling that is so dear to you. I have rented your small house. Adore Me and make reparation here. I will remain next to you while you live here on earth. I do not want to set you aside for one moment. I see the doubts that have arisen in your soul because of this. What did I tell you a long time ago? If you feel a strong resistance when you listen to My words, you can know that the words clearly come from Me. Elizabeth, believe! Oh, little nothing, what would you be without My love?"

YOUR CONFESSOR'S WORD

July 17, 1965

Jesus: "Feel in your heart, My little sister, the reward favored with graces for having accepted My order that I gave you through your confessor. Now, you see and feel the power that caused the doubts, which come in varied and disturbing ways, to cease in your soul.

You gained this reward only through obedience. You can now recognize that I gave you peace not because the absolution was truly valid, but rather through a command of your confessor. If you had not accepted this command, your soul would have been shipwrecked once and for all. My words are serious and firm. Does this surprise you? Think of what I emphasized to you on other occasions, namely that your confessor's word is My word and to not accept it is to revolt against God. Therefore, I had to be firm with you. Now, I will change your sufferings. I will no longer send you the torments of doubts. Once and for all, until the end of your life, the fire of charity will burn you. In your longing for souls, this fire will consume the strength of your body."

Because the Lord Jesus had not yet given me this new suffering, I did not understand His words about the fire of charity that will burn me, and the strength of my body that will be consumed in my longing for souls.

After a few days, I felt as if a burning arrow had been thrust into my soul. By this suffering, souls must be saved from damnation. Since then, I do not even know myself. How can I understand? I am this burning fire of charity but I cannot describe it. Some feelings are exclusive secrets between the soul and God. To speak of them is impossible and I do not intend to do so. I know that you, Father, will understand by the grace of God what is hidden between these lines. It is the business of the Lord. Here, my own effort would only ruin everything. Because it is only in the silence of the soul that one can hear the love of the Lord. But at that time, we did not even speak of this. According to the words of the Lord Jesus, "The fire of charity burns," and as natural combustion cannot be explained in words, so too this fire…

I do not want you to think that I am possessed by melancholy. This would go against my happy nature. Nevertheless, a silent withdrawal dominates my soul and I feel as if I did not belong to the earth. This happened on other occasions also, but the Lord Jesus said that now it will continue until the end of my life. Since then, I have used greater surrender and greater fidelity in keeping the fasts requested by the Lord. As to the night vigil, which before cost me the most, I have now doubled it.

The Lord Jesus had first asked me to make a one hour vigil twice. Now, by the grace of God, since the fire of charity is burning me, I have neither night nor day. All that I could do for the Lord seemed so small. I spend each night in prayer from midnight to 5:00 a.m. Then I go to church where I continue my adoration. Then, at the Holy Mass of 7:00 a.m., I receive the Sacred Body of the Lord. I spend the day helping my family. All during this time, the Lord's presence fills me to such a degree that my soul is lifted above my bodily activities, because my soul remains next to the Lord without any interruption. During my work, I frequently enter my small room to adore and make reparation to the Lord Jesus who is present. These are secrets of my heart that I reveal to you.

THE DESIRE TO SAVE SOULS

July 20, 1965

I continue having the bodily weakness and pains which the doctor diagnosed. Many times during the day, they come with such intensity that I have to lie down for fifteen minutes every hour.

Otherwise, I would faint because of the pain. Today, as I returned from Holy Mass, this extraordinary and painful weakness came over me again. I wanted to adore the Lord Jesus and to offer Him reparation in my little dwelling. Instead, I had to lie down. However, desiring souls for Him, I offered my sufferings to the Lord Jesus. With great emotion, the Lord Jesus began to speak intimately.

Jesus: "How kind you are to desire souls for Me. Could you want anything better? This is what I am hoping for from you all. You see, Elizabeth, you poor souls can give something to God. The heavenly Father welcomes your longings with love and sends them back as an outpouring of grace upon you and upon those souls for whom you plead. Believe Me, you cannot say anything greater or more pleasing to Me. For this I came down from Heaven to redeem souls, so they would have eternal life."

While saying this, He quenched in my heart the thirst for souls and He poured the fire of His burning charity over me in the greatest measure. This caused me to tremble. Meanwhile, He spoke softly.

Jesus: "Beloved, more than ever, be humble. God has come down to you."

After this, my heart throbbed intensely for a long time.

GOD COMES DOWN

July 24, 1965 - Saturday

Today, the Most Holy Virgin came with her gentle words. Immediately, the power of her fullness of grace radiated in my soul while she also spoke words of praise.

Mary: "By the effect of grace of my Flame of Love, you have gained, my Carmelite daughter, that God come down to you and that the fire of charity burning for His work of Redemption greatly consume your soul. To possess this is a very great privilege. This is why your heart should be permeated with a deep humility."

Very often, I feel a great inhibition while writing... Very often, it paralyzes me completely. On these occasions, my strength leaves me and I stop writing. For days and even weeks, I do not take it in my hands. I resume writing only when, by His presence, He shows me with great firmness that He wants me to write these things.

Not long ago, I once more asked the Lord if what I had written was truly His Holy Will. He gave a very definite response.

Jesus: "Do you know why I make you write about the different events in your life? Because these are reflections of My graces in your soul that you – I know it well – would never tell others. In this manner, I oblige you to write so all will see the Divine Work that I have done in your soul since your childhood."

These words from Him reassure me and I continue writing all this.

TO SAVE EVERYONE

August 13, 1965

I reflected on the Lord's words spoken at an earlier date, "I cannot renounce you." I was amazed and thought surely that I had misunderstood. The Lord Jesus intervened.

Jesus: "You did not misunderstand the words. Why do you wonder that I cannot renounce you or any soul. Did I not shed all the drops of My Blood for you, for all? My Will is to save everyone. Elizabeth, you also must will it with all your strength at every moment of your life."

August 18, 1965

In the morning, while prostrating before Him during Holy Mass, I pleaded with a deep sorrow for my sins. The Lord showed me that He was deeply moved and made me feel the beating of His Sacred Heart. He said:

Jesus: "A long time ago, you received from My merciful Heart the full possession of the love which forgives. I accept this profound repentance with which you prostrated yourself before Me for the sake of others, and I grant them My pardon."

And while He pronounced these words, He filled me with so much of His charity that I began to tremble. I cannot express this experience in words... Because the fire of charity now inflames me, I experience ecstasy much more frequently, often in unexpected moments.

TO SAVE THE DYING

August 27-28, 1965

"It hurts me so much, my adored Jesus, that because of tiredness, I cannot pray tonight for the souls of the dying. But you see in my soul my great desire to do so." In my great pain, He consoled me with these words:

Jesus: "I accept your soul's great desire which you offer for the dying. Yes, I will grant this also in favor of the souls of the dying."

I was calmed and went to bed. During the night, I woke up often and I immediately began to implore for the dying. However, I did not have the strength to get up to pray. During the same night, the Lord Jesus assured me that He accepted "my desire to keep vigil," as He expressed it Himself.

The next day, on the morning of August 28, before and during Holy Mass:

Jesus: "Now, My Elizabeth, I continue the conversation that did not take place last night. I thank you for your effort, but now, pay attention and remember what I say."

So that others can understand the conversation, first I must write about what happened in the family. In a short period of time, two grandchildren were born. One on August 22, feast of the Immaculate Heart of Mary, and the other on September 8.

And so, for my little strength, the work was excessive. I felt that I could not carry on. I begged the Lord in His kindness to give me strength because I could not manage to help my two daughters-in-law. When I awoke the next day, I possessed an amazing vitality. I worked all day with no tiredness. This lasted for two weeks. This extraordinary strength, I realized, distanced me from the Lord. I even thought that if it continued this way and if I remained in this great physical shape, I could even go back to work. I entertained these thoughts because I had regained my bodily strength. Then the Lord Jesus spoke.

Jesus: "Now, you will understand even better why I stripped you of your bodily strength. You see, while you were weak, you served Me with all your strength. Now that I have increased your strength, you do not serve Me as before. Your thoughts are distracted and you give Me less time. Moreover, you do not stay with Me as you did before. As to the length of time and strength, it affects Me much less. This strength will remain just a few days before I take it away. I only gave it for the good of your family."

FAST UNTIL THE CAUSE REACHES THE POPE

September 18, 1965

The Lord Jesus said:

Jesus: "I want to ask something great of you, My Elizabeth. Will you commit yourself to that? Fast on bread and water until the Holy Cause reaches the Holy Father."

He repeated this request a few days later. This request confused me greatly, because I did not think I could fulfill it due to my weak strength. However, I did not have any distressing doubt as to whether it was the request and Will of the Lord. The fire of charity is burning me and I want only what the Lord wants. I have no fear of being deceived by the Evil One. The Lord's request left me dismayed and I could not immediately give an affirmative reply. Something went on that never happened before in my life. For days, I was going back and forth concerning this decision. Generally, when I think about doing something, I decide quickly what I want to do and I get it done. But this did not emanate from my thought, and hearing these words, my womanly weakness reacted. I opposed this with all my strength, knowing that because of my lack of energy and will power, I would be unable to do it. For three days, I fought a battle within. On the fourth day, I mentally accepted it. It is only after the arduous struggles of the fifth and the sixth days that

I fully accepted it. On the seventh day, my soul was filled with joy. Having fully accepted the Lord's Will, I went to the Sister assigned to me. I told her all that happened in my soul. She was getting ready to go to my confessor. I begged her to ask him to allow me to keep this fast. On the ninth day, counting from the day the Lord asked me, I received the answer that he forbade me to do so. For two days, I had peace in my soul until the Lord Jesus repeated His request.

Jesus: "I stand by My request. You must repeat it several times to your confessor."

I felt very confused and I abandoned myself to the Lord Jesus concerning the interdiction of my confessor.

NEGATIVE ANSWER BY THE PRIEST

At the end of September 1965, I went to my confessor at the appointed time. Because of these difficulties, I was shaking. I repeated to him the Lord's request. My confessor repeated his negative reply and showed me how absurd it was.

In spite of this refusal, I repeated the request because the Lord had asked me. My confessor continued to explain why he considered this absurd. Although he can only exercise the rights given by God, he could not grant this because it would be contrary to the fifth commandment. If the Lord Jesus would manifest the request to him, he would not oppose it and would immediately grant permission.

When I left my confessor, the suffering in my soul caused by the refusal ceased for a few hours. Then the sufferings came over me with great power and I could hardly walk for days. When I thought about food, I got dizzy. At breakfast and at the late afternoon snack, this ceased because I took only bread and water at the request of the Lord Jesus. He had told me that only at lunch I should eat other foods, not for their taste but only to feed my body. On Monday and Thursday, I live only on bread and water. I do likewise on Friday. It is only after 6:00 p.m. that I take other nourishment. Thus, on those days, the suffering that I feel in my soul ceases when I take other food also... Since then, I have had indescribable suffering, a continual interior anguish, distress and nausea. One day, the Lord Jesus said:

Jesus: "Do you see how much I love you? I reward your perseverance to do good and convert it into blessing for My work of Redemption. I need your sacrifices so you ceaselessly give momentum to our messages and offer reparation to My offended Sacred Heart."

He spoke for a long time. And once again, emphasizing His request, He sent me back to my confessor.

Jesus: "Repeat My request to him. Do not fear. Tell him that I want you to fulfill My request until the petitions entrusted to you arrive at the Holy Father. Tell your confessor that I change your sufferings according to whatever My Divine Wisdom and My work of Redemption demand. He should not be afraid and should abandon himself to Me.

Elizabeth, you need patience and perseverance. Whenever I send you, you must go humbly and promptly. Be careful, you cannot disobey the command of your confessor, not even for My Divine Request."

I dared to ask the Lord if He was using this request to test me.

Jesus: "No. If your confessor had not ignored My request but had accepted it and abandoned himself to Me, then your acceptance of sacrifices, with My help, would have achieved the result intended by My Divine Plans. I know very well that he would have received the momentum, and that with all his strength, he would have succeeded in making the Cause reach the Holy Father. Your acceptance of the strict fast as a sacrifice would have continually urged him to take additional measures."

EXPERIENCING TRANSUBSTANTIATION

October 17, 1965

This event took place during the elevation of the Host. When the priest pronounced the words of consecration, the Lord Jesus allowed me to experience in a wonderful way the Transubstantiation of His Sacred Body. He said:

Jesus: "I did this for you and for all the souls. It is due to the working of special graces of My Divine Love that your soul was able to deeply feel this sublime moment."

Several hours passed and my heart was still pounding from this amazing experience of Transubstantiation. Then I started to think: "How could the apostles withstand the miracle of Transubstantiation in their body and soul, being so close to the Lord Jesus?" Because even in these few minutes – no, I have not written it right – in these few moments, I felt as if I was going to die on the spot. If the Lord Jesus had not lessened the extraordinary effect of Transubstantiation in me, I would have had no strength. Even now, the effects of this experience are difficult to bear.

NOVEMBER, MONTH OF THE SUFFERING SOULS

November 1-2, 1965

The Lord Jesus flooded me with extraordinary sufferings which grew greater at night. I was bent over when I walked. Also, a fear of death took hold of me. I had never experienced this in all my life. Before going to rest, I was preparing for death with all my strength, as if now, at any moment, I would have to present myself before the Holy Face of God. I offered these great sufferings to the Lord Jesus. Meanwhile, He said:

Jesus: "Do not grow tired of them."

The next morning, I felt a relief which increased throughout the day. Suddenly, the Lord Jesus spoke again.

Jesus: "My soul, do you believe that I love you very much? I used this violent suffering which you have endured for the suffering souls. Now, I smile upon you."

At that moment, I felt as if my soul separated from my body. The Lord Jesus spoke again.

Jesus: "God smiles upon you. You see, with My Divine Smile, you can easily endure the great and violent sufferings. The souls in

Purgatory need your sufferings so much because you now share in the work of the Church Suffering. Suffer with a smile! Let no one know, let no one see, this is a secret between the two of us. Only God grants this and I give it only to the souls who know how to endure ceaseless sufferings with a smile."

SORROW FOR SIN

November 27, 1965

On many occasions, the Lord Jesus said:

Jesus: "Keep nothing for yourself! You must ensure that even the contrition of your sins yield interest here on earth because you will not be able to do this after your death."

Then, as if I was flooded with light, my soul was immersed in an indescribable bliss. After Holy Mass and all during the day, a feeling of unspeakable gratitude was poured upon my soul and these words came to my lips: "Lord, my adorable Jesus, You have given me a sorrow for my sins so I can share in your work of Redemption..." And while I was still thinking of His Divine Goodness, His longing for souls was burning in my soul with a fire which was constantly growing. At its flame, He allowed me to feel that He even uses our sorrow for sins for the redemption of souls. Then He interrupted my thoughts.

Jesus: "The current of My graces, powerful like an overflowing river, would act in your souls in an uninterrupted way and with a constant intensity, if your repentance, like a powerful river, was rushing toward Me and surrendering to Me!"

THE EXAMPLE OF THE SAINTS

December 1, 1965

Just as I was meditating on how to imitate the example of the saints, the Lord Jesus began to instruct me.

Jesus: "My little one, you can see why, from the very beginning, I asked you to renounce yourself. I asked this many times because you can only share in My work of Redemption if you live totally united with Me at every moment. I now repeat to you these words that long ago you returned to me as a prayer: 'Do not spare any effort, My little one, know no limit. Do not remove yourself from My work of Redemption for even one instant. If you did, I should feel that the love you have for Me has lessened. How much I desire your love!' Today also, these words have to be continuously present. This is how you can imitate the saints. On this, all the cooperators in My work of Redemption agree, no matter the circumstances of their lives. I do not change this condition for anyone called to follow Me. Let him take up his cross and follow Me. Now you can see that there is not one saint that you cannot imitate. It is sure that I place you in different circumstances, but the requirement is one and the same.

Then your example to imitate is always the same: renounce yourselves and do not spare any effort, know no limit and never withdraw for even one instant from My work of Redemption. If you did, I should feel that your love for Me has lessened. Is it not simple, My Elizabeth, to follow in My footsteps? I do it that way so that no one feel rejected nor consider My request as impossible to accomplish."

I reflected on the Lord's teaching. His simple words permeated my soul like silent drops of rain on arid soil. While praying, I placed the Lord's words in my soul and I asked Him: "My adorable Jesus, make it such that not a single word of yours drop out of my heart nor the hearts of those wanting your teaching and wanting to participate in your work of Redemption."

INVITE ME TO YOUR TABLE

December 1965

The second Friday of December 1965 was a clear day. I did the autumn work of cleaning my garden. When it became noon, I wanted to continue my work, so I put bread in my apron pocket so I could eat it while I was working.

The Lord Jesus intervened:

Jesus: "How will you say the blessing of the table? And how will you invite Me to be your guest? Tell Me, if a guest arrives, will you offer him the bread from your pocket, and will you receive him while working?"

His words dismayed me. I stopped my work, and while I washed my hands, He flooded me with His pardoning love and said:

Jesus: "Today, I want to honor you in a special way."

Meanwhile, I covered the little table of my room with a cloth, white as the snow. On a white plate, I put slices of bread and prayed, "Come, Jesus, be our table companion..." I prayed kneeling, not standing. The presence of the Lord Jesus was so heavy upon me that I could not rise. For a time, He stood in front of me and He blessed my bread. Then He helped me to get up and said:

Jesus: "This is how you must invite Me to your table."

YOU ARE THE LIGHT OF THE WORLD

December 17, 1965

After Holy Communion, He instructed me again and filled my soul with His Divine Light. I will record some of His words.

Jesus: "My light permeates you and surrounds you. Through Me, you enlighten in the obscure Advent these souls awaiting Me. The sacrifices of your life, united with My merits, will be light for them. I said, 'You are the light of the world' to those whom I filled with the special light of My grace. You and others must give light to the dark parts of the earth which are in the shadow of sin, such that My Divine Light attracts towards the true road those souls teetering in the shadow of sin and death."

Today, I meditated all day on the Lord's words, and I thought especially of these: "The sacrifices of your life, united with My merits, will be light for them."

"O, my adorable Jesus, I, the small grain of dust! The only light that shines within me is what I have received from You. Oh, how infinitely good You are and how immeasurably great is Your light. It shines continuously over us and will never be extinguished from the beginning of the world until its end." I thought that I was apathetic and negligent when I did not see clearly the flame of this light burning within me. "My adorable Jesus, I beg you, forgive my sins and my indifference by which, I, also, have offended You. Pour out Your pardoning charity over all those for whom I make my little sacrifices united to Your infinite merits. Reward my burning desire for the salvation of souls with the splendor of Your light. Let those souls who have not received Your light feel Your yearning for them."

Chapter six

1966

POWER OF REPENTANCE

January 3, 1966

Early in the morning, my soul was filled with a profound sorrow for my sins. On the way to morning adoration and Holy Mass, the Lord was talking with me. I could only record these few words which left a living mark on my soul. I continued to sorrow for my sins.

Jesus: "You see, beloved, how immensely powerful repentance is! You can even disarm the power of God on the verge of chastising the world. Listen, Elizabeth, you and all who make reparation for others force Me to forgive even though My raised hand is ready to punish. I extended My hands nailed to the Cross before My heavenly Father to defend you and save you from eternal damnation. I offered satisfaction to My Father. You must do likewise, this is what it means to participate in My work of Redemption."

BLESSED ARE YOU

January 13, 1966

After Holy Communion, the Lord Jesus said:

Jesus: "Your repentance touches My Heart. I will imprint on your soul, little sister, a brilliant sign. Do you understand Me? I will mark your soul with a metallic sign of pure gold. You merited this for a long time because of your constant repentance. Even after your death, it will shine with light. Your soul's brightness shining from repentance radiates a light of repentance over the souls of others also."

This happened on the same day, in the evening, before going to bed. I always begin my prayer by stirring up a consciousness of sin because I feel that I can immerse myself truly in God's adoration only if, before the Lord, I first spread the very beautiful carpet of the breath of repentance over which I prostrate. The Lord said:

Jesus: "You are a blessed soul."

At that same instant, He lifted up my soul from the earth while the sound of His words kept ringing in me. He added:

Jesus: "It is only the soul purified of its sins that I raise to Me in this way."

On this, I cannot write any more. This elevation to God cannot be expressed in words.

The next day, at Holy Mass, I meditated on the words from the conversation of the preceding night, "You are a good and blessed soul." The Lord Jesus was constantly asking me to write down the words I was addressing Him. I put into a prayer what He told me, "My adored Jesus! Would I be blessed if You did not bless me? Would I be good without Your grace?

O my Jesus, blessed be Your Holy Name by which I came to be blessed. I, a lowly nothing! My Lord, my adored Jesus, it is also Your infinite goodness that proclaims Your glory. How good You are to keep my soul in constant humility!

My Lord, Your glory showed itself even more for having praised me. I am annihilated. Like a grain of dust, I fall at Your feet."

BE A MATCH

January 16, 1966

In the afternoon, I lit a match to make a fire. The Lord Jesus surprised me again with His words.

Jesus: "You see, beloved, you are like this match. My Divine Hands have lit you because I wanted this, and you will ignite the whole world like a single match because God wants it so. You are a small instrument, just like the little match that you hold in your hand. Do not be surprised by what I tell you. With one strike of the match, I will enkindle in millions of souls the Flame of Love of My Mother. Satan's fire will be unable to extinguish this Flame. In vain, he prepares his burning iniquities coming from his terrible hatred. One single match that My Mother strikes will blind him, and you will serve as My Mother's instrument."

YOU ARE NOT ALONE

January 25, 1966

Coming back home that night, I got off the bus. Because I could hardly walk on the icy snow, a depressing loneliness came over me. Looking around, the other passengers were rapidly dispersing. Most of them had companions. I was fearful of walking on the dark and icy road. On setting out, the Lord Jesus surprised me, first only with His words and then with His increasingly felt presence. He asked me:

Jesus: "Tell Me, little sister, why do you consider yourself alone since I am the One leading you? Have no fear, I will not let go of you. Come, let us go together and let there be no other moment when you would feel alone."

As He spoke, the feeling of His presence grew ever stronger in my soul. He kept speaking.

Jesus: "Elizabeth, a long time ago, when you did not think of Me, I was always there. I kept you from falling on the icy and slippery road of life. At that time, you did not believe that I was protecting you from so many falls. Still, it was like this because I was watching closely each footstep you were taking. My loved one, just your thinking that you are alone hurts Me. Our souls are in harmony and our thoughts are in unison. Reject every idea that you are alone, this is impossible between us. It would hurt Me very much if you still think this way. Don't ever have such thoughts again. The beating of My Heart echoes in yours and if you are alone, you will hear it even more. You see how the suffering becomes immediately burdensome if for one instant you do not think about Me. I know this very well. This is the eternal guarantee of My love. Now, I ask you, do you want anything?"

"...Yes, I do. Before all else, I desire souls for You! I want all the souls to possess God, You, infinitely good and merciful Love."

Meanwhile, I was immersed in Him. He breathed silently in my soul.

Jesus: "Thank you, Elizabeth! This is what I expected from you. I see that My grace does not fall in vain upon your soul."

THE MOST BEAUTIFUL GIFT

January 26, 1966

At morning Holy Mass, when the organ played a line from a Christmas carol, the Lord brought me into ecstasy. When this happens, I do not see nor hear anything. I just hear the Lord's words. Taking total possession of my soul, He again began to speak.

Jesus: "Yes, My beloved, carrying with us in our hearts a beautiful gift... Do you know what the most beautiful gift is?"

I repented for my sins and said: "My Divine Master, I do not know what sublime answer You would want from someone else. I have only sorrow for my sins. I bring You this gift in my heart and I carry it in my soul with humble faith and hope. I offer it to You again and again with thankful love, my Divine Master."

In these moments of ecstasy, the Lord Jesus exchanged His Heart and Soul with me, and He allowed me to feel the Divine Heart beating within me while His Soul penetrated my inner being. Moreover, there is no way of writing down what happened in my soul; it is sharing in the infinite goodness of God.

MAKE REPARATION FOR SINNERS

March 4, 1966

The Lord Jesus spoke again. This conversation lasted the whole morning. If someone reads these lines, he should know that this conversation was often interrupted. While it was going on, the Lord Jesus overwhelmed me. He increased the feeling of His presence. From time to time, He would say a few words. He knows very well that I listen to each of His words as a prayer. I constantly reflect on His teaching. Today, it happened the same way. At nightfall, He said:

Jesus: "On the chords of your soul, I play the melody of repentance. Upon hearing this melody, even the obstinate sinner will convert. This melody comes from all the suffering you accept. It is the melody of your accepted sacrifices whose sound penetrates souls, and through it, you make reparation for sinners."

BE HUMBLE

March 16, 1966

Jesus: "You are the prompter in the Divine Drama. I tell you this so you do not falter in this task. By My grace, this Divine Principle has become yours. Always see it as holy and true.

The Evil One wants to make you fall into despair. He will use a ruse to ruin your humility. The Evil One knows that if he removed the water of your humility, he can smuggle in all his perversities. Just be humble! Do the members of the audience need to know the prompter? No. Why? The prompter's job is to make the show go well, but he can neither shine nor appear on the stage. Many times, he does not have a moment's peace. This is your situation, daughter. See to all what the dramatic work requires; breathe it out to wherever it is necessary. I, your Master, have instructed you in all that you need. If you keep My teachings, you need not fear. Naturally, this does not mean that you can rest whenever you want, but only if the show allows it. I know, I see your thoughts, your efforts, by which you want to satisfy My Divine Request and Will. This is enough for Me. I never seek results from you, Elizabeth. I tell you this so you are humbled. In these days and in these difficult times, you have a need for greater and more frequent humiliations. I know this. Therefore, I send you everything to bathe your soul in humiliation because without it, I could not guarantee the purity of your soul."

THE HEART'S LONGING

March 17, 1966

Before Communion, I told the Lord of my profound sorrow for sins. "O my adored Master, how I suffer from all that I have offended You! Your infinite goodness fills me with admiration because You have forgiven me all this." The Lord Jesus answered:

Jesus: "Tell Me. What else afflicts you and what causes you sorrow?"

For a few brief moments, I reflected on the Lord's question and I answered: "O my adorable Jesus, I am saddened because others offend You and do not lament their sins." Again, the Lord Jesus spoke.

Jesus: "What else afflicts you? Tell Me, My sweet soul. I like to hear you speak. Your words are a melody for Me. They fill My Divine Heart with joy. Please continue. Tell Me, to whom should I award My abundant riches? I want to hear the longing of your heart."

During this time, the wonderful outpouring of His presence pervaded my body and soul and projected from my heart the answer to the question of the Lord Jesus concerning what is afflicting me. "O my Jesus, my heart aches for those who, from pride, reject the graces that You offer them, and because of that, the terrible danger of damnation threatens them.

O my adorable Jesus, give them Your abundant Divine Riches. Because You asked me, I humbly seek graces for them, also. My Jesus, You have told me that I am a sweet soul for You and that You enjoy hearing me speak and that my words are a melody for You, filling Your Divine Heart with joy.

O infinite Goodness and Mercy! Now You have made me even bolder.

Give me Your abundant riches so my every prayer would be a melody. Then Your Divine Grace will penetrate the souls who reject You and they will continue this melody which You so love."

At Holy Communion, a profound silence came upon my soul. As the Lord Jesus entered my soul, even the beating of my heart grew less. His words resounded in my ears. However, at the moment of Divine Union, every stirring in my soul was one with God. How great is that miracle that is repeated every day and washes again my soul with His Precious Blood and nourishes it by the power of His Sacred Body. Thanks to Him, I can keep the ruses of the Evil One far from my soul.

SEEING THE ROAD

April 9, 1966

While adoring the Lord at the altar of repose (of Good Friday), I pondered the great torment that He suffered for me. The Lord, with a silent sigh, began to speak.

Jesus: "Look, the Word became Flesh."

No matter what I tried, I was not able to grasp the significance. The Lord Jesus drew my attention to this reality. "Even now, adorable Jesus, I cannot grasp this miracle." The Lord Jesus continued:

Jesus: "I am not surprised, My little one. I reassure you, no one has understood this great miracle until now except My Mother; for to understand it, it is necessary to accept suffering also. It is only through suffering that the soul can understand the great miracle of the Incarnation of the Word. Through the consummation of the sacrifice, will be clarified in your soul what I did for you, for all."

"O adorable Jesus, You have made these profound thoughts very clear to me. My Divine Master, I cannot understand. I have the feeling that it is only through the sorrow for my sins that I can thank You. I have no other words to say, nor any request to make, except pronounce the words of the Good Thief: 'Lord, remember me when

You come into Your Kingdom.'" As I was praying the Lord Jesus, the Blessed Virgin said:

Mary: "Yes, my little Carmelite, address yourselves with a repentant soul to my Divine Son and to me whenever you think of the Kingdom of my Divine Son, and that you do everything so it would come for you all. For this reason, I want my Flame of Love to overflow upon the earth so all can see the road that leads to the Kingdom of my Divine Son."

Then the Lord Jesus spoke again.

Jesus: "I say to you what I said to the Good Thief: The day of your death you will be with Me in Paradise. You neither, you may not sigh more for Me than I for you, given that our hearts beat to the same rhythm. Listen to the beating of My Heart resounding in yours."

Immediately after writing these lines, I knelt down. The beating of His Heart forced me to kneel and I couldn't keep on writing.

I PAY YOU

April 14, 1966

In my night prayer, I repeated many times: "Thank you. Thank you very much, my Lord Jesus, for Your infinite goodness."

Meanwhile, I was trying to think of a better word to express this. Suddenly, I remembered that when anyone does me a favor, I say, "May God repay you." "My sweet Jesus, you are almighty God, I can only thank You." Then I grew silent and thought, "No one can pay God." But, I am a daring person. "My Jesus, do not think it is because I am rude or proud that I dare to think that I will repay You with the sorrow for my sins. I give You what You do not have and what I do have." Then the Lord Jesus spoke to me.

Jesus: "You know, My Elizabeth, not long ago, I exchanged My Heart and My Soul with you. This means that I bought your sins at the price of My Precious Blood. But for your offering not to be without value, I accept it now so that it would be you who will pay the others in My Name. Do you understand? By your repentance, a perfect sorrow for sins will be enkindled in a multitude of souls."

April 18, 1966

At morning Holy Mass, the Blessed Virgin said:

Mary: "My Flame of Love and your repentance work together. Through this, many souls return to my Divine Son."

DIVINE MYSTERIES

April 19, 1966

Jesus: "Do you wonder how you can see and comprehend the Divine Mysteries with so much clarity? Only can see them is the one whose sight is one with My Divine Gaze, and whose thought is one with My thoughts. My Elizabeth, many of the Divine Mysteries you have been experiencing on account of My Divine Clarity in periods of ecstasy, strengthen you across the suffering that you must bear for the salvation of souls. I know that you suffer with joy, and I will continually strengthen your availability for sacrifices since I know that you will need it and those I have sent you to, with respect to our holy communications. You must make sacrifices on their behalf. That is why I often repeat this so it may become your continually renewed prayer."

April 24, 1966

Before morning Holy Mass, I prostrated before Him and greeted Him with these words: "You are my adored Jesus, the apple of my eyes." After that, I knelt for a long time, unable to say anything because Jesus welcomed me with these words:

Jesus: "You tell Me this so rarely. Yet, because of My human nature, I also desire to be pampered."

TEARS OF REPENTANCE

May 8, 1966

As I got home, after the night adoration, the Lord Jesus said:

Jesus: "Each tear drop that the suffering draws from your eyes will fall upon the souls of sinners and bring forth their tears of repentance."

THE FLAME OF LOVE WILL FLOOD YOUR CONFESSOR

June 3, 1966

A few days ago, I reported to the Blessed Virgin what my confessor had said: "Until such time the Lord Jesus or you, my Mother, make your requirements known to him, he will do nothing." Today, the Blessed Virgin responded:

Mary: "My little one, my Flame of Love makes no exception, even with his soul. I will flood him with the gentle light which he cannot resist, and I will do the same for all who are called to spread my graces. Just as I poured out a gentle light in your soul, I will also do the same for others.

I must tell you, my little one, that the purer the soul, the more fully the grace of my Flame of Love will shine, because purity makes the soul receptive. Then, with my maternal love, I bring forth tears of repentance."

At these words of the Blessed Virgin, a great peace came to my soul.

ADMINISTRATOR OF MY GRACES

June 12, 1966

In the morning, while adoring Him before the altar and revealing my poverty of soul, He said:

Jesus: "Now, My beloved, I cover the misery of your soul. And I want you also to feel it, so that you draw strength.

You see that I have covered your soul's misery. Now, only beauty shines forth from you. Although you feel the misery of your soul, others will not. The richness of My Divinity will radiate from your soul and you will be able to distribute it to others. In one word, I have made you an administrator of My graces."

Chapter seven

1969

I WILL SEND YOU A PRIEST

November 7, 1969

On November 7, 1969, while in my small room, immersed in adoring the Most Holy Trinity, I heard these words in my heart:

Jesus: "Soon I will send you a priest who will take your soul and our Holy Cause into his hands."

Chapter eight

1971

SPEECH IS A GIFT OF GOD

July 26, 1971

Both the Lord Jesus and the Blessed Virgin took turns speaking in my soul.

Jesus: "Speech is a gift of God, and one day, we must give an account of our words. Through words, souls communicate with one another. Also through words, people get to know us.

Therefore, we have no right to wrap ourselves in silence, but we also must remember that we are responsible for every spoken word. Therefore, we should walk and live in God's presence, pondering each word that we say. Our Father gave the gift of speech and you must make use of your gift. Do not be afraid to speak!

Shaking others out of their lethargy is a serious responsibility. Nevertheless, you cannot leave them in their homes with empty hands and empty hearts. You must speak!"

Mary: "You can only explain my Flame of Love to others by speaking about it. You have no right to be silent because of cowardice, pride, negligence or fear of sacrifice.

Let the words you say about me be alive so the mystery of Heaven has an impact on souls. If, eventually, you ask to speak and it is granted to you, may my power be with you! Let each word be like a seed planted so those listening produce an abundant harvest."

Jesus: "Get the timid and passive priests to leave their homes. They must not stand idle and deprive humanity of the Flame of Love of the Immaculate Heart of My Mother. Let them not abuse the confidence by which I have bonded them to Me. They must speak out and announce My abundant riches, so I can pour out My forgiveness upon the whole world.

Be on a war footing! Satan, by his cunning and deceitful machinations, is trying to produce a muddy morality to ruin the good. The Christian conscience cannot be satisfied with just helping here or there because the souls to whom you should have spoken will accuse you.

Trust in My Mother! She wipes away all doubt and removes fear by her boundless, motherly love. She marks you with a sign and will protect those who trust her. If you trust her, the depraved will be humiliated and thrown into the depth of hell. The future world is in preparation:

The smile of My Mother will light up the whole earth."

Chapter nine

1975

TEACHINGS

July 11, 1975

- First Teaching

Mary: "My children, many suffer, – so to speak – being captive and blinded by material things. In spite of their goodwill, many cannot come closer to God because material goods act like a wall between God and the soul.

Even among yourselves, some well-intentioned souls make serious sacrifices from time to time. Yet, they are blind because of earthly goods and material interest. As a result, they cannot receive the singular graces that they so much want. At every moment, these souls receive inspirations telling them what to do. However, they do not want to believe that this inspiration comes from God, their guardian angel or their patron saint."

The heavenly Father does not want us to convince or influence these persons in any way because He expects a voluntary renunciation on their part. Also because Divine Providence, Divine Tactfulness, sees that the interested party could not renounce, despite counsels, and could even sin by distrust.

- *Second Teaching*

Jesus: "If someone gave up a particular good, let him not give it to some location where his name will be listed forever as a donor and shine for his own glory, but let him give it without being noticed, anonymously, because it is only thus that the Father of Heaven can reward him."

- *Third Teaching*

Elizabeth Kindelmann: "For the teachings and inspirations of the Lord Jesus (of God the Holy Spirit), the Flame of Love of the Blessed Virgin prepares a road in our souls. If we refer to the Flame of Love, the Lord Jesus will enlighten our intellect to know what we must do, for example, how we can choose between two things and which is the most perfect and represents the Will of God.

Whoever receives this light, let him follow it and transmit it to others. They must water this gift like a flower. Otherwise it fades and is covered with dust."

- *Fourth Teaching*

"Love God very much. Love Him more every day." The heavenly Father says: "Inasmuch as you love Me, by the same measure the world will be freed from sin and adversity.

You are responsible for one another. You are responsible for your family, for your nation, and for the entire world. May all of you feel responsible for the fate of all humanity.

You must remind each other: you will receive My inspirations in the measure that you love Me."

Mary: "I grant to all the grace to see the results of their labors on behalf of my Flame of Love in each soul, in your country and in the entire world. You, who are laboring and making sacrifices for the prompt outpouring of my Flame of Love, you are going to get to see it."

Chapter ten

1977

DESTROYING THE WRITINGS

Note: The following is not taken from the notes of the Spiritual Diary. This confession is drawn from a letter written by the chosen of God to one of her acquaintances, Doctor N. Its authenticity can be proved from the style, the words and the originality of the images...

In the summer of 1969, the torments and doubts surprised me very much. I came to know that all that I had written did not come from God. All was my scribbling. This thought left me no peace and I made an inner decision, so I will be free from these terrible torments. I decided to destroy the material, which now consumes many volumes, by burning it in the earthenware stove in my small room which is 2 x 2 meters. I had all the material in my hands and was ready to tear it up and throw it into the fire, but the Lord Jesus paralyzed my hand. The messages of the Lord Jesus fell from my hands and I collapsed. I could not move or even light the match. My eldest daughter, Cecilia, suddenly came and found me. She understood what I was going to do, so she took the writings from my hands. When she did this, I regained my strength and said: "No, no. I want to burn them and free myself from these torments because I can no longer bear them."

My daughter took the material back to her room (which was in the same house), and I, regaining movement in my paralyzed hand, ran after her and took the messages of the Lord Jesus with the intention of burning and destroying them.

When I came back to my little dwelling, I knelt down on one knee in front of the door of the stove. The paralysis of the fingers of my hand returned. Right in front of the stove, I experienced the same inability to act. From this, I realized that I was doing wrong and He (the Lord) did not want the destruction of His words that must be given to the world.

SEEK A SIGN

In the spring of 1971, I woke up with a terrible suffering coming from grave doubts. I was getting ready for Holy Mass, but because of the torment of doubts, I could not even move. I asked: "Why am I going to Holy Mass if I receive no relief and no peace for my soul?" I begged the Lord to dispel this great confusion in my soul caused by the doubts. What do I have in me? I want to see it and know it. Why does it torment me so cruelly? If all is true and authentic and if it is the Will of God, why must I live with such dark and troubled torments? I broke down. In my little dwelling, I collapsed before a small piece of furniture, and in my torment, I began to hit the surface with my fist: "I seek a sign. I seek a sign, a sure and acceptable sign, so I can withstand these torments!" With a terrible lack of respect, I demanded a sign from God. This made me laugh even before I expressed it in words: "Ah, I asked God what He surely cannot give me."

I demanded that He send me a priest, the one who had already heard my confession a few times, but ceased to do so later on because his assignment had changed, such that he could no longer come. Thus, this contact also has been interrupted for the past year. And that person, I demanded him from God. If that person comes to me today at noon time sharp, I will take it as a sign that the Cause is authentic and I will accept it.

As if I had just done a good work, I grew calm and walked to Holy Mass in the Máriaremete Sanctuary.

On the way, a feeling of shame came over me. How could I act this way with God? I wished that this had never happened. Thinking about this, I arrived at church. My first steps led me to the confessional. I told the priest my terrible spiritual state and my disrespectful dispute with God. My confessor strongly reproved me. "How can anyone act this way toward God?" For a penance, he told me to beg the Lord Jesus that this 'hard head' would finally be converted (an acquaintance of the confessor, an insensitive person).

Before leaving the confessional, I did not resist the temptation of saying to Father: "I would like to see, if you were in this state of soul, would you not also discuss things with God?" After saying that, I left the confessional and collapsed before the Lord Jesus. I could only say my penance, "My adorable Jesus, convert this 'hard head...'"

After saying my penance, the darkness that ruled in my soul was gone. After Holy Mass and Communion, I returned home, quite peacefully. I sat in my little house mending the clothes of my three grandchildren of whom I took care. My soul, in God's peace, was filled with thoughts about the good God. I did not even remember my blindness of this morning, I had completely forgotten it.

Suddenly, someone stopped at the door of my small room. He pressed the latch and called at the door. "Come in," I answered. It was noon and the Angelus bells rang. Almost frozen in my place, I asked the one who was entering why he was coming. Who had called him?

It was the priest whom, this very morning, laughing to myself, I had asked God to send as proof, as evidence. I asked him: "Who sent you? And why did you come?" He answered that he did not know, he just felt a strong internal feeling that he had to come immediately. In great detail, I told him what had happened.

As a parenthesis, the 'hard head' for whom I prayed for as a penance, has returned to God.

DOUBTS AND CRISIS

Doubts, similar to the ones I have just mentioned and exposed, arose in many diverse ways, stirred in my soul and struck me for years. They kept occurring even in my sixty-four years of life [in 1977].

The story of one of my most serious doubts and crises, with respect to consequences, I reveal it with what follows:

On one occasion, when these strong doubts came upon me, I once again sought peace of soul. To gain this peace, I decided to retract the words and the messages of the Lord Jesus and the Blessed Virgin before all those to whom I had given them. I acted on this decision. I went to twelve Hungarian priests and said to each one: "Do not believe what I have told you because it all comes from me. They are lies I invented." While crying and sobbing, I asked them for their absolution. They reacted in different ways and gave their opinion. I told them, without hiding anything, that my terrible torments were forcing me to retract. I said, humbly prostrated to the ground, that I retracted my messages given until then and I asked them for general absolution exactly how the good God sees things in respect to my person.

The great moment of Calvary caused by the torment of my doubts arrived when, after I had retracted, the Lord Jesus made me see my confessor and all the other priests before whom I had retracted the words of the Lord Jesus and the Blessed Virgin. The response that I most remember was formulated by a priest who said: "After you had retracted, the Lord Jesus spoke again to you. Do not be ashamed. This proves, with the greatest clarity, that we are face to face with God's Will."

Chapter eleven

1980

THE MONDAY FAST

August 15, 1980

Both the Lord Jesus and the Blessed Virgin took turns speaking. The Blessed Virgin's words sounded in my soul with firm, but loving power. She asked the clergy, the consecrated religious, and the faithful Christians of the whole world to fast on bread and water on Mondays, when they are able to do so.

Jesus: "The Church and the whole world is in grave danger. Even with your strength, you cannot change this situation. The Most Holy Trinity alone can help you, through the concerted intercession of the Most Blessed Virgin, all the angels, all the saints, and those souls whom you have freed from Purgatory."

According to the message of the Blessed Virgin:

Mary: "When priests observe the Monday fast, in all the Holy Masses that they celebrate that week, at the moment of Consecration, they will free an innumerable* number of souls from Purgatory.

When those persons consecrated to God and the faithful keep the Monday fast, they will free a multitude of souls from Purgatory each time they receive Communion during that week, at the very moment they receive the Holy Body of Our Lord Jesus Christ."

* Elizabeth asked later what the word 'innumerable' meant, whether it was a thousand or a million souls.
Jesus said: "More."
Elizabeth asked: "How many exactly?"
Jesus answered: "Many souls, so many that it cannot be expressed with human numbers!"

ADVICE OF OUR LADY ON FASTING

While fasting, we can eat bread abundantly and drink water. We can put salt on the bread. We can take vitamins, medicines and whatever is necessary to our condition. However, we should not enjoy it.

Mary: "Whoever usually keeps the fast, it suffices to keep it until 6:00 p.m. In this case, they should recite this very day five decades of the Rosary for the souls."

Note: To see how effective fasting is, we find examples in the Gospel. Think of the curative action of the disciples, in St. Mark 9:14. The disciples asked Jesus: "Why were we not able to expel the demon?" He told them: "This kind of demon can only be driven out by prayer and fasting." (9:28) In these times, this kind of demon wants to undermine souls.

Chapter twelve

1981

PRAYER COMMUNITIES

January 1, 1981

Jesus: "Reach beyond your limits. Look at the Three Wise Men, who made superhuman sacrifice. They left behind their limitations. First and foremost, this is what is expected of the clergy and others consecrated to God and all the believers."

(We must increase beyond the usual measure the intensity of our prayers and sacrifices for peace in the world and for the salvation of souls. We have to reach new heights.)

"Every parish must urgently organize communities of prayers of atonement, blessing one another with the sign of the Cross" (including strangers).

THIRD ORDER OF CARMEL

Spring 1981 (Middle of March)

The Blessed Virgin asked that we urge the competent authorities for the restoration of the Third Order of Carmel throughout the world. This must happen quickly and everywhere. Humanity needs lay people who have a spirit of prayer.

Mary: "Because the Flame of Love of my heart was ignited here in Hungary, for this reason I want to put into action many of my desires from here. Humanity must fulfill my request with the greatest devotion."

While the Blessed Virgin was speaking about the Carmel, Jesus interrupted: "Because the Flame of Love of the heart of My Mother is Noah's Ark."[10]

The Lord Jesus repeated this on various occasions in his conversations.

DO NOT IMPEDE THE EFFUSION OF GRACE

April 12, 1981

Our Blessed Mother implores that we allow her to spread as quickly as possible the effusion of grace of her Flame of Love over humanity. Let us not impede her work because she depends on us.

Mary: "All those who impede and act irresponsibly to delay this outpouring of grace have a great responsibility."

November 20, 1981

I meditated profoundly on the words of the Lord Jesus and the Blessed Virgin. Because of these words, the knowledge of my responsibility weighed upon my soul. The Lord Jesus then assured me.

Jesus: "Do not fear. We are beside you, beside all of you. The grace spreads in a great degree over the souls of all who share in My work of Redemption. Just do not delay in fulfilling our requests."

That day, while I was preparing food for the chickens, I heard the words of the Lord Jesus and the Blessed Virgin pronounced simultaneously in the depth of my soul.

---

10. Let us remember the promise of the Blessed Virgin to spread the effect of grace of her Flame of Love to all the souls who are marked with the sign of the blessed Cross of her Divine Son. The Sign of the Cross blinds and expels Satan just as the prayer received from the Blessed Virgin: "Spread the effect of grace..." or that of the Lord Jesus: "May our feet journey together..."

GREAT MOBILIZATION

November 20, 1981

Jesus and Mary: "We greet you. We know that you suffer much. But today, we ask the whole world, through you, for a great mobilization. Give our petition to your spiritual director.

In every part of the world, multitudes of people should petition the Holy Father for an official declaration of the effusion of the Flame of Love of our Hearts for the whole world. We do not ask, deliberately, for an examination that will take time, as we have already said in a previous request. Everyone feels it in their own heart, in their soul.

Our petition is urgent. There is no time for delays. Let the faithful together with the priests satisfy our petition in a great spiritual oneness. The effusion of graces will also reach the souls of the non-baptized with its effect of grace."

PRAY FOR ONE ANOTHER

December 12, 1981

The Blessed Virgin said:

Mary: "My little one and all of you my beloved children, be on the alert. Satan wants to remove the ground of hope from beneath your feet. He knows very well that if he succeeds in doing this, he will have removed everything from your souls. If you lose hope, he does not even need to tempt you to sin. He who has lost hope is in terrible darkness. He no longer sees with the eyes of faith. For him, all virtue, everything that is good, loses its value. Oh, my children, pray constantly for each other. Allow the outpouring of my graces to take effect in your souls."

SUMMARY

For greater clarity, we now summarize the promises of graces and the requests of the Virgin Mary given to men all over the world: the Pope, priests and laity.

The Blessed Virgin, during the period of time between 1961 and 1981, requests and implores incessantly. She begs gently but decisively.

"You ask me? It is I who am asking you! You cry? I am sobbing!"

(May 12, 1974)

THE GIFT OF GRACE THAT THE BLESSED VIRGIN OFFERS US

1. "I would like to place in your hands a new instrument... It is the Flame of Love of my heart... With this Flame full of graces that I give you from my heart, ignite all the hearts in the entire country. Let this Flame go from heart to heart. This is the miracle becoming the blaze whose dazzling light will blind Satan. This is the fire of love of union which I obtained from the heavenly Father through the merits of the wounds of my Divine Son."

(April 13, 1962)

"We will put out fire with fire: the fire of hatred with the fire of love."

(December 6, 1964)

2. "My Flame of Love has become so incandescent that I want to spread on you not only its light, but also its warmth with all its power. My Flame of Love is so great that I can no longer keep it within me; it leaps out at you with explosive force. My love that is spreading will overcome the satanic hatred that contaminates the world, so that the greatest number of souls is saved from damnation."

(October 19, 1962)

3. "Just as the whole world knows my name, so I want the Flame of Love of my heart performing miracles in the depths of the hearts to also be known."

(October 19, 1962)

4. "My little one, I extend the effect of grace of the Flame of Love of my heart over all the peoples and nations, not only over those living in the Holy Mother Church, but over all the souls marked with the sign of the blessed Cross of my Divine Son. Also over those who are not baptized!"

(September 16, 1963)

GRACES PROMISED BY THE VIRGIN MARY

She encourages us to make reparation to her Divine Son so often offended, to venerate His Holy Wounds, to immerse ourselves frequently in His sorrowful Passion, and also to venerate and adore the Most Blessed Sacrament.

1. "My little one, Thursdays and Fridays should be considered as great days of grace. Those who offer reparation to my Divine Son on these days will receive a great grace. During the hours of reparation, the power of Satan will weaken to the degree that those making reparation pray for sinners..."

(September 29, 1962)

2. "Whenever someone does adoration in a spirit of atonement or visits the Blessed Sacrament, as long as it lasts, Satan loses his

dominion on the parish souls. Blinded, he ceases to reign on souls."

(November 6-7, 1962)

3. "If you attend Holy Mass while under no obligation to do so and you are in a state of grace before God, during that time I will pour out the Flame of Love of my heart and blind Satan. My graces will flow abundantly to the souls for whom you offer the Holy Mass... The participation in the Holy Mass is what helps the most to blind Satan."

(November 22, 1962)

WHAT ARE THE LORD JESUS AND THE VIRGIN MARY ASKING OF US?

Conversion, spiritual renewal, applying oneself to achieve holiness of life, zeal for the salvation of souls.

1. The Flame of Love of the Blessed Mother and families

The Blessed Virgin says that the spiritual renewal must begin with the families:

"With my Flame of Love, I want to make the home come alive again with love. I want to unite families that are scattered."

(August 8, 1962)

To this end, she is asking for reparation:

"On Thursday and Friday, I ask you, my daughter, to offer a very special reparation to my Divine Son. This will be an hour for the family to make reparation. Begin this hour with a spiritual reading, followed by the Rosary or other prayers in an atmosphere of recollection and fervor.

Let there be at least two or three, because my Divine Son is present where two or three are gathered. Start by making the sign of the Cross five times offering yourselves to the Eternal Father through the wounds of my Divine Son. Do the same at the conclusion. Sign yourselves this way when you get up and when you go to bed, and during the day. This will bring you closer to the Eternal Father through my Divine Son, filling your heart with graces."

(April 13, 1962)

2. Request of the Blessed Virgin to the Holy Father

"I ask the Holy Father to make the feast of the Flame of Love on February 2, the feast of Candlemas. I do not want a special feast."

(August 1, 1962)

3. Request of Jesus to His priests and souls consecrated to Him

"Turn to Me and be sacrificed on the sacred altar of inner recollection and martyrdom. Do not forget that this inner martyrdom is My Will and Satan cannot stop it. This battle in the depth of your souls brings about abundant fruit, just as does martyrdom... Set the earth ablaze with your burning desires. Use your sacrifice made from pure love to burn away all sin. Do you not believe this is possible? Just trust Me."

(August 7, 1962)

"You should stand where I put you, firm and full of the spirit of sacrifice… Take upon yourself the Cross that I also have embraced and thus offer yourselves as victims as I have done. Otherwise, you will not have eternal life."

(October 4, 1962)

- What is the Lord Jesus asking of His beloved priests?

That they give a good example (December 22, 1963); that they follow the inspirations of the Lord and make souls see the importance of that (January 1, 1964); that they shake the lethargic souls and give raise to courage in souls (April 17, 1962); that they make good use of their time (October 19, 1964); that they allow themselves to be guided by Divine Grace to a sacrificed and apostolic life (November 23, 1962); and that they make adoration and incite the faithful to do the same (July 25, 1963).

"Ask My sons to direct souls towards My beloved Mother. They should never give a homily without exhorting the faithful to have a profound devotion for her."

(April 17, 1962)

"While I was hanging on the Cross, I cried out in a loud voice: 'I am thirsty.' I say these same words to all, especially to the souls consecrated to Me."

(August 18, 1964)

4. The Flame of Love of the Blessed Virgin and sinners

In these messages, the sacred cause of the salvation of souls holds a central position, because the essence and purpose of the action of the Flame of Love is the salvation of souls, their return to God, and their renewal.

The Lord Jesus:

"Let us have just one thought: the salvation of souls."

(May 17, 1963)

"Oh, how I long for sinners!"

(August 15, 1964)

"No soul I have entrusted to the care of My priests ought to be damned."

(August 6, 1962)

That is why He instructs us:

"Let all of you take part in My work of Redemption!"

And He also indicates the heavenly instrument:

"Hell is swallowing those souls created in the image and likeness of My heavenly Father. They fall into the clutches of Satan. The Flame of Love of My Mother can soothe the sorrow of My Heart."

(July 26, 1963)

The Blessed Virgin also said:

"I want that not one soul be damned. You should want this together with me. For this purpose, I place in your hands a beam of light that is the Flame of Love of my heart."

(January 15, 1964)

But it also depends on us:

"Satan is sweeping souls away in a terrifying way. Why don't you all try your best to stop him and do it as soon as possible?"

(May 14, 1962)

She added:

"You must dedicate yourselves to blind Satan. The coordinated forces of the entire world are necessary to accomplish this. Do not delay because someday you will be called to account for the work entrusted to you, for the fate of a multitude of souls... Satan will be blinded inasmuch as you work against him."

(November 27, 1963)

- The means to save souls:

"Sacrifice and prayer! These are your instruments."

(July 22-23, 1963)

All kinds of sacrifices such as bearing with patience bodily and spiritual sufferings, uniting them to the Passion of Jesus (May 24, 1963), as well as fasting, keeping night vigil (during part of the night), etc. Each one, according to his ability, can practice them at all times and in all places. Even with the offering of our daily work and chores, we can save souls (November 30, 1962). The sorrow of remembering our sins is also fruitful for souls (August 15, 1964). Even the desire for the salvation of souls helps to blind Satan (November 30, 1962), because, "The will of the soul is already love" (September 15, 1962).

The Blessed Virgin:

"The greater the number of souls who sacrifice and watch in prayer, the greater the power of my Flame of Love on earth will be... Because it is with the power of sacrifice and prayer that the flash of hellish hatred will be overcome."

(December 6, 1964)

"I will support your work with miracles as never seen before, and that the reparation to my Divine Son will accomplish imperceptibly, gently and silently."

(August 1, 1962)

And the Lord Jesus:

"If you ask for souls, can I refuse your petitions? No. Otherwise, I would be acting against My work of Salvation. I always hear your persevering prayer."

(June 24, 1963)

5. *The Flame of Love of the Blessed Virgin and the dying*

"Once the Flame of Love of my heart lights up on the earth, its effect of grace will also spread out to the dying. Satan will be blinded, and through your prayer at the nighttime vigil, the terrible struggle of the dying against Satan will end. Coming under the gentle light of my Flame of Love, even the most hardened sinner will convert."

(September 12, 1963)

"I want the holy night vigils – by which I want to save the souls of the dying – to be organized in every parish, so there is not even one moment without someone praying in a vigil."

(July 9, 1965)

6. *Request of the Blessed Virgin to all her children*

"When you say the prayer that honors me, the Hail Mary, include this petition in the following manner:

'Hail Mary, full of grace… pray for us sinners, spread the effect of grace of thy Flame of Love over all of humanity, now and at the hour of our death. Amen.'

This is not a new prayer formula; it must be a constant petition."[11]

(October 1962 and February 2, 1982)

"This is the instrument that I place in your hands. By this, you and your companions will save the souls of the dying from eternal damnation. By the light of my Flame of Love, Satan will remain blind."

(July 9, 1965)

7. *The Flame of Love of the Blessed Virgin and the souls in Purgatory*

Mary: "My Flame of Love which I desire to spread from my heart over all of you in a greater measure extends even to the souls in Purgatory."

a) "For those families observing a holy hour of reparation on Thursday or Friday, if someone happens to die in the family, the deceased is freed from Purgatory after a single day of strict fasting observed by anyone member of the family." (Let's understand: if he died in a state of grace.)

(September 24, 1963)

b) "Anyone fasting on bread and water on Monday will free each time the soul of a priest from the place of suffering. Whoever practices this will receive the grace of being liberated from the place of suffering within eight days after their death."

(Monday's Agenda)

New privileges for those who keep a strict fast on Mondays.

"When priests observe the Monday fast, in all the Holy Masses that they celebrate that week, at the moment of Consecration, they will free an innumerable number of souls from Purgatory."

"When those persons consecrated to God and the faithful keep the Monday fast, they will free a multitude of souls from Purgatory

11. Let us pray the Rosary and add this invocation to each Ave Maria.

each time they receive Communion during that week, at the very moment they receive the Holy Body of Our Lord Jesus Christ."

(August 15, 1980)

c) "My little one, your compassion for the poor souls has so moved my motherly heart that I grant the grace that you sought. If at any moment, while invoking my Flame of Love, any of you pray in my honor three Hail Mary's, a soul is released from Purgatory. The suffering souls must also feel the effect of grace of the Flame of Love of my maternal heart."

(October 13, 1962)

LETTERS OF THE BISHOPS

These letters were written as the result of the measures taken by those responsible for the Flame of Love Movement intended for the bishops of the respective countries. In view of their importance to the Cause of the Flame of Love, we publish some of them on the pages that follow.

Arzobispado de Guayaquil
Apartado [illegible] - Teléfonos [illegible]
GUAYAQUIL - ECUADOR

GOBIERNO ECLESIASTICO DE LA ARQUIDIOCESIS DE GUAYAQUIL

Puede imprimirse el folleto intitulado "LLAMA DE AMOR DEL INMACULADO CORAZON DE MARIA", traducido al español por el R.P. Gabriel Rona, S.J.

Guayaquil, 15 de Agosto de 1987, festividad de la Asunción de la S. Virgen María.

Gabriel Días Cueva
Obispo Auxiliar

Archdiocese of Guayaquil
Guayaquil, Ecuador

The ecclesial Government for the Archdiocese of Guayaquil

Permission is hereby granted for the printing of the booklet entitled "Flame of Love of the Immaculate Heart of Mary", translated into Spanish by Father Gabriel Róna, S.J.

Guayaquil, August 15, 1987, on the feast of the Assumption of the Blessed Virgin Mary.

+ Gabriel Dias Cueva
Auxiliary bishop

+ Antonio Troyo Calderón
OBISPO AUXILIAR DE SAN JOSE
Teléfonos: (506) 233-6029 · 233-5713 · Fax: (506) 221-2427 · 253-8184
Apartado: 3187-1000 San José, Costa Rica.

San José, Costa Rica, 17 de abril de 1998.

Señoras
Mercedes de Ulloa y Ana Isabel Soto Q.

Queridas Hermanas en Cristo Señor:

A la luz del Espíritu Santo , y después de leer el " **Diario Espiritual de la Llama de Amor del Corazón Inmaculado de María"**, he reflexionado y meditado profundamente en su contenido, y no encuentro en él nada que atente contra la moral y la Doctrina de la Fe. Por el contrario, considero que es un libro que servirá para profundizar en los deberes de la vida cristiana, calentando con esa Llama de Amor, Llama que que ilumina y calienta en el Corazón de María a todos sus hijos.

Por lo tanto, apruebo la publicación de tan bello mensaje, que servirá para la edificación de muchas almas, iluminándolas con esa eterna Llama de Amor, que no es otra cosa, que el Amor de Jesús, en el Corazón del Inmaculado Corazón de María.

Les saluda y bendice su hermano y servidor,

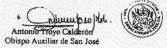

+ Antonio Troyo Calderón
Obispo Auxiliar de San José

San José, Costa Rica, April 17, 1998
Mrs. Mercedes de Ulloa and Ana Isabel Solo Q.

Dear sisters in Jesus Christ Our Lord:

Under the inspiration of the Holy Spirit, and after reading the Spiritual Diary of the Flame of Love of the Immaculate Heart of Mary, I reflected and meditated thoroughly upon its contents. I find nothing in it which could affect negatively morals or the doctrine of the Faith. On the contrary, I believe that this book will be useful to learn more about the duties of the Christian life, a book burning with this Flame of Love, a flame which brings light and comfort for all Mary's children in her heart.

Accordingly, I approve the publication of such a beautiful message, which will enhance the spiritual well-being of many a soul, enlightening them by this eternal Flame of Love, which is nothing short of the love of Jesus in the Immaculate Heart of Mary.

Please receive my greetings and my blessing. Your brother and servant.

Antonio Troyo Calderon
Auxiliary bishop of San Jose

OBISPADO DE CIUDAD GUZMAN
Portal Ramón Corona # 26
Apartado 86 Teléfono 2-05-28
Diócesis de Ciudad Guzmán, Jal. México.
C.P. 49000

Cd. Guzmán, Jal. a 14 de septiembre de 2000.

Dra. Ana María Trujillo de Moreno:
Salina Cruz No. 39
Col. Roma Sur
06760 México, D.F.

Dra. Ana María trujillo de Moreno:

La saludo con toda estimación en el Señor y le deseo todo bienestar y salud.

Recibí su muy amable y atenta carta del 16 de agosto de los corrientes. He leído con atención los informes adjuntos.

Felicito de todo corazón al Movimiento "La Llama de Amor" por sus trabajos en favor de la propagación de esta Llama de Amor de Nuestra Madre Santísima. Que Ella continúe impulsando, con el Amor de su Inmaculado Corazón, los generosos esfuerzos que Ud., junto con los demás integrantes, prodiga.

En unión de oraciones quedo de Ud. su Afmo. servidor en Cristo Jesús.

+ Rafael León Villegas
Obispo de Cd. Guzmán, Jal.

Cd. Guzman, Jal., September 14, 2000

Dr Ana Maria Trujillo de Moreno

I send you a warm greeting in the Lord Jesus. I wish you well-being and health.

I received your kind and distinguished letter dated August 16. I read carefully all the information enclosed. I congratulate with all my heart the Association "Flame of Love" for all the efforts put towards the spreading of this endeavor of our Holy Mother. May she continue to inspire through the love of her Immaculate Heart the tremendous efforts that you and the other members are doing.

United in prayer, I remain sincerely yours in Jesus Christ.

Rafael León Villegas
Bishop of Ciudad Guzman, Jal.

PARROQUIA "CRISTO SALVADOR"
PADRES FRANCISCANOS CAPUCHINOS
[illegible]

Chama, 23 de noviembre de 1999

Señora
NILDA DE MEJIA
MOVIMIENTO DE LA LLAMA
DE AMOR DEL CORAZÓN
INMACULADO DE MARÍA
Ciudad

Estimada hermana Nilda:

Por intermedio de la presente saludo a usted y a los hermanos integrantes del Movimiento de la Llama de Amor del Corazón Inmaculado de María.

Respondiendo a su gentil carta y deseando con ustedes que este movimiento pueda seguir creciendo en todos los lugares, les autorizo incluir esta hermosa jaculatoria de La Llama de Amor en su comunidad:

"SANTA MARÍA MADRE DE DIOS Y MADRE NUESTRA, RUEGA POR NOSOTROS PECADORES, DERRAMA EL EFECTO DE GRACIA DE TU LLAMA DE AMOR SOBRE TODA LA HUMANIDAD, AHORA Y EN LA HORA DE NUESTRA MUERTE. AMEN."

Según el pedido de la Santísima Virgen para vuestro movimiento, y así pueda seguir creciendo la devoción auténtica a la Virgen María y por el Espíritu Santo el amor de Dios se derrame en el mundo.

Paz y Bendiciones,

P. Angelo Costa OFM Cap.
Párroco

Parish Christ the Savior
Franciscan Fathers Friars
Lima, Peru

Chama, November 23, 1999

Mrs. Nilda de Mejia
The Flame of Love of the Immaculate Heart of Mary Movement

Dear sister Nilda,

By the present, I am greeting you as well as my brothers members of the Association "Flame of Love of the Immaculate Heart of Mary". While I am responding to your letter, I have the great desire that this Movement continue to grow and extend. In the same spirit, I authorize you to introduce this beautiful invocation within your community:

"Holy Mary, Mother of God and our Mother, pray for us sinners, spread the effect of grace of Thy Flame of Love over all of humanity, now and at the hour of our death."

All in your Movement must be done according to the demands of the Most Holy Virgin Mary. In this way, the authentic devotion to the Virgin Mary might grow. May the love of God, through His Holy Spirit, fill the earth!

P. Angelo Costa, OFM, Cap., priest

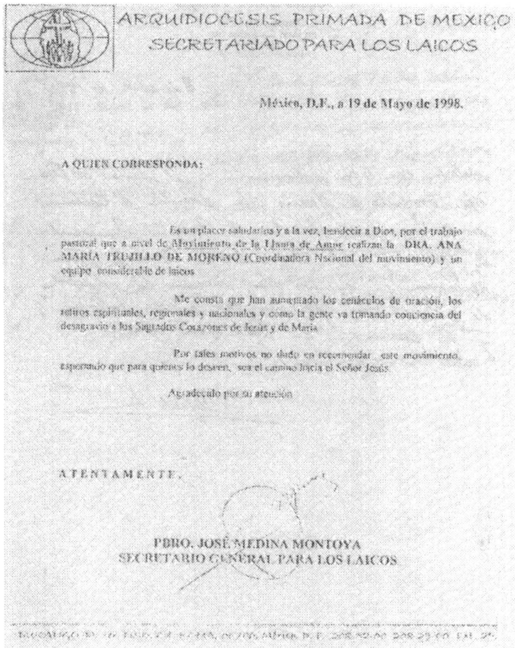

ARQUIDIOCESIS PRIMADA DE MEXICO
SECRETARIADO PARA LOS LAICOS

México, D.F., a 19 de Mayo de 1998.

A QUIEN CORRESPONDA:

Es un placer saludarlos y a la vez, bendecir a Dios, por el trabajo pastoral que a nivel de Movimiento de la Llama de Amor realizan la DRA. ANA MARÍA TRUJILLO DE MORENO (Coordinadora Nacional del movimiento) y un equipo considerable de laicos.

Me consta que han aumentado los cenáculos de oración, los retiros espirituales, regionales y nacionales y como la gente va tomando conciencia del desagravio a los Sagrados Corazones de Jesús y de María.

Por tales motivos no dudo en recomendar este movimiento, esperando que para quienes lo deseen, sea el camino hacia el Señor Jesús.

Agradecido por su atención.

ATENTAMENTE,

PBRO. JOSÉ MEDINA MONTOYA
SECRETARIO GENERAL PARA LOS LAICOS

Archdiocese of Mexico
Office of the Laity - Mexico, D.F., May 19, 1988

To whom it may concern:

It is with great pleasure that I greet you and bless the Lord for the great pastoral task that is being carried out by Dr. Ana Maria Trujillo de Moreno (National Coordinator of the Movement) and a considerable team of laity of the Flame of Love of the Immaculate Heart of Mary Movement.

I was informed that prayer groups and spiritual retreats, whether local or national, have increased, and also that people seem to be more and more conscious of the necessity to compensate for the harm caused to the holy Hearts of Jesus and Mary.

That is why I do not hesitate to recommend this Movement and I wish that it becomes the road leading to the Lord Jesus for those who desire it.

Thank you.

Yours sincerely,

Pbro José Medina Montoya
General Secretary for the Laity

CARLOS QUINTERO ARCE

ARZOBISPO DE HERMOSILLO

ENERO 8 DE 1992.

DRA. ANA MARIA TRUJILLO DE MORENO
SALINA CRUZ NO 39 COL. ROMA SUR
06760 MEXICO, D.F.

Estimada en Cristo:

Que Dios en este Año Nuevo, le conceda crecer en el amor a la Santísima Virgen María y la felicito porque se editará ya el Diario de la Llama de Amor, que bendigo de corazón.

Deseo que el Mensaje Celestial que nos dá la Llama de Amor sea difundido entre todos nuestros Católicos.

Espero que las personas a quienes yo recomendé le contesten en una próxima ocasión.

Reciba mis Bendiciones Afectuosas.

+CARLOS QUINTERO ARCE
ARZOBISPO DE HERMOSILLO

January 8, 1992

Dr. Ana Maria Trujillo de Moreno

Dear sister in Christ Jesus,

As the year begins, may God strengthen your love for the Most Blessed Virgin Mary! I congratulate you on the new edition of the Diary of the Flame of Love which I truly bless.

I sincerely hope that this heavenly message will be spread throughout the whole Catholic community.

I also hope that the people to whom I recommended you will respond to you on the first occasion.

Accept my friendship and my blessings.

+ Carlos Quintero Arce
Archbishop of Hermosillo

+ J. Ulises Macias S.
ARZOBISPO DE HERMOSILLO

SRA. ANA MA. TRUJILLO DE MORENO
Salina Cruz No.39, Col. Roma Sur
06760 México, D.F.

Estimada en Cristo:

Reciba un cordial saludo y mi más sincera felicitación por la edición del Diario de la Llama de Amor.

Envío mis Bendiciones para usted y todos los integrantes de este Apostolado, para que nuestro Señor Jesucristo y la Santísima Virgen María, les concedan crecer en su amor y a difundir el Mensaje Celestial que nos dá la Llama de Amor.

Afectísimo en Cristo, La Bendice.

+ J. ULISES MACIAS SALCEDO
ARZOBISPO DE HERMOSILLO

Hermosillo, Son., 09 de Enero de 1997.

Mrs. Ana Maria Trujillo de Moreno

Beloved sister in Jesus Christ,

Receive my warm regards and my most sincere congratulations for the publication of the Diary "The Flame of Love".

I give you and the members of this apostolate my blessings and I ask our Lord Jesus Christ as well as the Virgin Mary to allow us to grow in their love by spreading out this heavenly message of the Flame of Love.

Yours truly,

+ J. Ulises Macias Salcedo
Archbishop of Hermosillo

Hermosillo, Son., January 9, 1997

DETAILED TABLE OF CONTENT

Chapter One

1961-1962

Chapter two

1962

Chapter 3

1963

Chapter four

1964

Chapter five

1965

Chapter six

1966

Chapter seven

1969

Chapter eight

1971

Chapter nine

1975

Chapter ten

1977

Chapter eleven

1980

Chapter twelve

1981

Elizabeth in 1932

Elizabeth, her husband Karoly Kindelmann, and their six children, in 1940

1980

1982

1983

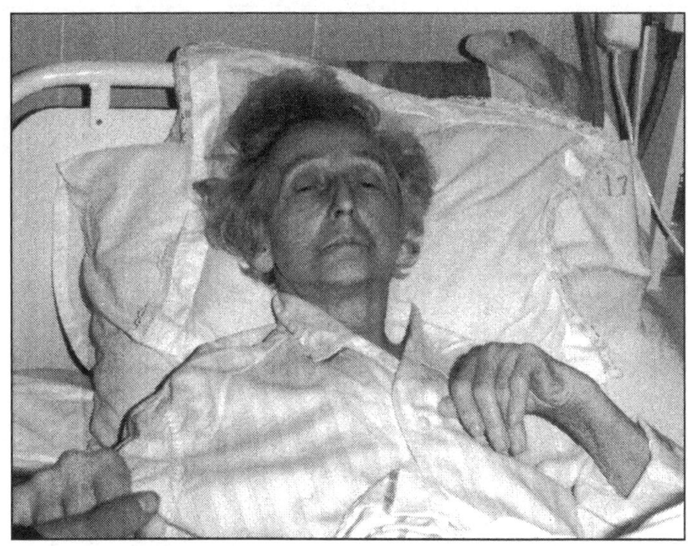

Elizabeth on her hospital bed in 1985

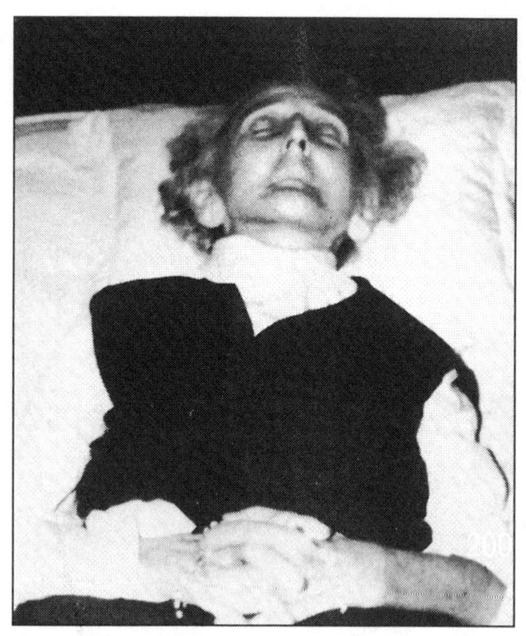

Elizabeth in the peace of God, April 11, 1985

Her funeral, April 16, 1985